America's Best Presidents

AMERICA'S BEST PRESIDENTS

Bruce Myers Gilbert

LIBERTY HILL PUBLISHING

Liberty Hill Press
2301 Lucien Way #415
Maitland, FL 32751
407.339.4217
www.libertyhillpublishing.com

© 2020 by Bruce Myers Gilbert

All rights reserved solely by the author. The author guarantees all contents are original and do not infringe upon the legal rights of any other person or work. No part of this book may be reproduced in any form without the permission of the author. The views expressed in this book are not necessarily those of the publisher.

Printed in the United States of America.

ISBN-13: 978-1-6312-9150-0

Table of Contents

Acknowledgments vii
Preface ix

1. Abraham Lincoln 1
2. George Washington 14
3. Theodore Roosevelt 38
4. Thomas Jefferson 49
5. Ronald Reagan 67
6. Ulysses S. Grant 76
7. Harry S. Truman 97
8. James Monroe 106
9. Andrew Jackson 120
10. Franklin D. Roosevelt 133
11. James K. Polk 151
12. Dwight D. Eisenhower 163
13. William McKinley 173
14. James Madison 181
15. George H.W. Bush 198
16. John Adams 204
17. Herbert Hoover 217
18. John Quincy Adams 234
19. Woodrow Wilson 244
20. James Garfield 253
21. Grover Cleveland 259
22. Calvin Coolidge 267

Appendix I 275
Appendix II 277
Appendix III 279
Appendix IV 283
Bibliography 285

Acknowledgments

I am grateful to the following individuals for taking the time to read earlier drafts of this book and providing recommendations which allowed me to improve certain chapters of the book — either in terms of additional content or stylistically. Marsha de la O made specific suggestions regarding the necessity for additional information on certain aspects of the careers of three Presidents. After doing the additional research those three chapters were enhanced by the additional facts and circumstances which she had recommended.

Similarly, Roberta Myers made an all-important suggestion very early on in the writing process, to wit: that the entire careers of the President should be considered, not merely their four to eight years in the Presidency. I had been contemplating the pluses and minuses of that issue, but she ultimately convinced me that each President's entire career should be evaluated and taken into consideration in the final rankings. She was right.

Phil Taggart made several valuable suggestions regarding issues of style and syntax that improved the text in those regards. Bill Todd made multiple suggestions regarding additional content for a number of chapters following his reading of the first draft of this book. Those suggestions were all valid and were followed up on.

Dr. Chuck Mosher provided me with a list of literary agents that he felt might be interested in a book about American Presidents and their successes and failures.

I am also grateful to the employees at Liberty Hill Publishing who worked with me on the various aspects of producing and marketing the book.

Last, but certainly not least, I am deeply thankful for the support and patience of my wife, Sharon Gilbert, throughout the 39 months of reading, researching, writing, and proofreading. In addition to her patience and understanding, she provided significant assistance when it came to issues of high technology — an area in which I am woefully lacking in even a modicum of skills.

Preface

THE FAUX EPIPHANY

In approximately the month of January, 2017, I came across a recent ranking of the forty-four American Presidents, a subject that has always held interest for me. I scanned the list, finding a number of Presidents with rankings that I felt were either quite too high, or significantly too low. "What's up with this list?" I thought to myself. This first thought was immediately followed with the knee-jerk thought of "I should make my own list!" I immediately went into our computer room and turned on the electronic gadgetry.

THE REAL EPIPHANY

While I was waiting for our aged "device" to spring into action, the real epiphany occurred. Like a powerful floodlight suddenly enlightening a massively dark section of the woods, I realized that a "seat-of-the-pants," instantaneous ranking list would be literally worthless. If I was serious about objectively ranking the American Presidents, I needed to read multiple biographies about all the Presidents I believed to be above average. Further, I felt it was necessary to read general histories of various salient periods of the American experience, as well as biographies of important non-Presidents who had interacted with their commanders-in-chief. Thus began what has flowered into over 81,100 words about *America's Best Presidents*.

The Ground Rules: Only Presidents who have been retired more than twenty years are considered for the list, as I believe that to fully evaluate Presidents one must wait a minimum of twenty years to determine how their various policies, both domestic and foreign, worked out, for better or worse. Thus, Bill Clinton, George W. Bush, Barak Obama and Donald Trump are not eligible for the Best Presidents List.

The Pre-list Preparations: Prior to making this list I read ninety-eight books (biographies and general histories) about my initial "top twenty-five" Presidents, as well as about key Americans who interacted in important ways with various Presidents. My original "top twenty-five list" was based on a long interest in American history prior to college, as well as obtaining a B.A. in history and a secondary teaching credential in history from the University of California at Irvine, plus earning a Juris Doctorate from the UCLA School of Law, and practicing criminal law for thirty-four years. Additionally, books I had read in the years since graduation were a factor in the initial "top twenty-five list." I attempted to obtain the best and most recent biographies/histories to read. Those ninety-eight books consisted of over 44,600 pages (an average of 455

Preface

pages per book). After reading the ninety-eight books and doing additional research, which included utilizing the two reference books listed in the bibliography, plus other sources, the bottom three Presidents were dropped from the rankings and only the top twenty-two are listed herein. I read two or more books on nearly all of the listed Presidents, and two or more on every one of the "top-ten" Presidents.

Statistical Coincidence: In the top eleven there are six Democrats, four Republicans, and one Federalist. In the second group of eleven (numbers twelve thru twenty-two), there are four Democrats, six Republicans and one Federalist. No attempt whatsoever was made to balance out the rankings between the two current parties. The rankings simply turned out the way they are listed. The rankings would have been quite different had I based them entirely on impressions from history classes and from articles and interviews I've read/seen in decades gone by. I found that taking the time over a thirty-one-month period to read the (mostly) highly detailed books, allowed my rankings to be based on fresh memories, and oftentimes fresh information, due to the vast amounts of recent research facilitated by the digital age.

Character Counts: I believe a person's character is of significant importance. I believe a President's character is of even greater importance, because millions and millions of people in this country, and to a certain extent, in many countries around the world, look to the leadership of the President of the United States. If the President engages in dishonest or sleazy behavior, then why shouldn't ordinary citizens engage in the same conduct? It is important for Presidents to lead by example. For the above reasons, character flaws of some of the Presidents have been taken into account, and have resulted in downward adjustments of their rankings. Two of the three Presidents considered for the list were not chosen due to massive and/or multiple malignant character flaws.

Other Important Factors: The three main factors I considered in making the rankings were the following: Character Flaws, if any, which has been discussed just above. The other two are equally important: How significant were his Accomplishments? How serious were his Mistakes? More specifically: How transformative was the President? How serious were the issues he faced? How well did he deal with those issues? Did he rise from a poor/troubled background—in other words, was he a self-made man? Did he eek out his election victory(s) for the presidency, or did he trounce his opposition? Did he communicate well with the citizenry? Did his administration have scandals? If so, how serious were they, and how did he deal with them? Finally, was he a visionary—that is, did he foresee future problems and/or potential opportunities and attempt to deal with them in significant ways during his years in office?

The Fourth Factor: Did he assist his country in significant ways prior to reaching the Presidency, or after leaving office, or both? That assistance could be on the battlefield, in the political founding of the country, in the cabinet, in the foreign service, in Congress, or overseas helping citizens of America's allies, or just helping massive numbers of people in general. This Fourth Factor is HUGE. The Rankings are based on the whole man, not merely his four to eight years in the Presidency. For instance, if this factor was not an element within the rankings, then Herbert Hoover, James Garfield and John Quincy Adams would not be on the list at all. Furthermore, James Madison and John Adams would be several notches lower in the rankings than they are now. Each of these five men made significant contributions to America's history and to the best interests of America, outside of their Presidential tenures. In my judgment, those contributions are fully worthy of being duly considered in the determination of their ultimate rankings as Great American Presidents.

Geography: The top twenty-two Presidents come from twelve different states. Four were from Virginia, three from Ohio and New York, two from Tennessee, Massachusetts and California, and one each from Illinois, New Jersey, Missouri, Texas, Vermont and Kansas. In determining what states the Presidents "come from" I am crediting the state with which they are most closely associated, not necessarily their birth state.

What is Not Included: I believe it to be unimportant what college or university a President attended, or if he even went to college. What I believe to be the most important factors in determining the successes of the various Presidents are the following characteristics: Decisiveness when tough issues must be dealt with, Integrity, Judgment regarding the selection of cabinet/staff members, Performing under pressure, Great Listening Skills, Common Sense, the Ability to work with members of opposing parties, Putting the best interests of the Country ahead of personal interests, Communication skills, Sensing the mood of the country, Magnanimity, Self-Confidence, and the Honesty and Courage to admit a mistake, correct it, and change course. Note: See Appendix IV for information showing the lack of correlation between performance in college and performance as America's President.

Caveat: The summaries of the careers of the twenty-two Presidents that I have provided are not meant to include all of their accomplishments, nor all of their shortcomings, but rather to attempt to provide significant information highlighting their major successes and occasional mistakes. Just as there are no perfect human beings, there are no perfect Presidents. Everyone, from Presidents on down, occasionally make mistakes or errors in judgment. Thus, this list of America's best Presidents seeks to weigh the importance of their myriad accomplishments, as mitigated by the seriousness of honest mistakes, as well as the nefariousness of corrupt or immoral decisions.

A Statement Regarding Bias: In making these rankings I have attempted to be as objective as I can, placing the various Presidents in the numerical position I believe they deserve, without regard to party or geography. I have voted in all twelve Presidential elections in which I was eligible to vote. I have voted for multiple Republicans, Democrats and third-party candidates. In the last three Presidential elections I have cast my vote once for a Republican, once for a Democrat, and once for a third-party candidate. I am not an ideologue.

Preface

A Statement Regarding Sources and Writing Style: During the course of reading the ninety-eight books, as well as doing additional research, I have occasionally come across conflicting information. When that happens I try to verify which source is correct, or more likely to be correct, and I use that information. One general area where there are often discrepancies are the statistics relating to battlefield fatalities, the number of wounded and the number captured. If exact numbers in these categories vary, I may use a "range of numbers" to convey the results of the battle, or I will indicate that the figures are approximations/estimates.

I have attempted to make all the information in this book as accurate and as objective as I possibly can. I have also endeavored to make the chapters as "readable" as possible, in terms of paragraph and sentence structure. I have also tried not to engage in the ostentatious use of obscure adjectives. In other words, there was no thumbing through the thesaurus.

The Mt. Rushmore Syndrome

I am well aware that my top four Presidents are the four who are featured on Mt. Rushmore in South Dakota (which, by the way, is an awe-inspiring experience to visit). I actually felt somewhat embarrassed by this, believing some readers might conclude I had automatically placed those four there without doing any serious analysis of their various strengths and weaknesses. I freely admit I actually gave some consideration to dropping Jefferson to slot number five, just to avoid having readers think I had "mailed in" the top four Presidents. I decided against that because I honestly believe, having done all the reading and research, that the four heads on Mt. Rushmore are, in fact, the four "best" Presidents America has yet experienced. I say this fully aware that Mt. Rushmore was constructed before Ronald Reagan, Harry Truman, and Franklin Roosevelt had served out their Presidential terms.

BIBLIOGRAPHY

Each of the ninety-eight books I read is listed in the bibliography, along with the author and the year of publication. I have also included brief summaries relating to the historical focus of the books, as well as my characterization of the books in terms of facts, details, readability, and in some cases, the vast number of pages. In two of the books, only certain chapters were read. Those two are also listed in the bibliography, along with a notation regarding the limited chapters read. Also listed are the titles and author/editor of the two general reference books on the American Presidents.

Chapter 1

Abraham Lincoln, upon taking office on March 4, 1861, faced the worst situation of any new President in American history. The majority of the Southern states had already seceded and were preparing their military strategies, as well as gathering supplies and military hardware. Some of the military hardware that the South already possessed had come directly from President James Buchanan's disgraced Secretary of War, John B. Floyd, who was a Virginian. Floyd had sent firearms to the South prior to resigning his position in late 1860. Floyd then went on to serve as a brigadier general in the Confederate Army during the Civil War.

Yet, Lincoln dealt with the tenuous and dangerous situation with unique brilliance. He selected for his cabinet the most outstanding Republicans in the country, including four men who had directly challenged him for the 1860 Republican Presidential nomination. Foremost among these was Secretary of State William Seward, arguably the greatest American cabinet officer ever. Lincoln also added four additional highly valuable cabinet officers, including Secretary of War Edwin Stanton, Secretary of Treasury (and future Supreme Court Chief Justice) Salmon P. Chase, Attorney General Edward Bates, and

Secretary of the Navy Gideon Wells. Lincoln wanted no "yes men" in his cabinet. He oftentimes solicited advice from his cabinet officers and would change or modify his own opinions if he felt his original position could be improved upon. He was not thin-skinned at all, and accepted their criticisms with surprising and genuine magnanimity.

Lincoln's capturing of the Presidency in November of 1860 was both unusual and fortuitous. It was unusual in that Lincoln's prior experience in government service consisted mainly of eight years in the Illinois State legislature (1834–1842). It should be noted that those sessions were exceedingly brief compared to the length of modern state legislative sessions. Lincoln also served one term in Congress (1847–1849). His military service was equally unimpressive, especially for a Presidential candidate in the nineteenth century, consisting as it did of just eighty days as a volunteer in the Black Hawk War, and having seen zero combat, as his unit was unable to locate Black Hawk and his warriors.

His Presidential campaign was fortuitous due to four relatively viable parties nominating candidates. Lincoln was the Republican nominee, while the Northern Democrats ran Stephen Douglas—the "Little Giant" of Lincoln-Douglas debate fame. Meanwhile, the Southern Democrats ran John C. Breckenridge of Kentucky, while the Constitutional Union Party nominated John Bell of Tennessee. If the Northern and Southern Democrats could have settled on just one candidate it may well have been the case that Lincoln would have finished second. After all, Douglas and Breckenridge combined to draw 220,000 more popular votes than did Lincoln. As it was though, Lincoln was the only candidate with relatively strong anti-slavery views, and he ended up winning easily, despite gathering just forty percent of the vote. Douglas drew twenty-nine percent, while Breckenridge (eighteen percent) and Bell (thirteen percent) trailed. In the electoral vote Lincoln captured every northern state and totaled 180 electoral votes, while Breckenridge (seventy-two), Bell (thirty-nine), and Douglas (twelve) combined for just 123 electoral votes.

In Lincoln's first Inaugural Address on March 4, 1861 (which was more than five weeks prior to the South's April 12, 1861, attack on Fort Sumter), Lincoln had pleaded with the seceding states for reconciliation and reunion, asserting that armed conflict could be avoided by "intelligence, patriotism, Christianity, and a firm reliance on Him, who has never yet forsaken this favored land." There was no response from the Confederate leaders.

Initially, the Civil War was about preserving the Union, but by the summer of 1862 Lincoln had come to believe it was time to emancipate the slaves in the eleven states that had seceded from the Union. However, he wanted to issue the order after a major Union victory. That victory turned out to be the Battle of Antietam in Maryland, which ended with Robert E. Lee's Confederate troops retreating south back across the Potomac River to Virginia on September 17, 1862. Five days later Lincoln issued his Emancipation Proclamation. Eight months thereafter, on May 22, 1863, Lincoln established the Bureau of Colored Troops, which yielded immediate results as tens of thousands of black men volunteered for service in the Union Army. Prior to the end of the Civil War, the number of African Americans who served in the Union

Army had reached a total of 179,000! On November 19, 1863, Lincoln delivered his historic and memorable Gettysburg Address. Eighteen months later, on April 11, 1865, in what turned out to be the final speech of his Presidency, Abraham Lincoln called for voting rights for those African-American men who were both literate and military veterans of the Civil War.

Lincoln had lobbied the House of Representatives to pass the Thirteenth Amendment to abolish slavery in early 1865, and on January 31, 1865, the House narrowly did so by a vote of 119-56, (it required a two-thirds majority to pass). The Amendment was quickly ratified by the required number of States and became the Law of the Land before the end of the year, but after Lincoln's assassination.

The Battle at Antietam is notable for more than just being the spark of good news that enabled the release of the Emancipation Proclamation. It was also the single bloodiest day in the history of American military conflicts, with 22,717 dead, wounded, or missing soldiers! More than twice as many Americans died in one day of fighting at Antietam than died in the War of 1812, the Mexican War, and the Spanish-American war combined. Also, the casualties at Antietam were more than four times greater than the American casualties on June 6, 1944, during the D-Day invasion of the beaches at Normandy.

The third noteworthy aspect of Antietam was a jaw-dropping piece of good luck that turned what could well have been a disastrous Union defeat into a confidence-boosting victory. Although, but for General George McClellan's continual dithering while General Robert E. Lee's battered army retreated, the narrow victory could

Chapter 1

instead have been a monumental and potentially decisive blow to the Confederates had McClellan continued the offensive against the retreating forces of the South.

Now for the stroke of unbelievable good luck: The 27th Indiana Volunteers regiment made camp on September 13, four days before the actual battle, in a field outside the town of Frederick, Maryland. It happened to be the exact spot where a portion of the Confederate Army had camped the day before. One of the Indiana volunteers noticed something white in the grass. He picked up what turned out to be an envelope containing two long sheets of paper wrapped around three cigars. Initially, the corporal kept the cigars and discarded the sheets of paper. A few minutes later he decided to take a look at the paperwork. The sheets of paper turned out to be Lee's detailed plans of what each Confederate division was expected to do, at what time, and at what locations! It even gave the names of the Generals. Thus informed, the Union Army, commanded by McClellan, had three full days in which to reposition their units in order to maximize their ability to repulse the invading Confederate army.

Prominent historian and professor James McPherson told the Associated Press there was "something spooky" about the lost orders, and went on to say that: "My own feeling is that this was a one-in-a-million chance." By "spooky" did McPherson mean "providential?"

There was also a fourth aspect of great importance about the Union's successful effort to force the Confederates back across the Potomac River at Antietam. In the summer of 1862, based on previous victories by the South, especially their second victory at Bull Run, both Great Britain and France were on the verge of granting official recognition to the Confederacy as an independent country. Further, they were planning to contact Lincoln in an attempt to negotiate a peace treaty between the North and the South. However, following Lee's retreat at Antietam, both Great Britain and France decided against official recognition of the Confederacy.

After just under three years of fighting, with multiple different Union generals having failed as Commander of the Army of the Potomac, on March 10, 1864 Lincoln made the controversial but daring and vitally important decision to bring in Ulysses S. Grant, who had been winning battle after battle after battle on the "Western Front." To the many complaints, which were overstated, that Grant drank too much, Lincoln reputedly said, "Find out what whiskey he's drinking and ship a barrel of it to all my other generals." Grant's appointments as General-in-Chief and General of the Potomac were the beginning of the end for the Confederacy. A mere thirteen months after Grant's dual appointments, Grant would accept Confederate General Robert E. Lee's surrender at the small town of Appomattox Court House in the softly rolling wooded hills of south-central Virginia.

Lincoln's only real mistake in running the war was in sticking far too long with General McClellan, who would repeatedly utilize excuse after excuse to avoid attacking Lee's troops. In May of 1862 Lincoln grew so frustrated with the lack of aggression by McClellan that Lincoln himself drew up a battle plan for an amphibious attack on a Rebel base at the port of Norfolk in Virginia. He personally watched the initial assault of the Union troops hitting the beach, but then returned to the White House. Later that night word reached Lincoln that the Union troops had overcome the Rebels, who had then surrendered.

McClellan, only 35, was an extremely handsome man (picture a young Robert Redford, but with dark brown hair) who came from a prominent family. He had graduated from West Point second in his class, despite being two years younger than most other members of the class. McClellan's father was a doctor and the founder of a medical college, while his great-grandfather had been a Revolutionary War General. Perhaps these attributes contributed to Lincoln's indecisiveness in relieving McClellan from his generalships. McClellan was ultimately removed from his position as General-in-Chief in March of 1862, and was then removed eight months later from his position as General of the Army of the Potomac in November of 1862, after that month's mid-term national elections. Lincoln called McClellan's repeated delays and failures to attack the enemy, "Unpardonable." Some members of the Joint Senate & House Committee on the Conduct of the War believed McClellan had committed treason and that he should have been court-martialed. Treasury Secretary Salmon P. Chase said privately that, "McClellan ought to be shot."

In 1864 McClellan sought to avenge his earlier removals from his Generalships by running for the Presidency on the Democratic ticket against Lincoln. However, Lincoln crushed McClellan in the electoral college vote, 212 to 21, and also bested the former General in the popular vote by more than 400,000 votes to easily retain the Presidency. Lincoln was especially gratified by the vote of the American military, which gave Lincoln eighty percent of their votes against their former general.

In addition to retaining the Presidency, voters gave Lincoln a larger majority of Republicans in the House of Representatives. McClellan spent the final few years of his life writing his autobiography, in which he vigorously attempted to defend his conduct in various battle campaigns during the Civil War.

Lincoln's other big mistake as President came in 1864 when he allowed the Republican convention delegates to select his Vice-Presidential running mate for the 1864 Presidential campaign against McClellan. However, it should be noted that it was not unusual in the nineteenth and early twentieth centuries for the convention delegates to select the Vice-Presidential candidates. Still, notwithstanding the customary practice, Lincoln should have made sure that the nominee was someone of character, intelligence, and sobriety. Instead, Lincoln played no role at all, with the unfortunate end result being that the convention chose Andrew Johnson, a Democratic Senator from Tennessee, who was the only Southern Senator that did not resign his position in the Senate and who remained loyal to the Union. Their reasoning was that the choice of Johnson would signal to the South that Lincoln would be fair and reasonable in dealing with them when they rejoined the Union. Tragically, Lincoln was assassinated six weeks into his second term, and Johnson proved to be far too lenient with the South, while also turning a blind eye on the oftentimes vicious and violent treatment that some southerners directed against the newly freed African Americans in the South.

In addition to dealing with the Confederacy, Lincoln suffered an extreme personal tragedy in February of 1862 when Willie, his 11-year-old son, passed away from

Chapter 1

what was believed to be typhoid fever. Earlier, in 1850, Lincoln's eldest son, Edward, had died in Illinois at the age of three.

In 1862, during the first full year of the Civil War, Lincoln signed into law two measures that would yield hugely positive impacts in the years following the Civil War: The Homestead Act and the Morrill Act. The Homestead Act provided title to 160 acres of free land for squatters, citizens and soon-to-be citizens upon their completion of settling on the land for five years. The Morrill Act granted to each state public lands, in proportion to their populations, which were to be sold to finance colleges specializing in training citizens for agricultural and/or mechanical education. On October 3, 1863 Lincoln issued a federal proclamation establishing an official National Thanksgiving Holiday, to be held every year on the fourth Thursday of November. Lincoln felt it was appropriate to establish the holiday in light of the crucial Union victory over the Confederates in the Battle of Gettysburg, which had taken place just three months earlier.

Also in 1862, in his first full year as President, Lincoln further demonstrated his immense visionary powers by signing the Pacific Railroad Bill of 1862, thus launching the most monumental building project of the nineteenth century. The bill provided financing and federal authorization for the Central Pacific and the Union Pacific railroad companies to build a transcontinental railroad system from the Omaha area of Nebraska to Sacramento, California. The C.P. started in Sacramento and built eastward, while the U.P. started near Omaha and built westward. On July 2, 1864, Lincoln, realizing the extreme geographic and weather-related problems that both the C.P. and the U.P. would be facing, signed into law the Pacific Railroad Act of 1864, a revision of the 1862 Act. Five months later Lincoln personally reviewed and approved the proposed route through the Rocky Mountains.

The revised Pacific Railroad Act provided that both companies could issue their own first-mortgage bonds. Additionally, the Act increased the amount that the federal government would pay the companies for each twenty-mile section of track that was completed. Also, the companies received additional mineral rights, as well as a doubling of the size of the land grants that had been previously established. As railroad historian Maury Klein has said, "The object was to induce private parties to build the road that everyone agreed must be built."

The two giant railroad companies completed their work in the spring of 1869, easily finishing the massive project well before the 1872 deadline originally established by Congress. The Union Pacific and the Central Pacific commemorated their historic joint accomplishment by together pounding in the final "Golden Spike" at Promontory Summit in what is now northern Utah on May 10, 1869. Three years later a railroad bridge over the Missouri River was completed, connecting Council Bluffs, Iowa, with Omaha, Nebraska. With the completion of the bridge, the United States then possessed a continuous railroad line that ran from New York City to Sacramento, California. It was the longest rail line anywhere in the world at that time (1872).

Lincoln's belief in the vast importance of constructing the Transcontinental Railroad went beyond the obviously huge financial benefits that would accrue to both

Chapter 1

the country and its citizens as a result of the gargantuan building project. Lincoln also believed the railroad had to be built "not only as a military necessity, but as a means of holding the Pacific Coast to the Union."

Also during the midst of the Civil War, on June 30, 1864, Lincoln found time to sign a bill establishing Yosemite Valley and the Mariposa Grove of Giant Sequoias as the first ever protected wilderness area in the western half of the country. This was only the second time in the history of the nation that federal land was set aside for public use and preservation. Since there was no National Park Service in 1864, Lincoln designated the State of California to protect and administer the new wilderness area.

It should be noted that Lincoln's father was a poor, somewhat unsuccessful farmer who was in great need of Lincoln helping out on the family farm. Thus it was that Lincoln only attended school sporadically, and for perhaps only a total of one year! Lincoln's mother had died when Abraham was just nine years old. However, his father married Sara Bush Johnson a year later. She strongly encouraged Lincoln to read, and Abraham enjoyed a far closer relationship with her than he did with his father. Lincoln loved books and became a voracious reader, who absolutely *consumed* every book he could get his hands on. Lincoln was quite fond of poetry and memorized many of his favorite poems. He also memorized his favorite lines from Shakespeare.

Lincoln performed significant physical labor during his teenage years and early twenties. He literally split thousands and thousands of logs, turning them into fence rails. He also made two separate trips on a flatboat, hauling goods down the Ohio and Mississippi Rivers to

New Orleans. Although Lincoln was "rail" thin, he was actually a very physically strong person, who did engage in the occasional wrestling match.

As author Michael Medved has succinctly and correctly written: "[Lincoln] had risen from poverty to power as the ultimate self-made man." Just as he had taught himself the law by reading multiple law books in his twenties and thirties back in Illinois, so it was that he taught himself about the nature of military combat by reading book after book about tactics, placement of troops, artillery, strategy and the importance of the geography of battlefields during his years in the White House. He put his knowledge of military matters to the test when he planned the above-mentioned, and highly successful, amphibian attack near Norfolk, Virginia in May of 1862.

Lincoln's law partner in Springfield, Illinois, William Herndon, said this about Lincoln: "…it was on the underlying principle of truth and justice that Lincoln's will was firm as steel and tenacious as iron…When justice, right, liberty, the government, the Constitution, the Union, [or] humanity were involved, then you may all stand aside. No man can move him. No set of men can."

Jefferson Davis, the President of the Confederacy, made the following highly revealing statement in 1875, ten years after the Civil War had ended: "Next to the destruction of the Confederacy, the death of Abraham Lincoln was the darkest day the South has ever known."

In an 1854 speech Lincoln made the following statement about slavery: "The monstrous injustice of slavery… deprives our Republican example of its just influence in the world [and] enables the enemies of free institutions, with plausibility, to taunt us as hypocrites."

Chapter 1

The East Coast establishment originally thought Lincoln to be a country bumpkin, based mostly on his tall and gangly physique, his lack of a college education, his somewhat squeaky and high-pitched voice, and his unusual edge-of-the-prairie style of attire. However, they eventually came to realize he was a man possessed of great wisdom, even greater political instincts, extraordinary magnanimity, a startling ability for evaluating people, and a brilliant gift for crafting memorable speeches. Perhaps most importantly, he possessed the self-confidence and personal courage, oftentimes in the face of extreme criticism, to repeatedly make the most difficult of decisions, with monumental consequences riding on those decisions, during his all-too-short four years and six weeks as President.

Chapter 2

George Washington lost more Revolutionary War battles than he won. However, the following facts need to be taken into account before a conclusion about his military talents may be drawn: He was faced with very steep odds in 1775 when he agreed to be the commanding general of the American Continental Army. His army was out-manned, out-armed, out-equipped, and out-provisioned. Plus, many colonists had enlisted for exceedingly short hitches, oftentimes just three months to a year. Another problem for Washington was that the Continental Congress routinely failed to pay the soldiers, leading to thousands of desertions. Additionally, the British navy was the most powerful in the world. Plus, the British had hired 31,000 German troops, nearly 19,000 of whom were Hessians, who specialized in hiring themselves out when other countries needed mercenaries to help put down a "rebellion." Interestingly, when the War ended just over 5,500 German fighters chose to remain in America, rather than join the 17,800 that returned to Germany — the other 7,600 having perished during the Revolution. Of those Germans who returned to Germany, several hundred later immigrated to America, bringing their families back with them.

Chapter 2

Another major problem Washington had to deal with were the tens of thousands of Americans who were "loyalists," many of whom provided information on Washington's troop movements to the British officers. Additionally, many thousands of the loyalists actually fought in battles and skirmishes against colonial forces — especially in the South. Another significant problem for Washington was the issue of experience. Washington's generals had an average of only two years of previous military service, whereas the British generals were largely professional career soldiers who had an average of thirty years of military service. Between 1755 and 1764 the British army had fought on five different continents with the end result being the defeat of every country they had campaigned against!

However, Washington was able to triumph over the Brits on multiple occasions by utilizing information provided to him by his own surprisingly effective cadre of spies, which he had developed early on in the War. For instance, information from his spies helped lead to the discovery of Benedict Arnold's treason, in which he was planning to turn over the American fort at West Point to the British army. The information also led to the arrest, trial and execution of the British spy John Andre, who had been working directly with Arnold in the effort to surrender the fort without a shot being fired (and for Arnold to join the British Army as a general, which actually did occur when Arnold escaped capture by the Continental forces).

Washington's spies also played a major role in providing information regarding the arrival of the French Navy in 1781. Being in possession of said information thus allowed Washington to deceive Henry Clinton, the British General-in-Chief, into thinking that Washington was preparing to attack Clinton's forces in New York City. In actuality, however, Washington, with the majority of his army, was able to sneak out of New York in the dead of night heading for Yorktown, Virginia, and a battle with British General Lord Cornwallis. By the time Clinton discovered he had been duped by Washington (who had sent a portion of his army, as well as landing craft, to two opposing positions that seemed to indicate upcoming dual attacks on the British military in New York), it was too late for Clinton to send additional forces to Yorktown to assist Cornwallis, who had unwittingly and prematurely settled into his 1781–82 winter camp, assuming that there would be no further fighting until the arrival of spring. Cornwallis also mistakenly believed the British Navy would be available for the evacuation of his army, if that became necessary.

Washington's tactics also included surprise attacks when the Brits least expected it, such as on Christmas night, 1776. It happened that on the evening of December 25, 1776, a major winter storm blew into the Trenton, New Jersey area. The Hessian commander responded by cancelling the previously scheduled pre-dawn patrol. However, Washington did just the opposite. He maintained his plans for the surprise attack on the Hessians and led his troops in the first boat to cross the Delaware River (at one of four crossing locations), and then surprised the Hessian soldiers just hours later in the first Battle of Trenton, which ended with a lopsided victory for the Continental Army. He followed up the Trenton victory just seven days later on January 2, 1777, by successfully repelling a British counterattack at Trenton, and again inflicting significant casualties on the British troops, which had been commanded by Lord Cornwallis.

Overnight, in the pre-dawn hours of January 3, Washington's troops quietly snuck out of the Trenton area, with some heading east and then north to Princeton, New Jersey, and others heading west and then north. While these surreptitious troop maneuvers were taking place, additional British troops were scurrying directly south to Trenton for what they thought would be a successful whipping of Washington's army the next day. However, after a twelve-mile march north in the darkness of night, Washington launched yet another surprise attack, this time on British troops stationed in Princeton. During a key point in the fighting, Washington rode amongst his troops, giving orders and leading the troops in a crucial counter-attack, which they executed with great success. Once again, although well within range of British rifles and muskets (an estimated thirty paces), Washington emerged uninjured.

Considering all three victories, the American forces had killed or captured an estimated 1,350 British/Hessian troops. On the American side the casualty figures were miniscule in comparison: approximately thirty–forty deaths and forty-five–fifty wounded. Notably, one of the wounded in the first Trenton battle was future President James Monroe, then just shy of his nineteenth birthday. Monroe suffered a major arterial wound in the area of his left shoulder. Luckily for him, a young Trenton physician named John Ryker had volunteered to provide medical services the night before the battle, and ultimately one of the American soldiers he treated was Monroe. With the aid and expert treatment from Ryker in clamping the artery and stopping the bleeding, Monroe was able to recover sufficiently to see further action in later Revolutionary War clashes. Monroe eventually served as the fifth American President from 1817 to 1825, albeit with bullet fragments still within his body.

Besides Washington's December 26th victory in the first Battle of Trenton, another major development occurred on December 26, 1776. The Continental Congress voted to give General Washington full authority to direct the War as he saw fit. They made this decision completely unaware of Washington's triumph at Trenton just hours before the Congressional vote.

In some ways, Washington's three victories at Trenton and Princeton in a nine-day span were the most important occurrences of the war prior to Yorktown. By December of 1776, Washington's army was down to just under 3,000 men. This is a known fact, as Lieutenant James Monroe, at Washington's direction, had counted the troops in early December as they marched south for their winter encampment on the west bank of the Delaware River. Due to deaths, captures, desertions and illnesses, Washington's army had lost roughly seventy-five percent of its members by early December, 1776. Making matters worse was that the enlistments of many of these men were due to expire on January 1. Washington was even considering the possibility he would have to flee farther west with his few remaining troops to beyond the Allegheny Mountains. He had lost four straight battles, five if one counts surrendering Fort Lee without a fight. He felt he had to gain a major victory immediately in order to draw more troops to his Army for the 1777 campaign. Thus it was that he made the critical and risky decision to play his cards aggressively at Trenton and Princeton—and came up with a trio of aces!

A full century later, famed British historian Sir George Trevelyan wrote a lengthy analysis of the American Revolution. Referring to Washington and his troops in the back-to-back-to-back wintery battles at Trenton and Princeton, Trevelyan wrote briefly but brilliantly: "It may be doubted whether so small a number of men ever employed so short a space of time with greater and more lasting effects upon the history of the world."

Another event in December of 1776 also had a hugely significant positive effect on the success of the American Revolution, although this event did not occur on the battlefield. Thomas Paine had previously published his highly acclaimed pamphlet, *Common Sense*, on January 10, 1776. Within five months over 150,000 copies had been sold in the colonies. In late November Paine felt it was time to publish another pamphlet, as the spirit of both the American soldiers and the American people seemed to be sinking into great despair, with many believing that perhaps the war was lost. The result was the publication of Paine's first essay of *The American Crisis* series on December 19, 1776.

The first phrase of the first essay contains the immortal words that remain in our collective memories to this day: "*These are the times that try men's souls.*" Paine continued the essay with the following words: "*The summer soldier and the sunshine patriot will, in this crisis, shrink from the service of his country; but he that stands it NOW, deserves the love and thanks of man and woman. Tyranny, like hell, is not easily conquered; yet we* [know] *that the harder the conflict, the more glorious the triumph."* On Christmas Day, 1776, prior to the first Trenton battle, Washington had astutely directed his officers to read Paine's essay to all of his soldiers, which they did. Following the publication of Paine's essay number 1, and Washington's three victories from December 26 through January 3, American spirits soared. Many soldiers re-enlisted, and many more enlisted for the first time. As a result, things were definitely looking up for the Continental Army as the 1777 campaign approached.

In addition to Washington's three major successes, the "Patriots" also achieved amazing results in a series of thirty guerrilla-type skirmishes that took place between January 4, 1777 and March 21, 1777, in what came to be known as the "Forage War." The Forage War consisted of attacks by small groups of local militias who would launch sudden assaults against unsuspecting British military units. These attacks resulted in more than 1,000 Redcoats being killed, wounded, captured, or listed as missing in action. The attacks also resulted in significant numbers of British wagons, weapons, horses, and other supplies such as cattle and sheep being captured. All thirty of the Forage War attacks occurred in New Jersey. By the end of March, 1777, British General-in-Chief Sir William Howe had seen his army diminished by more than half due to deaths in battle, deaths due to disease, capture, serious injury, or simply missing in action.

Another military advantage Washington enjoyed was his ability to utilize far superior mobility, oftentimes moving his troops at night. A primary example of this was his retreat from Brooklyn to Manhattan Island, wherein Washington was the last of 9,000 troops to get

Chapter 2

into the final boat to leave Brooklyn, in a situation where the British forces far out-numbered the Americans, and had administered a decisive victory over the Continental Army just three days before Washington's secretive withdrawal. Mother Nature had provided Washington a huge boost in this effort, as a violent Nor'easter blew in for two days immediately after the first-day whipping the Brits had administered to the Americans. The next day saw yet another favorable development for Washington as a thick pea-soup fog blanketed the entire area thereafter. Thus, with the assistance of the weather gods, Washington was able to engineer what was basically an eighteenth-century version of the twentieth-century British rescue of their forces from Dunkirk in 1940. Not a single soldier lost his life in Washington's seaborne withdrawal to Manhattan Island!

Another major advantage for Washington was his significant prior military experience, having fought with the British in the French & Indian War in the mid-to-late 1750s. He had defeated a small squad of French in the late spring of 1754, utilizing his equally small regiment to win the skirmish. The French suffered thirteen deaths, and their remaining twenty-one soldiers were taken prisoner. However, five weeks later a much larger French army attacked and defeated Washington and his men in the Battle of Fort Necessity. Washington may have been able to hold off the French attackers had he done a better job of locating his "fort." In his haste to construct the fort prior to the arrival of the French army, he had overlooked an important location that provided the French with a powerful offensive position. Thirty of Washington's troops perished in the battle, with another seventy being wounded. The French, generously and puzzlingly, allowed Washington and his men to march back to Virginia, while the French and their Indian allies set about burning the hastily constructed and short-lived Fort Necessity.

Washington's most memorable French & Indian wartime experience, and the one which made him a known commodity in the Colonies as well as to the British military, came in the 1755 Battle of Monongahela (which is also known as "Braddock's Defeat"), in which the French and their Indian allies, who were members of multiple tribes in the Upper Ohio Valley area, decimated the British troops. Virtually all of General Braddock's six to seven dozen British officers were either killed or wounded, including General Braddock, who died four days after the battle during the eastward retreat of the British forces. Washington, however, emerged from the fighting completely unscathed, although just barely!

After Braddock was injured he directed Washington to convey a series of orders to various British colonels and captains in the field as the Battle was still raging. While riding from point to point to deliver the orders, the then twenty-three-year-old had two horses shot out from underneath him, the crown of his hat was penetrated by a bullet, and a large flapping jacket that he was wearing had been pierced by four bullets! Still, Washington had delivered all of Braddock's orders. One survivor of the Battle said, "I expected every moment to see him fall. Nothing but the superintending hand of Providence could have saved him." Washington later sent a letter to his brother Jack regarding the battle, writing the following words:

Chapter 2

"The miraculous care of Providence protected me beyond all human expectation."

One salutary effect of the Brits having been mauled by the French & Indian forces was the suddenly altered opinion of the colonialists as to their previously held view of the near invincibility of the British Army. As the astute Benjamin Franklin put it: "This whole transaction gave us the first suspicion that our exalted ideas of the prowess of British regular troops had not been well founded." Additionally, the colonial troops under Washington's command had clearly out-performed the British troops under General Braddock's direction during the day-long battle. Among Washington's 800 colonial militia men was a young twenty-one-year-old from North Carolina by the name of Daniel Boone.

On November 29, 1775, Washington and his troops were the recipients of good fortune, as John Manley, who had been just recently commissioned directly by Washington as the captain of the schooner, the *USS Lee*, was able to deceive the British captain of the *Nancy*, an ordnance ship. Manley posed as a Boston pilot ship captain. Once the *Nancy* was turned over to Manley and his crew, they quickly gained physical control of both the *Nancy* and its valuable martial cargo: one mortar, 2,000 muskets, 100,000 flints, 32 tons of lead balls, as well as multiple barrels of gunpowder. This was critically important as the Continental Army was short on military supplies in general, and especially short on gunpowder. It was the exhaustion of their gunpowder that had forced the Colonial forces to withdraw from the Battle of Bunker Hill in June of 1775 (prior to Washington's arrival in Massachusetts), despite having administered a savage beating to the British troops. Nearly one-half of the 2,200 Redcoats in the Battle (1,054) were either slain or wounded! This casualty count is the highest suffered by Great Britain in any single-day Revolutionary War battle.

Washington's first major Revolutionary War military success occurred on March 4–5, 1776, when his troops, under the cover of darkness, obtained control of the Dorchester Heights, which loomed directly above the British troops, who thought themselves safe within the city of Boston. The next morning when the British woke up, they discovered to their horror that Washington's siege of Boston had now taken on a whole new and far deadlier dimension. Not only did Washington have armed troops on the heights, he also had twenty heavy cannons and thirty-eight mortars aimed directly down on Boston and the hated "Lobsterbacks." General William Howe, the British General in command, was stunned, saying, "My God, these fellows have done more work in one night than I could make my army do in three months."

Twelve days later on March 17, 1776 (St. Patrick's Day, but since 1776, also known in Boston as Evacuation Day), some 9,000 Redcoats, accompanied by an estimated 1,100 American loyalists and 1,200 women and children, all jammed onto 120 British ships and sailed off to Halifax in Nova Scotia.

Perhaps the most amazing aspect of the triumph at Dorchester Heights, was the transportation of the fifty-eight cannons and mortars, in the depths of a New England winter, to the outskirts of Boston. This feat had been accomplished by Colonel Henry Knox, later to become one of Washington's staff generals, and then ultimately President Washington's first Secretary of War.

Chapter 2

Knox, who had originally been a Boston bookseller (!) prior to the Revolutionary War, made significant use of sleighs in transporting the estimated 120,000 pounds of artillery from Fort Ticonderoga, which is located at the south end of Vermont's Lake Champlain, to the Boston area in just over seven weeks' time. Knox initially traveled south down the Hudson Valley with his sixty tons of military hardware until he reached the town of Kinderhook, New York (the hometown of America's eighth President, Martin Van Buren, although Van Buren was not born until 1782). Upon reaching Kinderhook, Knox turned and headed east through southern Massachusetts, eventually arriving in Cambridge on January 25, 1776.

Another major battlefield success for Washington was at the Battle of Monmouth on the blistering hot day of June 28, 1778. Learning that his troops were retreating, Washington rode into the midst of the retreat, turned his infantry around, and rallied the troops to counter-attack. The intense heat caused Washington's horse to collapse, but he quickly located another mount and continued spurring his forces onward, eventually driving the Brits from the field.

In Washington's siege of Yorktown in October of 1781, he enjoyed a "home field" advantage. He knew the Virginia terrain intimately, having lived in the region his whole life and having been a prolific, and government-certified, surveyor from the age of sixteen to the age of twenty. Washington had conducted surveys in both the Shenandoah Valley in western Virginia, as well as in eastern Virginia. Just how prolific was Washington's surveying? He surveyed nearly 200 separate tracts of land, totaling over 60,000 acres!

Washington was thus able to place British General Cornwallis and his entire army in an utterly untenable position in the final major Revolutionary War battle by trapping the Brits in what was literally an inescapable position near the end of a peninsula. The Redcoats were backed up against the wide York River on their north, with the equally wide James River a few miles to their south and southwest, and Chesapeake Bay to their east—which was blockaded by the newly arrived French Navy. After just more than a week of virtually non-stop pounding by Washington's artillery, aided by American and French ground forces, many of whom were commanded by Alexander Hamilton and the Marquis de Lafayette, as well as by French General Jean Rochambeau, Cornwallis realized the complete futility and utter weakness of his position. Thus, on October 17, Cornwallis requested terms of surrender from Washington and General Rochambeau. Coincidentally, October 17th was the exact four-year anniversary of British General John Burgoyne's surrender to American General Horatio Gates in the 1777 Battle of Saratoga. Two days later, Cornwallis agreed to Washington's terms and surrendered his entire army, nearly 8,000 soldiers, effectively ending the six-and-a-half-year struggle for American freedom.

Cornwallis had been highly successful on battlefields around the world, but he came up well short at Yorktown. Cornwallis had also been a member of Parliament and had opposed aggressive measures to punish the colonies. As historian David Hackett Fischer has pointed out, Cornwallis wrote that Americans were "free Englishmen, such as we, who are simply standing up for their rights." Cornwallis had also voted against the Declaratory Act, in which Parliament underscored their power to tax the colonies and, indeed, to pass whatever legislation they felt was merited. In light of the above information, one pauses to wonder if perhaps Cornwallis was not overly disappointed in having to surrender to Washington at Yorktown.

The French military assistance, both on land and at sea, in the Battle of Yorktown was the first major "boots on the ground" assistance the French had provided (other than Lafayette, who came to America of his own volition). Previously, though, in the fall of 1776, and again in the winter of 1777, the French had provided material and commercial assistance. Then, in February of 1778 came a major breakthrough: Benjamin Franklin was able to successfully conclude his negotiations with Louis XVI, in which the French king signed a treaty providing for both friendship and commerce between the two countries, and more significantly, the provision of military aid to the struggling colonies. The French king had come to the conclusion that the Americans would likely defeat the British — the arch enemies of the French. This conclusion was based on the American victory at Saratoga in October of 1777, following the string of successes Washington had enjoyed throughout 1777. The treaty was a major boost to the cause of American freedom — a boost which ultimately came to full and final fruition in the early autumn of 1781 near Yorktown, in the tidewater area of eastern Virginia.

Yale historian Edmund Morgan called Franklin's 1778 treaty with France "the greatest diplomatic victory the United States has ever achieved." In 1779 Franklin triumphed again, arranging for the American acquisition of a forty-gun man-of-war for Captain John Paul Jones.

It was the ship which, after a name change and a major reworking, became the *Bonhomme Richard*, named after Franklin's famous *nom de plume*, "Poor Richard." See Chapter 16 below, on John Adams, John Paul Jones, and the unbelievable-but-true, David-versus-Goliath story of the *Bonhomme Richard's epic defeat of the larger, virtually brand new British warship, Serapis.*

Although Yorktown was the last major battle of the war, there were multiple skirmishes still being fought on a smaller scale, especially in the Carolinas. More than twenty percent of all American casualties during the Revolutionary War occurred in South Carolina in the last two years of fighting! The final battle in South Carolina actually occurred a full year after Yorktown, in October of 1782.

The two most effective "Patriot" officers in the South Carolina fighting were Francis Marion, known to history as "The Swamp Fox," and General Nathanael Greene, who was one of Washington's favorite and most capable staff generals. Greene was a rare commodity in two ways: He was a Quaker, and he was from Rhode Island. Although Greene had no prior military experience, he was extremely well read on a variety of topics related to military matters. Greene was able to repeatedly disrupt many of the British attacks in the Carolinas, frustrating multiple offensives the British generals were attempting to execute, including Lord Cornwallis prior to his move north to Yorktown.

As for "The Swamp Fox," he was extremely knowledgeable about the Carolina swamps, the trails, and the river fords. He was an intelligent man who was also a highly successful strategist and fighter, as well as a charismatic leader of men. All of these elements were accurately featured in eight episodes of *Walt Disney Presents*, which ran on American television from 1959–1961. What was inaccurately depicted was how Marion was portrayed as tall and handsome (played by the prominent actor, Leslie Nielsen). In fact, Marion was quite short and was not at all regarded as being a turner of women's heads. Blame it on Hollywood.

In early 1776, Washington had begun accepting free African Americans into the embryonic Continental Army. By the end of the war the percentage of Blacks in the Continental Army stood at ten percent — a figure that was more than double their percentage of the overall population in the northern colonies! It should also be noted that the African-American troops were not in segregated units and were assigned to a wide variety of duties

On September 3, 1783, the Treaty of Paris was finally signed, officially ending the Revolutionary War. Washington was thus able to resign his commission and head home to Mount Vernon from New York. During his eight-plus years of service in the War, Washington had slept in 280 different locations!

One little known aspect of the Revolutionary War that Washington had to deal with was Ethan Allen and his "Green Mountain Boys." Although the GMB were extremely effective fighters, excellent marksmen and relatively fearless, they were also an administrative headache for Washington, both as the Commander of the Continental Army and later as President. The GMB, under the leadership of Seth Warren (not Ethan Allen, who was a second cousin to Warren), played a major role in diminishing the size and effectiveness of British

General John Burgoyne's army as it marched south down the Hudson Valley in 1777.

Burgoyne's army's most significant loss during their lengthy southward march occurred on August 16, 1777 in the Battle of Bennington when 2,000 New Hampshire militiamen led by John Stark and 350 Vermont militiamen led by Seth Warner attacked a large foraging party of approximately 1,400 men Burgoyne had ordered into the woods due to his army's severely diminished food supplies. Burgoyne's troops suffered 207 fatalities that day, with an additional 700 redcoats having been captured. The state militias suffered thirty deaths and forty wounded. The guerrilla tactics of both Stark (who had also fought heroically at the Battle of Bunker Hill back in 1775) and the GMB significantly slowed Burgoyne's march, which led to continuing shortages of weapons, food and other military supplies. All of these elements contributed to Burgoyne's subsequent defeats in two distinct battles on September 19 and October 7, 1777, which ultimately led to Burgoyne's stunning surrender of his entire army on October 17, some ten days after the second Battle of Saratoga. It had been a nightmarish two months and one day for General Burgoyne and his starving troops.

The problem for Washington was that the GMB, together with most citizens of Vermont, believed they should be admitted as the "14th Colony/State," and they were quite invigorated by the refusal of the other thirteen colonies to give Vermont equal political status. The fly in Vermont's admission ointment was powerful New York politicians and landowners who claimed "Vermont" was actually just the northeastern-most part of New York.

Chapter 2

Ultimately, this disagreement led to Ethan Allen and his brother Ira beginning negotiations with the British commander in Quebec for the intended purpose of withdrawing "Vermont" from the nascent American Union and becoming a province of the British Empire. Those negotiations basically ended with Cornwallis's sudden surrender at Yorktown in October of 1781.

However, the hard feelings of the Vermonters continued unabated for nearly a decade as the United States Congress refused to admit Vermont as the 14th State. Then, following the death of Ethan Allen in 1789 and with the support of Washington's Treasury Secretary, Alexander Hamilton, himself a New Yorker, Congress agreed to Vermont joining the Union in 1791. An additional problem for Vermont's statehood application had been that during the three-year period leading up to 1791, the Southern states were concerned about yet another "Northern" state being added to the Union, thus diminishing the political power of the South. This issue was subsequently solved by admitting Kentucky as a new "Southern" state in 1792 to balance out the admission of Vermont.

As a young man growing up in Virginia, Washington was quite the physical prodigy. He was 6' 3½" (as measured by the physician that prepared his body for burial in 1799) and in the neighborhood of 190-200 pounds. Washington was actually quite athletic. He was regarded by many as the best horseman in all of Northern Virginia, as well as one of the best dancers. Washington greatly enjoyed both activities. As Thomas Jefferson said regarding Washington's skill with horses: "[He was]...the best horseman of his age and the most graceful figure that could be seen on horseback." At age twenty Washington won a "running jump" contest with a leap of twenty-three feet. Although Washington certainly never threw a silver dollar across the Potomac River (or the Rappahannock), he did throw a rock over Virginia's Natural Bridge, which was/is 215 feet high! Another feat of strength by Washington occurred in 1772, when he was a middle-aged forty-year-old. Washington was walking around his property when he came upon the famed artist, Charles Wilson Peale, who was at Mount Vernon to paint Washington's portrait. Peale and his young friends were shirtless and were taking turns throwing a heavy iron bar. Washington was shown the pegs that marked the young men's best throws and, without removing his coat, heaved the iron bar far, far beyond the posted pegs. As Peale and his friends stood speechless and gawking, Washington said to them, "When you beat my pitch, young gentlemen, I'll try again."

Due largely to the mostly unworkable nature of the Articles of Confederation, the leaders of the revolutionary movement called for a Constitutional Convention in 1787, although not using that term. Washington, not surprisingly, was chosen to preside over the Convention. Once the new constitution was agreed to, after four months of oftentimes emotional and rancorous debate, and after eleven states had ratified the agreement, Washington was unanimously elected President by the "electors." The voting for President had begun on December 15, 1788, with the final votes being cast on January 10, 1789. Ten months after Washington's election, North Carolina finally ratified the new Constitution and joined the young nation. Rhode Island, however, did not ratify the new Constitution until May of 1790, thus completing the initial 13 states. More than two years later, in voting that took place between November 2, and December 5, 1792, Washington was again unanimously chosen for his second term.

In 1789, following the passage of the Judiciary Act, Washington appointed the nation's first Supreme Court: six justices from five different states were selected by the President, who valued regional balance. Also in 1789, Washington signed a proclamation establishing the first Thanksgiving Day, selecting November 26. It should be noted, though, that for the next seven decades the holiday was only intermittently observed.

In the summer of 1790 Washington signed into law the Residence Act and the Assumption Act, as a negotiated package deal between the Federalists and the Jeffersonian Democratic-Republicans. The Assumption Act provided that the new federal government would assume all the war debts that had been incurred by the various thirteen states, which Washington's Treasury Secretary, Alexander Hamilton, had strenuously argued was an absolute requirement for the newly formed United States in order to establish a solid footing for its commercial trading credit with the major European countries. The Residence Act provided that a new Federal District, ten miles square (later to be called Washington, D.C.), would be built astride the Potomac River on land then belonging to Virginia and Maryland. The Act further required that the new Federal District be completed in time to be occupied by 1800. In the meantime the temporary Capitol would be in Philadelphia, following its first eighteen months in New York City.

In the mid-summer of 1794, Washington had to deal with the "Whiskey Rebellion" in western Pennsylvania. Farmers and whiskey distillers in that region were violently protesting new federal taxes on the production of alcoholic beverages. There had been at least one death and six injured in the various protests. At the request of the Pennsylvania governor, 12,000 state militia troops were sent to the area, with Washington leading them as far as the city of Carlisle. It was the first and last time that a sitting President led armed troops. The issue was solved with relatively little violence amid the arrest of 150 suspected rebels. Two of the suspects were tried, convicted of treason, and sentenced to death. Later, though, Washington pardoned the two men. The remaining arrestees were either not tried or were acquitted. Eight years later, in 1802, during the Presidency of Thomas Jefferson, the whiskey tax was repealed.

In 1793 Washington issued his strict "Neutrality Proclamation" pertaining to foreign affairs. He was opposed to both a standing army and a permanent navy. However, just months later the American consul in Lisbon reported that Algeria had recently constructed and floated a new attack fleet of eight ships to increase their raiding of European and American merchant vessels. This news prompted both houses of Congress to pass the Act to Provide Naval Armaments which, notwithstanding his Neutrality Proclamation, Washington signed into law in late March, 1794. It provided that six military frigates would be constructed in order to provide security for American shipping merchants and sailors. In 1797 the first three frigates slid down the ways and were officially launched.

Chapter 2

In the years just prior to 1795, many Kentucky residents were threatening to secede due to Spain's restrictions on the shipping of goods down the Mississippi River. Thus, Washington appointed a special envoy to Spain, Thomas Pinckney, who successfully concluded the Treaty of San Lorenzo, which gave Americans the full right to use of the Mississippi River, as well as to trade at the port of New Orleans.

In retiring from the Presidency after two terms, Washington established the tradition of an eight-year limit on Presidents. The tradition lasted for 144 years, until it was broken by Franklin Roosevelt in 1940, and then again in 1944. The constitution was then amended in 1951 so that it now specifically provides that no President may serve a third term.

Washington passed away in December of 1799, two months short of his 68th birthday. In his hand-written will, which he had authored just three months earlier, he provided for all of his slaves to be freed upon his own death or his wife Martha's death, whichever came last. Martha ended up passing away twenty-nine months after Washington. They had been married for just under forty-one years. They had no children in common, probably due to Washington having contracted smallpox in Barbados at the age of nineteen, resulting in him most likely being unable to father children. That Washington chose to free his slaves is really not surprising. Back in 1774 Washington had endorsed the Fairfax Resolves, which among other things advocated for the elimination of any further importation of slaves into any of the thirteen colonies.

In addition to freeing his (and Martha's) slaves, his will provided that the freed slaves that were either too old or too young to support themselves must be supported for as long as necessary. Additionally, all of the freed young slaves were to be taught how to read and write, and also to be prepared for "some useful occupation." He also provided a specific clause in the will that none of the freed slaves were to be taken out of Virginia "under any pretense whatsoever."

Of the slave-owning "Founding Father" Presidents, Washington was the only one who provided for the manumission of his slaves upon his death. Although, in fairness, it should be noted that Washington had no natural children and was extremely wealthy. That was contrary to most Virginia planters, who were land-rich and cash-poor, which was exactly the situation that Thomas Jefferson and James Madison found themselves in toward the ends of their lives. Jefferson's financial situation was far more severe than Madison's as the latter had no natural children. Jefferson, however, had one living child as well as multiple grandchildren. In addition, Jefferson was a life-long spendthrift, who could not resist buying literally thousands of books on a wide variety of topics, as well as purchasing a diverse collection of tools and scientific instruments.

During his first term, Washington had proven to be a supremely important balance in the political middle between Alexander Hamilton's extreme, almost monarchical brand of federalism, and Thomas Jefferson and James Madison's Democratic-Republicanism, which placed great trust in the collective wisdom of the everyday, working American people. Jefferson and Madison greatly valued the personal freedom and rights that citizens should enjoy. However, in his second term Washington came to rely more and more on Hamilton's advice and on his own philosophy of the importance of a powerful central government. The result of Washington's ideological shift towards a more stringent form of Federalism led to a significant and permanent gulf developing between Washington and the Jefferson/Madison Democratic-Republicans. This led to Jefferson submitting his resignation as Secretary of State at the end of 1793, as he was diametrically opposed to Hamilton's program and strongly believed it would inevitably lead to the creation of an American monarchy.

Thus, it was not surprising that Washington, on September 19, 1796, released to all the various American newspapers for printing, his last official message, which was largely written by Hamilton, but based on Washington's outline of four major points he wished to stress. In his written statement Washington declared the following: 1.) His absolute intention to retire from the Presidency; 2.) He stressed the importance of strict neutrality in foreign affairs; 3.) He warned the country against the dangers of weakening the Constitution; 4.) He also strongly warned against the dangers he foresaw from strict loyalty to political parties. His fourth warning was an important and timely message not only in 1796, but also in twenty-first-century America — what with our current situation of rabid, profane, and occasionally violent far-left and far-right demonstrators and politicians.

Chapter 3

Theodore Roosevelt was the grandson of Cornelius Roosevelt, one of the wealthiest of all New Yorkers. Teddy grew up in opulent surroundings, and traveled extensively in Europe and the Middle East with his entire family as a child. As a young boy he became obsessed with animals, especially birds. He would dissect them, compare them, and make detailed anatomical drawings of a wide variety of birds. This intense interest in wildlife and the outdoors unquestionably led to his historic, eye-popping accomplishments several decades later as America's first conservationist and preservationist President.

Succeeding to the Presidency following the assassination of William McKinley in early September of 1901, Roosevelt served until March 4, 1909, becoming the foremost nature lover, conservationist, and preservationist of both animals and federal lands among all forty-four Presidents to date. Roosevelt created or enlarged 150 National Forests, fifty-one Federal Bird Reservations, four National Game Preserves, six National Parks, and eighteen National Monuments. In seven-and-a-half years as President he preserved over 234 million acres of wilderness for the enjoyment and education of future

Chapter 3

generations of Americans. In May of 1908 Roosevelt tried to bring the importance of conservation to the attention of the national media and the American public, as well as to state officials, by hosting the first conservation conference in American history at the White House (Previously, in July of 1902, Roosevelt had issued an executive order which officially changed the name of the "Executive Mansion" to the "White House"). Forty-five state and territorial governors were among the 360 persons who attended the four-day conference, which dealt with the importance of preserving the country's unique and beautiful mountains, canyons, lakes, plains and deserts, as well as the plants and animals that lived thereon.

Just one month into his Presidency, Roosevelt invited the prominent African-American educator and agrarian Booker T. Washington to join him for dinner in the White House. It had been 20 years since Washington had founded the Tuskegee Institute (now Tuskegee University). Washington, quite naturally, accepted. Unfortunately, and shockingly, Roosevelt's respectful gesture resulted in Southern racists violently attacking blacks at various locations in the South.

Six years later in 1907, the Territory of Oklahoma was seeking statehood. However, before Roosevelt would sign off on the application he forced the Oklahoma governor to remove a white supremacist plank from the proposed Oklahoma state constitution. Only after the offending provision was removed did Roosevelt sign legislation allowing Oklahoma to become the 46th state on November 16, 1907.

Roosevelt was clearly not a racist, but he did mishandle a racial riot that occurred in Brownsville, Texas in 1907. The melee involved white citizens and twenty to thirty black soldiers from the nearby Army base. One citizen was killed and at least one was injured. When an Army inquiry into the incident was held, all of the non-involved black soldiers refused to testify about what, if anything, they knew about the incident. Ultimately, Roosevelt ordered all of the uncooperative soldiers to be dishonorably discharged, including at least one soldier who was a widely recognized military hero. Although a subsequent and lengthy investigation by a United States Senate committee ultimately supported Roosevelt's decision by a 9-4 vote, there were clearly other, and more appropriate, disciplinary options Roosevelt should have utilized in order to bring the incident to a more satisfactory and just conclusion.

In 1902 Roosevelt appointed Oliver Wendell Holmes to the nation's Supreme Court. Holmes went on to become perhaps the most highly regarded associate justice in the nearly 230- year history of the Court. Holmes not only knew the law, but he was a brilliant writer — a master of the memorable phrase. He was also not at all hesitant to dissent from the beliefs of the Court's majority. He ended up serving for thirty years on the Supreme Court.

In the autumn of 1902, as the weather in the Northeast turned ever colder and colder, and as the public became increasingly worried about possibly freezing to death in the fast-onrushing winter if they could not heat their homes due to a strike, Roosevelt concluded he had to act. He injected himself into the lengthy and bitter anthracite coal strike, which had been dragging on for seven months. Roosevelt was able to successfully mediate the strike by getting both sides to agree to a Coal Strike Commission, as well as to agree to the members of the commission whom Roosevelt had personally selected. The coal miners went back to work immediately, families were able to heat their homes that winter, and Roosevelt's Commission subsequently established a new and binding, multi-year contract between the mine operators and the miners which, among other things, raised wages and improved working and health conditions for the miners.

Not only was Roosevelt hugely popular with the families of the North as a result of his successful settlement of the coal strike, but he also received world-wide approval of his actions. He was given a public acclamation by the French Chamber of Deputies, and was also lauded thusly by the staid *Times of London:* "In a most quiet and unobtrusive manner, the President has done a very big and entirely new thing. We are witnessing not merely the ending of the coal strike, but the definite entry of a powerful government upon a novel sphere of operation."

Just two months after the anthracite coal strike issue, in December of 1902 Roosevelt was yet again confronted with another major issue: Germany's, and to a lesser extent Great Britain's, threats against the South American country of Venezuela, which owed large sums of money to both countries, (especially to Germany — 62 million bolivars). Germany and Britain thus launched a blockade of the Venezuelan coast, and threatened to establish military bases in Venezuela if the debts were not paid. The German Navy actually skirmished with the Venezuelans, seizing four of their gun boats and sinking three of them.

Roosevelt responded by invoking the Monroe Doctrine and by sending Admiral Dewey, who was both respected and feared worldwide after his utterly one-sided and devastating defeat of the Spanish Navy in the 1898 battle of Manila Bay, to the Caribbean with a fleet of fifty-three warships. The American fleet vastly outnumbered the combined German and British total of twenty-seven warships. Roosevelt advised the German ambassador that there would be war with the United States unless Germany, within ten days, ceased their blockade of Venezuelan ports and withdrew their navy from the area. He further proposed that the three countries should settle their problems by submitting to arbitration. Great Britain and Venezuela were willing to resort to arbitration but Germany initially refused. Ultimately, just hours before Roosevelt's timetable for Germany to agree to arbitration would have expired, Germany backed down, and further proposed that Roosevelt himself mediate the disagreement! Roosevelt declined to personally engage in the mediation, but proposed a panel of mediators, which Germany then accepted. By February of 1903 the threat of war was over, and both Roosevelt and the Monroe Doctrine stood stronger and firmer than ever.

Roosevelt also was the first President to engage in a serious way in "trust busting" the giant corporations of the Gilded Age. Among those "busted" were the following: John D. Rockefeller's Standard Oil, J.P. Morgan and Edward Harriman's Northern Securities Company (a consolidation of three major railroad systems), the American Tobacco Company, and Du Pont. To deal with the giant trusts, Roosevelt advocated for the creation of a new cabinet position, the Department of Commerce and Labor, which was created by Congress in 1903. Additionally, in 1906 Roosevelt signed into law the Meat Inspection Act and the Pure Food and Drug Act.

Chapter 3

Roosevelt also played THE major role from 1903–08 in America's building of the Panama Canal, following the utter failure of the French to get it built. Roosevelt accomplished this by backing a Panamanian revolutionary movement. Following the success of the literally bloodless "revolution," Roosevelt recognized Panama's sovereignty and sent an American warship to make sure that Colombia did not attempt to retake their former colony. Shortly thereafter the new Panama government signed the lease that the Colombian government had haughtily rejected and the American construction of the canal began. The canal was dubbed by many when it was finished in 1914 as the Eighth Wonder of the World (Read David McCullough's excellent page-turner, *The Path Between the Seas*, for all the details, problems and intrigues, as well as Chapter 11 below on President James K. Polk's role in laying the legal groundwork in 1846 for Roosevelt's Panama Canal).

Contrary to what some believe, Roosevelt's support of the Panamanian Revolution wasn't just bullying Columbia in order to build the canal. He actually had a valid legal basis for his canal maneuvering, to wit: the 1846 Treaty of New Granada between the United States and Columbia (then known as New Granada), which was signed into law by President James K. Polk. The treaty guaranteed the U.S. government and its citizens free transit across the Isthmus "upon any modes of communication that now exist, or that may hereafter be constructed." For nearly six decades, and on multiple occasions, American Presidents had upheld their treaty obligations by saving Columbia from both outside attacks and internal revolts, with the first such effort being the sending of American troops to New Granada/Colombia in 1852 by then President Millard Fillmore.

Prior to supporting the Panamanian Revolution, Roosevelt had told Ohio Senator Mark Hanna, who was one of the leading voices in the Senate in support of building the canal, "I feel we are certainly justified in morals, and therefore justified in law, under the treaty of 1846, in interfering summarily and saying that the canal is to be built, and they must not stop it." On February 23, 1904, the United States Senate voted in favor of the Hay-Bunau Varilla Treaty regarding the building of the Panama Canal by the significant margin of 66 to 14. Sadly and ironically, Hanna's vote was not among the "Yes" votes, as he had passed away eight days prior to the scheduled vote.

Roosevelt was so energetic and so wildly popular, and his Presidency had been both vigorous and daringly successful, that he handily won election for a full term in 1904, with 57.4 percent of the vote. His chief opponent, Alton B. Parker, who was the Chief Justice of the New York State Court of Appeals, drew only 37.6 percent, while the socialist candidate, Eugene Debs, received a miniscule 3.0 percent. The prohibition candidate, the ironically named Silas Swallow, gathered in 1.9 percent of the vote. Roosevelt's 57.4 percent of the vote was the highest figure since James Monroe, more than eighty years earlier.

Out west in Dayton, Ohio, Wilbur Wright, who with his brother Orville were the first men to successfully fly an airplane, celebrated Roosevelt's election by flying four laps around Huffman Prairie, the Wrights' eighty-four-acre testing grounds. Four years later, in the final year of Roosevelt's Presidency, the Wrights would begin negotiations with Roosevelt's War Department to build airplanes for the American military. The negotiations ultimately led to the signing of a contract in 1909, during the early months of the Taft Administration.

In 1898, while he was serving as President McKinley's Assistant Secretary of the Navy, Roosevelt had resigned his administrative position and joined the Army as a colonel. He then recruited his troops, mostly from the American Southwest, and formed his famous Rough Riders cavalry unit. He later led the Rough Riders in three separate battles in Cuba during the Spanish-American War. The fighting had been both intense and deadly, as nearly one-third of the Rough Riders were either wounded or died in the war, with many dying as a result of tropical diseases.

In 1905 Roosevelt was requested by both Russia and Japan to mediate an end to the savage and bitter Russo-Japanese War, which he agreed to undertake. Initially, it looked hopeless as each country was adamant that the other side should be the one to relinquish its position. Ultimately, Roosevelt was able to convince the combatants that it was in the best interests of both sides to reach an agreement. His efforts resulted in his subsequent receipt of the Nobel Peace Prize.

In 1907–1909, for the purpose of demonstrating America's growing military might, and as a warning to both the European powers and to Japan, Roosevelt sent a huge armada of American naval ships, called the Great White Fleet due to the color the ships had been painted, on a highly successful world-wide tour. Hundreds of thousands of people all around the globe came out to gape at the American Navy vessels as they visited numerous prominent ports in their circumnavigation of the globe.

Due to Roosevelt's strengthening of the American Navy, it had risen from only the fifth strongest in the world in 1901 to the second most powerful fleet in the world by the time Roosevelt left office.

Just as did Lincoln and Jefferson, Roosevelt also experienced personal tragedy, although not while he was the sitting President. In July of 1918, the youngest of his six children, Quentin, an army pilot, was shot down by German forces in the skies over France, just four months before World War I ended. Quentin had been Roosevelt's favorite child, and just like the President, he possessed boundless energy — basically in perpetual motion as a child and teenager.

On November 10, 1978, Theodore Roosevelt National Park was established near Medora, North Dakota. Today, forty-one years later, Roosevelt remains the only President to have a National Park named after him. The Park includes the area where Roosevelt maintained a ranch, and where he had lived off and on for four years in the mid-1880s following the tragic death of his young wife due to complications from the birth of their daughter, Alice. Making his wife's death all the more heartbreaking for the twenty-five-year-old future President was the fact that Roosevelt's mother had passed away on that very same day due to typhoid fever. Additionally, both deaths had occurred in the family home.

Despite all his fully justified bona fides in federal land and wildlife preservation, in 1908 Roosevelt *inexplicably* failed to protect the Hetch Hetchy Valley, which is located entirely within the confines of Yosemite National Park. The now uber-liberal city of San Francisco was seeking to build a dam in the Park and turn the beautiful valley

Chapter 3

into a lake, for later piping to Bay Area residents. Despite the pleadings and protestations of John Muir, who had spent three days camping and hiking in Yosemite with Roosevelt just five years earlier, Teddy turned a deaf ear to Muir and failed to take any action at all to permanently protect Hetch Hetchy Valley. Thus it was that in 1913 Woodrow Wilson gave final approval to the building of the dam, which resulted in the permanent loss and the flooding of the Hetch Hetchy Valley, *which Muir regarded as "every bit the equal of Yosemite Valley."* Many environmentalists and outdoor enthusiasts regard the damming of the Tuolumne River and the subsequent flooding of Hetch Hetchy as the single worst event to ever occur in a National Park!

Despite all of his interests in politics, hunting, hiking, travelling, sailing, and his six children, Roosevelt found time to be a prolific writer, penning nineteen books, one of which featured four volumes! Many of the books were hugely popular with the reading public, and two were highly acclaimed by historians: *The Naval War of 1812*, and *The Winning of the West, 1769–1807* (four volumes).

During Roosevelt's final weeks as President, the Enlarged Homestead Act of February 19, 1909, was passed into law. The measure increased the maximum number of acres of non-irrigable land that could be homesteaded to 320, although it applied only to eight Western states. The law was in response to the dry-land farming boom that had begun shortly after the turn of the century. One salutary side effect of the dry-land farming boom was the significant increase in the number of single women who applied for and received homestead acreage.

Elihu Root, a United States Senator, a Secretary of State, a Secretary of War and a Nobel Peace Prize winner, wrote this about Theodore Roosevelt in 1904: "Men say he is not safe. [Well,] he is not safe for the men who wish to prosecute selfish schemes to the public detriment… who wish government to be conducted with greater reference to campaign contributions than to the public good… who wish to draw the President of the United States into a corner and make whispered arrangements which they dare not [to] have known by their constituents."

Famed journalist William Allen White wrote these words in 1946, some 27 years after the death of Theodore Roosevelt: "I had never known such a man as he, and never shall again. He overcame me…He poured into my heart such visions, such ideals, such hopes, such a new attitude toward life and patriotism and the meaning of things, as I had never dreamed men had."

Maurice Francis Egan, a writer, English professor, diplomat and friend of Theodore Roosevelt, wrote these words in May of 1919, some four months after Roosevelt's death on January 6, 1919: "During the coal-famine [strike], to be near him, to be in his circle, was to feel that you were in the presence of a man who had the heart of Lincoln and the virtue and the common sense of Washington."

Chapter 4

Thomas Jefferson was quite likely the most knowledgeable and most gifted wordsmith of all the American Presidents. At a dinner given by President Kennedy in the early 1960s where he was honoring Nobel laureates, Kennedy called his honorees "the most extraordinary collection of talents that has ever been gathered together at the White House, with the possible exception of when Thomas Jefferson dined alone."

Jefferson, in 1774 at age thirty-one, wrote *A Summary View of the Rights of British America*. Without his knowledge or permission the book was published on both sides of the Atlantic, and was so well received (in the colonies) that it moved Jefferson to the forefront of American patriot scholarship. That literary success undoubtedly contributed greatly to Jefferson, at age thirty-three, being assigned the task of being the principal author of the American Declaration of Independence, a document that many scholars regard as perhaps the most important writing since the Magna Carta in 1215.

Although other members of the Continental Congress made roughly eighty changes to Jefferson's original draft, most of the changes were minor issues of grammar or syntax. One significant change, however, was the deletion of one of the major grievances against King George III that Jefferson had detailed in considerable depth. It dealt with the British Monarchy having established and preserved the slave trade in the American colonies for the benefit of the British economy, which Jefferson described as having caused numerous societal problems for the colonies, and which (he predicted) would continue to cause major problems long into the future. He was 100 percent right, of course. Jefferson's passages blasting King George III for maintaining the slave trade were deleted at the insistence of the representatives from South Carolina and Georgia.

When the Declaration was released to the public on July 4, 1776, all 1,337 words were printed by newspapers across the thirteen colonies (it fit perfectly on one long page). Numerous celebrations occurred throughout the colonies. As for General Washington, he ordered his officers to read the Declaration aloud to all their troops.

Later, in 1781, Jefferson wrote a book called *Notes on the State of Virginia,* which dealt in part with both the "miserable conditions of the slaves" and the evils that slavery inflicted on the slaveholders themselves. Jefferson had also drafted a law providing for the gradual elimination of slavery in the Virginia House of Burgesses prior to the period of the Revolution. Although no record of this proposed law has been found, this is most probably due to the destruction and/or loss of many written records during the periods when the British military twice invaded Central Virginia during the Revolutionary War. The records could also have been lost or misplaced prior to those invasions when the records were moved from

Chapter 4

Williamsburg to Richmond, due to the collective belief they would be more secure farther inland.

In the 1776-77 Virginia legislative session Jefferson proposed a three-tiered, publicly funded school system for Virginia, as well as an act for "true religious freedom." He also offered bills to dispose of the old English concepts of primogeniture and entail. He proposed an overhaul of the system of punishment for lawbreakers, arguing the punishments should be more in line with the degree of seriousness of the various offenses. He also argued for extending the right to vote to all residents with an intention to permanently reside in the country (state). All of his proposals eventually became law, though it was many years later for some. He also proposed ending the importation of slaves, which the Virginia Assembly agreed to in 1778.

As early as 1780, in his second year as the Governor of Virginia, Jefferson was considering the benefits of the Mississippi River and New Orleans. He wrote to the Spanish Governor of Louisiana to advise him of George Rogers Clark's presence on the Mississippi, and pointing out the mutual advantages of commerce and trade between Virginia and Louisiana.

Jefferson served as Virginia's governor for three years. On June 3, 1781, one day after his term as governor expired, British military forces invaded Virginia, causing significant damage. Jefferson had anticipated an attack and had moved the capital inland to Charlottesville. He had also requested troops from General Washington, but none were available. The Brits attempted to capture Jefferson himself at Monticello, his famous hilltop home. The thirty-eight-year-old Jefferson was able to escape on horseback into the nearby woods, which he knew intimately, and evade the British searchers. Strangely, the British troops did not damage his home, other than consuming and taking with them as much food as they could carry.

Jefferson came under much criticism due to the British attack. One state legislator called for an inquiry into Jefferson's failure to anticipate the attack. Jefferson himself also requested an inquiry into the matter. Five months later, and two months after the death of Jefferson's thirty-three-year-old wife, and one month after Washington's monumental victory at Yorktown and the capitulation of Lord Cornwallis, the inquiry was finally held. The result was entirely supportive of Jefferson. Both branches of the Virginia Legislature unanimously found in Jefferson's favor. No censure was issued.

In 1783 Jefferson called for a Constitutional Convention for the State of Virginia. Among a bevy of other ideas, Jefferson proposed a gradual emancipation for existing slaves; an absolute restriction on the importation of new slaves into the state, and a provision that all children born on and after January 1, 1801, would be absolutely free. Regrettably, Jefferson's call for a new Constitution went unheeded by most of his fellow Virginians. In 1785–86 Jefferson, together with James Madison, successfully advocated for passage of the Virginia Statute for Religious Freedom. Virginia's Religious Freedom statute was copied by five other states in the succeeding years, as well as by all the new states admitted to the Union after 1790, none of which ever provided for a specific religious establishment. Additionally, the Virginia state statute undoubtedly contributed to the later passage of the Federal First Amendment in 1791.

Jefferson wrote the Northwest Ordinance of 1784, and chaired the committee which wrote the Land Ordinance of 1785. Both of these new laws provided the rules and regulations that would control the future expansion of the country over the Appalachians and across the plains and valleys of the West. Jefferson believed that lands should be available to all persons, not just the wealthy. He also believed in the importance of multiple small states, as opposed to a handful of large, powerful states. However, one provision in Jefferson's original draft of the Ordinance was defeated by a single vote in the Confederation Congress— Jefferson's provision there would be no slavery after 1800 in the new states of the West.

However, two years later Jefferson, James Madison and James Monroe collaborated on the Northwest Ordinance of 1787, which established the various requirements for the formation and admission of new states, and which also included a specific clause restricting the expansion of slavery into any regions of the Northwest Territory. The ordinance also provided for religious freedom, the establishment of a public university, and "schools and the means of education shall forever be encouraged." Ultimately, five non-slavery states were admitted to the Union out of the original Northwest Territory: Ohio, Illinois, Indiana, Michigan and Wisconsin. Seventy-four years later in 1861 when the Civil War broke out, the five states from the former Northwest Territory combined to send more than a million men to fight for the Union Army.

Jefferson served in Congress, and then as Washington's Minister to France. He then returned to America and became Washington's Secretary of State. In June of 1790, Jefferson stepped out of his role as Secretary of State to mediate an agreement on two seemingly insoluble issues Congress was attempting to deal with. Jefferson hosted a dinner with Alexander Hamilton, Washington's Secretary of the Treasury and the most powerful Federalist politician in the country other than Washington, and with James Madison, the most powerful Democratic-Republican in Congress. The two major issues the two sides had been unable to reach agreement on were: 1.) where the new federal capital should be located, and, 2.) whether or not the federal government should "assume" the debts of the thirteen states, which had built up largely during the Revolutionary War. Thanks to Jefferson's conciliatory skills and to Hamilton's agreement to "adjust" the numbers a bit regarding Virginia's share of the collective debt, by evening's end Madison and Hamilton had agreed that the Assumption Bill would be put forward without Madison's opposition, in exchange for the location of the capital being placed astride the Potomac River in Maryland and Virginia. The deal struck by Madison and Hamilton exactly reflected Jefferson's positions on the two issues.

After serving as Secretary of State for four years Jefferson resigned, as Washington began increasingly aligning himself with Alexander Hamilton. After a three-year break from public service, Jefferson lost a narrow election for President in 1796 to John Adams, by a vote of 71-68. However, having received the second-most votes, under the rules of the time, he became the Vice-President for the next four years under Adams, even though each man was loyal to a different political party. As Vice-President, Jefferson wrote and published *Jefferson's Manual,* establishing parliamentary procedures for the U.S. Senate. The rules, with some modifications, continued in use until 1977, and are still in use in the House of Representatives (along with additional rules). In 1800 Jefferson turned the tables on Adams, defeating him for the Presidency, 73-65 (Unbelievably, Adams and Jefferson, both signatories of the Declaration of Independence, would each pass away on July 4, 1826, the fiftieth anniversary of the Declaration!) Jefferson's Democratic-Republican Party also captured the House of Representatives by a significant margin, 65-41, as well as the Senate by a narrow 17-15 tally. By 1805 Jefferson would enjoy a 27-7 advantage in the Senate.

Both Jefferson personally, and his Declaration of Independence, had been extremely popular in France, and the Declaration clearly contributed to some of the ideas behind the French Revolution of 1789. Fast forward to 1803 and Napoleon is now the Emperor of France, the French Revolution having gone savagely and tragically off track. He needs money to finance his vast plans of military conquest in both Europe and the Middle East. He realizes his plans to settle Louisiana will ultimately not come to fruition, due in significant part to the number of Americans already west of the Appalachians. He also believes that with the Americans in possession of New Orleans, as well as the rest of the Louisiana Territory, that those circumstances will combine to weaken the British — his hated rivals. Thus Napoleon offers to sell Jefferson the Louisiana Territory.

Jefferson quickly sends James Monroe to Europe to finalize the negotiations for Louisiana as Monroe and his wife had both been extremely popular with the French citizenry, as well as with governmental officials, during Monroe's three-year term as George Washington's Ambassador to France in the mid-1790s. Jefferson says to Monroe, "…on the event of this mission depends the future destinies of the republic."

Eventually, Monroe, together with then-current American Ambassador Robert Livingston, were able to negotiate a purchase price of $11,250,000, plus the assumption of French debts owed to American citizens in the amount of $3,750,000. Monroe wisely provided Napoleon with the transfer of $2,000,000 of American stock as a down payment to lessen the chance that Napoleon might have a last-minute change of heart and back out of the deal.

Once finalized, the Louisiana Purchase had cost Jefferson just over three cents an acre! This was a bit more than Jefferson had thought it would cost, but still Jefferson was beside himself with glee. The deal nearly doubled the size of the United States in one fell swoop. The "Louisiana Territory" extended north through most of the Great Plains region, and thence west to the northern crest of the Rocky Mountains. The property was 828,000 square miles, covering all or parts of fourteen current states. The transaction obtaining the Louisiana Territory remains the single largest purchase of land in all of human history! Jefferson's acquisition of the Louisiana Territory is one of the five most significant occurrences in all of American history.

Chapter 4

Famed western historian Frederick Jackson Turner wrote in 1920 that "From this event dates the rise of the United States into a position of world power." Nineteenth-century historian Henry Adams, the grandson of President John Quincy Adams, believed the Louisiana Purchase was the equivalent of the Declaration of Independence and the successful adoption of the American Constitution. Pulitzer Prize-winning historian Joseph J. Ellis wrote in 2007 that "Politically, the Louisiana Purchase was the most consequential executive decision in American history, rivaled only by Harry Truman's decision to drop the atomic bomb in 1945."

In actuality, Jefferson had been thinking about an exploration of the continent from the Mississippi River to the Pacific Coast as early as 1793, when he had engaged George Rogers Clark in a discussion about his idea. Nine years later in 1802 and now President, Jefferson again began planning an exploration of the Great Plains and the Rockies, this time with Meriwether Lewis. Just months later, in January of 1803, Jefferson acted on his idea by obtaining $2,500 from Congress to fund an expedition for the exploration of the American Continent from the Mississippi to the Pacific. This was five months *before* the purchase from Napoleon had even been consummated, and nine months before the Senate overwhelmingly approved the treaty that finalized the purchase by a vote of 24-7.

The news of the American acquisition of the Louisiana Territory was released to the single major Washington newspaper on July 4, 1803, and was met with huge excitement there, as well as in most of the rest of the country as the news spread across the nation. On the very next day, July 5, Meriwether Lewis left the capitol heading to St. Louis, but first stopping to pick up William Clark in Indiana (Clark was the younger brother of the prominent George Rogers Clark, who had been America's highest ranking military officer west of the Appalachians during the Revolutionary War). The exploration of the Northern Plains, the Northern Rockies, and the Pacific Northwest took twenty-eight months, leaving St. Louis in May, 1804, and returning in September, 1806. Amazingly, only one member of the Corps of Discovery died during the journey of exploration, and that was from peritonitis due to an infected appendix.

Lewis, who had been personally schooled by Jefferson in zoology and botany for weeks prior to the start of the journey, ended up identifying 178 new species of plants, and 122 new species or subspecies of animals. Lewis had also received training in geography, astronomy, geology and medicine from the experts at the Philadelphia Museum. The publicity about the trip, as well as the dramatic descriptions of the beauty and geography of the American West contained in the journals of both Lewis and Clark, plus the enthusiastic statements by Lewis regarding the massive potential for America in the fur trade, prompted a significant westward migration of Americans in the succeeding decades.

It also prompted John Jacob Astor, the richest man in America, to meet with Jefferson and Madison in the spring of 1808 regarding the establishment of an American fur-trading company near the mouth of the Columbia River in extreme northwest Oregon. Jefferson advised Astor that the federal government could not be involved in the fur trade, but he did provide strong encouragement

Chapter 4

to Astor to pursue his plan privately. Two years later, in 1810, during the Madison Presidency, Astor did just that. See further details on Astor's fur venture in northwest Oregon in Chapter #14, below, on James Madison.

In 1802 Jefferson established the Military Academy at West Point, New York, which during and since the Revolutionary War had been the site of a key American fort. In 1804–1805, and again in 1815, after continuing problems with the "Barbary Pirates" (which included Tripoli and its dey), two highly successful naval campaigns were led by Captain Edward Prebl (1805), and Lieutenant Stephen Decatur (1804). Additionally, there was an 1805 ground campaign led by soldier/diplomat William Eaton, which captured the Tripolitan city of Derne, with the assistance of eight U.S. Marines led by Lieutenant Presley O'Bannon, all of which caused the dey to beg for a treaty of peace.

Decatur's strategy and courage as captain of the *Intrepid* in an 1804 nighttime recapture of an American ship, the *Philadelphia*, that was moored in a Tripolitan harbor and manned by Tripolitan pirates, was so remarkable and improbable that it drew the following comment from Admiral Lord Nelson, arguably the foremost British Admiral in the long history of the British Navy, who called Decatur's retaking of the *Philadelphia* "the most bold and daring act of the age." Evidently the American Navy agreed with Nelson as Decatur was promoted to Captain even though he was only twenty-five, making him the youngest Captain in the history of the U.S. Navy.

One of the sailors that joined Decatur in his bold and dangerous recapturing of the *Philadelphia* was a young twenty-one-year-old midshipman named Thomas

Macdonough, who overwhelmed one of the pirates in hand-to-hand combat, killing the Tripolitan with his own gun. Macdonough would go down in American Naval History in an even greater way ten years later in the 1814 Battle of Lake Champlain. For all the details regarding Macdonough's historic victory in 1814, see Chapter 14 below on James Madison.

The treaty with the Tripolitan dey included the freedom of the seas for American shipping, the release of nearly 300 previously captured American sailors, plus restitution for damaged American property. The U.S. did have to pay $60,000 in ransom for previously captured seamen, per an unfortunate deal made by the American consul to Tripoli, Tobias Lear, who was unaware of the dey's extreme fear of future attacks by the American Navy, and mistakenly thought he was driving a "hard" bargain. The involvement of the Marines in the capture of Derne, Tripoli's second largest city at the time, was the first time the Corps had fought on foreign soil. Their success in the capture of Derne has been forever after memorialized in the Marine Corps hymn: "…to the shores of Tripoli…"

In 1815, during the Madison Administration, Decatur returned to the Mediterranean and defeated two Algiers gunboats, in two separate encounters, each of which lasted less than a half hour. The two battles resulted in the capture of over 500 Algiers pirates/sailors. He then negotiated a treaty in less than 48 hours that provided for freedom of the seas for American merchants, $10,000 in restitution, and the release of ten captured American sailors. In the succeeding weeks he then obtained nearly identical treaties from both Tunis and Tripoli (a previous treaty with Morocco had been obtained in 1805 by Prebl).

In Tunis the restitution was $60,000, while in Tripoli the restitution was $30,000. Significantly, in Tripoli, Decatur required the dey to release all captured sailors from all nations, not just captured Americans.

In terms of domestic policy, Jefferson cut taxes, cut the Federal budget, and paid down a substantial portion of the Federal deficit he had inherited from Adams and Washington. Jefferson trimmed $26 million dollars off the federal debt, which was more than thirty-one percent of the total debt. Jefferson also made the sale of federal lands to farmers/settlers far more accessible to the common man. He did this by reducing the minimum amount of land that could be purchased, from 640 acres to 160 acres. He also provided credit to the purchasers for up to four years, and opened three new federal land offices to speed the process along.

Jefferson also successfully lobbied Congress to repeal Adams's Judiciary Act of 1801, which had been passed during the "lame duck" final weeks of the Adams Presidency. The repeal of the Act resulted in the dissolving of the positions of numerous "midnight judges" Adams had appointed in the final days of his administration, after he was defeated in the 1800 election. The result of all the above was a massive Presidential landslide for Jefferson in 1804, winning 162 electoral votes to a mere fourteen for the Federalist candidate, C.C. Pinckney. Jefferson won eight of the ten Northern states and all seven Southern states. Pinckney captured only Connecticut and Delaware. Additionally, Jefferson's Democratic-Republicans captured huge majorities in both houses of Congress. They now enjoyed a 27-7 advantage in the Senate, along with dominating the House by a 116 to 35 margin.

In Jefferson's second inaugural address he dealt in part with the major issue of slavery. Fifty-eight years later in 1863, when Lincoln made his decision to emancipate the slaves, he referred back to Jefferson's writings regarding personally having wrestled with the issue of slavery, and even utilized some of Jefferson's actual language/comments.

In Jefferson's annual address to Congress nine months later in December of 1805, he recommended that Congress fund the building of large substantial warships, as the current fleet of smallish gunboats would be inadequate if a war with a major European power were to occur. Both Secretary of State James Madison and Secretary of the Treasury Albert Gallatin supported Jefferson's proposal, but the Democratic-Republican leaders of Congress could not be swayed. They refused the President's request! That refusal, in part, would lead to major consequences for the young American nation between 1812 and 1814.

Jefferson passionately believed in complete religious freedom, and further that the government had no legitimate concern whatsoever regarding an individual's religious beliefs. Today, more than 200 years later, Jefferson's strong stance on religious freedom remains a bedrock principle of American life and liberty.

One major problem for Jefferson was that the British Navy had been engaged in impressments of American ships and sailors for years, but the situation finally came to a head in May of 1807 when the fifty-gun British warship *Leopard* fired on the American frigate *Chesapeake* after the American captain refused to allow his ship to be boarded for an impressment search. Jefferson made the wise decision to reject the calls for war that many

Chapter 4

Americans were passionately advocating. Jefferson believed both that the young country was not militarily prepared, and that the ultimate result would be defeat at the hands of the powerful British military.

In fact, the American military was not prepared for war with the Brits, in large part due to the failure of Congress in 1805 to fund the building of large ships of war, as Jefferson had recommended. Additionally, Jefferson had cut the military budget in half based on Adams's treaty with the French in 1800, which was also partly about the impressments issue. Instead, Jefferson signed into law the Embargo Act of 1807. Although well-intended, the Embargo Act was Jefferson's biggest mistake as President. The act was a failure, hurting American merchants more than it hurt the British. It should be noted, though, that the economic loss suffered by Americans due to the Embargo Act was significantly less than what the cost of a war with England would have been, without even taking into account the cost of lives lost and physical injuries suffered.

In contradistinction to the Embargo Act, another act that Jefferson signed into law in 1807 was both enlightened and successful: The Slave Trade Act (officially, *An Act for the Abolition of the Slave Trade*), which outlawed any further importation of slaves into *any* American state or territory. The Act took effect on January 1, 1808.

Although largely successful as President, Jefferson experienced great personal tragedy in the White House as Polly, his adult daughter, who had basically served him as the First Lady (since Jefferson's wife died more than twenty years before, and Jefferson did not remarry), herself passed away from complications shortly after giving birth to the President's grandson. It was the last of many personal tragedies in Jefferson's life, as four of his and his wife's six children had perished prior to reaching the age of two years.

Just prior to Jefferson's wife passing away in 1782 at age thirty-three, while on her death bed she had begged her thirty-nine-year-old husband to promise her he would never marry again. Jefferson promised. This discussion was witnessed by multiple servants present in the bedroom. In fact, Jefferson did remain a widower for the remainder of his life, dying at age eighty-three. Although he never remarried, it appears quite likely he did have a long-term relationship with one of his slaves, Sally Hemings, who was three-quarters Caucasian and one-quarter African American. From both DNA testing (although some scientists contest the findings) and oral histories from Sally's descendants, it appears Jefferson fathered perhaps as many as six children by Sally Hemings. These children were born between 1795, when Jefferson was fifty-two, and 1808, when Jefferson was sixty-five. Sally's ages at the times of the births of her children ranged from twenty-two to thirty-five.

There is an oral history in the Hemings family that relates while Sally and others were in Paris with Jefferson from 1785 to 1789, while he was the American ambassador to France, she struck a deal with Jefferson. To wit: Since slavery was outlawed in France, Sally had the right to become totally free if she wished. This provided her with the leverage to propose to Jefferson the following arrangement: She would agree to return to Virginia with Jefferson and remain a slave in exchange for "extraordinary privileges" for herself, and freedom for any yet-to-be born children she may have. Per the oral family history, Jefferson accepted Sally's proposal and subsequently honored the agreement, freeing all of Sally's children, two in 1822 while he was still alive, and the remaining two through the provisions of his will, following his death in 1826. It should be noted he never freed any other nuclear family unit that lived at Monticello.

Jefferson's eight years as President were largely successful, and he was sufficiently popular with the citizenry that his political "coattails" extended for 16 years (!) as the next four Presidential elections were all won by members of Jefferson's Democratic-Republican party. Additionally, the four elections were won by Jefferson's two protégés, both from his home State of Virginia—James Madison and James Monroe.

In retirement, Jefferson was the primary force behind the establishment in 1817 of the University of Virginia in Charlottesville, which was just eight miles from Monticello, his hilltop home. Ironically, the new university would be built on property once owned by Jefferson's protégé, James Monroe. Jefferson also played a major role in designing the layout of the campus, as well as many of the original buildings, some of which still stand. In the 1976 Bicentennial Celebration proceedings, the American Institute of Architects recognized the design of the buildings on the University of Virginia campus as "the proudest achievement of American architecture in the past 200 years."

Pulitzer Prize-winning Historian Joseph J. Ellis has called Jefferson's first inaugural address on March 4, 1801 "one of the two or three most significant inaugural addresses in American history...and most artful and eloquent…" Ellis has further written that Jefferson's "mastery of language was unmatched by any subsequent American President, save Lincoln."

Pulitzer Prize-winning historian Gordon S. Wood wrote the following words about Thomas Jefferson in his dual biography, *Friends Divided*: "Jefferson had the most spacious and encyclopedic mind of any of his fellow Americans, including even Benjamin Franklin. He was interested in more things and knew more about more things than any other American. He amassed nearly 7,000 books and consulted them constantly; he wanted both his library and his mind to embrace virtually all of human knowledge, and he came as close to that embrace as an eighteenth-century American could. Every aspect of natural history and science fascinated him…He was an inveterate tinkerer and inventor and was constantly thinking of newer and better ways of doing things…He loved the arts…and he became quite proficient playing the violin. He loved to sing…and apparently had a fine clear voice. He was also passionate about architecture and became, according to one historian, 'America's first great native-born architect.'"

In the early 1780s after Yorktown, a French visitor, the Marquis de Chastellux, characterized Jefferson as "an American who, without having quitted his own country, is a Musician, Draftsman, Surveyor, Astronomer, Natural Philosopher, Jurist, and Statesman."

Little did the Marquis know, although he probably would not have been surprised to find out, what was yet to come from Mr. Jefferson in the decades that lay ahead.

Chapter 5

Ronald Reagan—Despite growing up in poverty in rural Illinois, moving from town to town seemingly every other year (he lived in eleven different homes prior to leaving for college at age seventeen), and despite being raised by an alcoholic father who had a hard time holding down jobs in the 1910s and 1920s, Reagan rose to become the most popular President of the Post-World War II era, now seventy-four years along as of 2019.

When Reagan became President in 1981 the country was in the midst of an economic calamity that featured double-digit inflation, double-digit interest rates and an unemployment rate above seven percent (note: by 1989 when Reagan's eight years in office ended, unemployment had fallen to 5.3 percent and inflation was down to 4.7percent). Under Jimmy Carter, America's foreign policy was a massive embarrassment, what with fifty-two Americans having been held hostage in Iran for more than a year. An attempt to rescue the hostages had been a mortifying failure, which had also cost the lives of eight American servicemen. It was a depressing, disappointing and hugely maddening continuation of the many failings of the 1960s and the first half of the 1970s. There was a real sense in the country ever since the 1960s that "American Exceptionalism" was at an end—that the United States was no longer a world power. A malaise had long since blanketed the country following the Bay of Pigs disaster in 1961, the riots and the assassinations of the mid-to-late 1960s, followed by the oftentimes violent demonstrations against the Vietnam War in the late 60s, as well as the escalation of the War along with the concomitant elevation in American casualty figures. The 1970s continued the ongoing pattern of negativity that saw American withdrawal from Vietnam, as well as the vast and seemingly never-ending Watergate scandal, which finally did end in August of 1974 with the long anticipated and long over-due resignation of President Richard Nixon.

In less than four years after taking office, Reagan had completely turned around both America's spirit and her economy. He had originally won the Presidency in 1980 by crushing the incumbent President, Jimmy Carter, 489 to 49 in the electoral college. It wasn't just Carter that he beat, his "coattails" extended to Congress, where for the first time in 25 years the Republicans were able to gain control of the United States Senate.

Four years later his victory over Walter Mondale was even more eye-popping: 525 to 13—still to this day the largest electoral vote margin in Presidential history! In the popular vote Reagan beat Mondale by nearly 17 million votes. Reagan lost only one state in 1984—Mondale's home state of Minnesota—and it was lost by less than 3,800 votes. Reagan knew he could have won all 50 states, and he had been urged by his campaign staff to go personally to Minnesota and meet and speak to the citizens there, and to run campaign ads on local television.

Chapter 5

However, Reagan refused to campaign in Minnesota, saying "Mondale is a decent and honorable man who deserves to win his home state." *It was, indeed, a rare act of class in American politics!*

As President, Reagan made four appointments to the U.S. Supreme Court—all of whom are regarded as having been outstanding justices. The appointments were Sandra Day O'Connor in 1981, the first woman ever appointed to the Supreme Court; William Rehnquist, elevated to Chief Justice in 1986; Antonin Scalia in 1986, arguably the most brilliant Justice of the last sixty years; and California's Anthony Kennedy in 1988, who retired in 2018 after a highly respected thirty years on the Court.

In 1981 Reagan also appointed the first woman to serve as America's Ambassador to the United Nations—Jeanne Kirkpatrick, a Democrat at the time, who served until 1985. In addition, Reagan appointed three women cabinet officers: Elizabeth Dole (Secretary of Transportation), Margaret Heckler (Secretary of Health & Human Services), and Ann McLaughlin (Secretary of Labor).

For nearly 200 years America's Supreme Court had been composed entirely of men! Reagan quickly put an end to that moldy tradition with his nomination of O'Connor in July of 1981, just six months into his Presidency, and one month after Justice Potter Stewart's retirement. O'Connor went on to serve until 2006, having been a highly respected, dignified, thoughtful and extremely important force for moderation on the Court. Interestingly, O'Connor and Rehnquist each attended the Stanford University Law School, with both having graduated in the Class of 1952.

In the forty-eight years immediately prior to the Reagan Presidency, twenty-six Supreme Court Justices had been nominated—all men. Franklin Roosevelt appointed nine men to the Court, followed chronologically by Harry Truman (four), Dwight Eisenhower (four), John Kennedy (two), Lyndon Johnson (two), Richard Nixon (four), and Gerald Ford (one). During the 1980 Presidential campaign Ronald Reagan had promised the American voters he would make it a priority to appoint a woman to the Supreme Court as early in his Presidency as he could. He kept his word.

During the Senate hearings on the nomination of O'Connor, she spoke the following words regarding the duty of a Judge: "...the proper role of the Judiciary is one of interpreting and applying the law, not making it." Quite obviously, the United States Senate was more than satisfied with Reagan's choice of O'Connor to replace Stewart, approving the nomination by a vote of 99-0!

There was one notable scandal during Reagan's presidency—the Iran/Contra affair. It involved guns being sold to Iran, which was trying to defend itself in a war with Saddam Hussein's Iraq. Upon receipt of the weapons, three American hostages were then freed by Iran. A portion of the money Iran paid for the guns was then funneled to the Nicaraguan Contras, who were attempting to prevent their country from being taken over by Marxist Sandinistas, who were being supported by Fidel Castro's Communist government in Cuba. Two members of the White House staff, Admiral John Poindexter and Colonel Oliver North, were originally convicted of criminal offenses as a result of their actions, however both convictions were subsequently overturned on appeal due to the

Chapter 5

trial court having improperly allowed certain evidence to be heard by the jury. The special prosecutor ultimately declined to re-try Poindexter and North based on the evidentiary rulings of the reversing Appellate Court. A third federal official, Robert MacFarlane, a national security adviser, pled guilty to four misdemeanor counts, and was sentenced to probation and a fine.

On March 30, 1981, just barely more than two months into his first year as President, having just finished a speech at a Washington hotel, and while walking out to the Presidential limousine, a mentally disturbed twenty-five-year-old man fired six rounds from a .22 revolver at Reagan and other federal employees that were with him. Reagan was shot once in the chest, the bullet missing his heart by one inch! Reagan's Press Secretary, James Brady, was shot in the head, and remained disabled for the remainder of his life. Additionally, a Washington, D.C. policeman and a Secret Service agent also received bullet wounds. The shooter, John W. Hinckley, Jr., had attempted to kill Reagan in order to impress actress Jodie Foster, the star of the movie *Taxi Driver*, which Hinckley, Jr. had seen fifteen times. Hinckley, Jr., who had described his shocking assassination attempt as the greatest love offering in history, was eventually found by a jury to be not guilty by reason of insanity. He was then committed to a mental institution in Washington, D.C., where he spent thirty-five years. He was released from the facility in 2016 and, as of 2018, was living in Virginia.

In 1983 Reagan signed a new Social Security Act into law. It was proposed and passed with the goal that the numerous corrective measures written into the new law would render the Social Security fund solvent at least until the year 2050. The 1983 Act was passed with bi-partisan support, and by significant margins. In the Senate the vote was fifty-eight to fourteen in favor of the Act, while in the House the vote was 243 to 102. The willingness of both houses of Congress to pass the Act was undoubtedly due in part to the support of both President Reagan and prominent economist Allen Greenspan, who served as the Chairman of the special Presidential Commission that studied the issue. Among those on the Commission were Republican Kansas Senator Bob Dole and Democratic New York Senator Daniel Patrick Moynihan. The 1983 Act was the last major Social Security legislation of the twentieth century.

Also in 1983, in mid-October, President Reagan ordered the invasion of the Caribbean Island nation of Grenada following the attempted takeover of the island by a violent leftist group consisting of Marxists and supported by more than 700 Cuban military personnel, as well as a relatively small number of Soviet operatives. In addition to the citizens of Grenada who were threatened by the military coup, there were nearly 1,000 American citizens present on the island as well, including over 600 medical students. The American military quickly overcame the Marxist forces, although nineteen American soldiers lost their lives. The Marxist forces suffered forty-five killed and 337 wounded, while the Cubans had twenty-five casualties, fifty-nine wounded, and 638 captured. Two Soviet operatives also were among the casualties. There were also twenty-four civilian fatalities. The American military forces were back home prior to Christmas Day, just as Reagan had promised. The Grenada government, which was a parliamentary representative democracy,

Chapter 5

was reinstated, and it has been maintained to the present day. Interestingly, the date of the American invasion is now a national holiday in Grenada: Thanksgiving Day!

Having turned the economy around in his first term, as well as having launched his Strategic Defense Initiative (SDI) in 1983, commonly referred to as Star Wars, Reagan turned to foreign affairs in his second term. From 1985 through 1988, Reagan conducted a series of five summit meetings with Mikhail Gorbachev, the Soviet Union's new leader, who was extremely concerned over SDI, knowing the Soviets could never match it for both technological and financial reasons. In late 1987 the two leaders signed the Intermediate Range Nuclear Arms Treaty, which required both countries to destroy a specific number of warheads. In May, 1988, in their final summit held in Moscow, Reagan spoke to 1,200 Russian Moscow University students in a packed auditorium. He spoke of freedom and of the positive future for both Americans and Russians. When he was finished the 1,200 students gave the American President a long and loud standing ovation.

Earlier, in the spring of 1987, Reagan had traveled to the historic Brandenburg Gate in Berlin, where he gave the famous speech that ended with these immortal words: "Mr. Gorbachev, tear down this wall!" In 1989, just nine months after Reagan left office, Mr. Gorbachev did indeed allow the tearing down of the wall, leading to the uniting of East and West Germany into a single country. Two years later, in December of 1991, after more than seventy years of violence and terror, the Soviet Union broke up, becoming fourteen separate and independent countries. As British Prime Minister Margaret Thatcher famously said in late 1991: "Ronald Reagan won the Cold War without firing a single shot."

That Reagan had political "coattails" was made clear in 1988 when Reagan's Vice President, George H.W. Bush, cruised to an impressive victory over the Democratic nominee, Massachusetts governor Michael Dukakis. Bush won forty of the fifty states, and defeated Dukakis in the popular vote by more than 7,000,000 votes.

That Reagan was hugely popular with a large share of the American public was, without question, true. When Reagan left office in January of 1989 his approval rating stood at a nearly unbelievable level: a whopping seventy percent!

As Professor and Historian James T. Patterson wrote in *To the Best of My Ability, The American Presidents* (published in 2001): "First, Reagan worked skillfully to accomplish his major goals of lower taxes, a stronger military, and the marginalization of Communism. Second, he had fixed convictions that distinguished him from many other politicians. Third, his infectious optimism made Americans feel better about themselves. He was more than (just) a 'communicator.'"

Upon Reagan's death in 2004, Gorbachev wrote "A President Who Listened," an op-ed in the *New York Times* that included the following words: "The personal rapport that emerged between us over the years helped me to appreciate Ronald Reagan's human qualities. A true leader, a man of his word and an optimist, he traveled the journey of his life with dignity and faced courageously the cruel disease that darkened his final years. He has earned a place in history and in people's hearts."

Chapter 5

Also upon Reagan's death in 2004, Colin Powell, who had served as Reagan's National Security Advisor from 1987-1989, and who had previously served from 1983-1986 as Senior Military Assistant to Reagan's Secretary of Defense, Caspar Weinberger, and then later served as George H.W. Bush's Secretary of Defense said this: "I was privileged to serve as [Reagan's] National Security Advisor, and I was proud to be a soldier during his Presidency, as he restored the morale and fighting prowess of our armed forces."

In 1984, United Nations Ambassador Jeane Kirkpatrick, a lifelong Democrat until 1985, said this: "Ronald Reagan brought to the Presidency confidence in the American experience…The Reagan administration has restored the American economy. It is restoring our military strength. It has liberated the people of Grenada from terror and tyranny. With NATO, it has installed missiles to defend the cities of Europe."

In 1988, during Reagan's eighth year as President, British Prime Minister Margaret Thatcher said this about Reagan: "Let us above all thank President Reagan for ending the West's retreat from world responsibility, for restoring the pride and leadership of the United States, and for giving the West back its confidence. He has left America stronger, prouder, greater than ever before, and we thank him for it."

Chapter 6

Ulysses S. Grant—In the year 1900, Theodore Roosevelt, then the Governor of New York, spoke these words: "Mightiest among the mighty dead loom the three great figures of Washington, Lincoln, and Grant." Roosevelt then proceeded to list Benjamin Franklin, Thomas Jefferson, Alexander Hamilton and Andrew Jackson in his second rank. This wasn't a gratuitous comment upon hearing of Grant's death, as Grant had passed away some fifteen years earlier, in 1885. A year-and-a-half later, in September of 1901, Roosevelt would become America's 26th President.

Similarly, famed nineteenth-century African-American leader Frederick Douglass, who campaigned in 1871–72 for Grant's re-election to the Presidency, later elaborated about Grant, saying, "To Grant more than any other man, the Negro owes his enfranchisement, and the Indian his humane policy…He was accessible to all men…The black soldier was welcome in his tent, and the freedmen in his house."

Historian Sean Wilentz backs up Douglass on the issue of Grant's humanity, writing the following: "The evidence clearly shows that Grant created the most auspicious record on racial equality and civil rights of any

Chapter 6

president from Lincoln to Lyndon B. Johnson." This is a 100+ year period from 1861–1865 and 1963–1969.

Further evidence of Grant's views on racial equality can be found in his employment of Ely S. Parker, a full-blooded member of the Seneca tribe. Parker served as one of General Grant's military secretaries during the Civil War, and then was appointed by President Grant as Commissioner of Indian Affairs in March of 1869, the highest appointment ever for a Native American at that point in American history.

Grant was the standout military figure in the Civil War. His brilliance as a field general and tactician was surpassed by no one. Not by Robert E. Lee, not by William Tecumseh Sherman, not by Stonewall Jackson, and not by Phil Sheridan, great generals though they all were. Military historian John Keegan wrote the following about Grant's generalship and the modernity of his methods: "[Grant was] the towering military genius of the Civil War [and] was the greatest general of the war, one who would have excelled at any time in any army."(!)

Grant's fairness, class and humanity were shown by his treatment of Robert E. Lee and his officers when Lee surrendered to Grant at Appomattox Courthouse, Virginia, on April 9, 1865. He treated the defeated South with honor and dignity. That this is true is clearly shown by the results of the 1872 Presidential election, in which Grant was seeking a second term. He won eight of the eleven states that had made up the Old Confederacy! He won 31 of 37 states overall, and won the electoral college 286 to 66, defeating the newspaper gadfly Horace Greeley, who had been nominated by the Democrats. Technically, Grant defeated Greeley 286-0, as Greeley died shortly after the popular election and before the electors met to cast their votes. Thus the Democratic electors ended up splitting their sixty-six votes four ways, with Thomas Hendricks of Illinois leading the way with forty-two votes.

Grant collected 55.6 percent of the popular vote against Greeley, which was the highest percentage of the popular vote since Andrew Jackson in 1828, who received 56 percent of the vote. Going forward in time, no President would again receive 56 percent of the vote until 1904, when Teddy Roosevelt retained the Presidency, with 57.4 percent of the vote. Grant also had long coattails in 1872, as the Republicans extended their domination of the House of Representatives from a margin of 141 to 102 in 1870 to a whopping 203 to 89 in 1872.

Grant had first won election to the White House in 1868, defeating the two-time New York Governor, Horatio Seymour, 214 to 80. Grant's election to the Presidency in 1868, at age forty-six, made him the youngest President in American history at that point in time.

The Fifteenth Amendment was ratified by the various states by February 3, 1870, with Grant's full support. The amendment prohibited the denial of the right to vote due to a man's race, color, or previous condition of servitude. Grant called it, "the most important event that has occurred, since the nation came into life." Later that year, on May 31, 1870, Grant signed into law the Force Act, which was designed to put some muscle power behind the Fifteenth Amendment. This act sought to prevent the intimidation, attacking or threatening of African Americans, so as to protect, as much as possible, their Constitutional freedom to the right to vote.

Chapter 6

Grant was also an early environmentalist, issuing an order in 1869, just months after he had assumed the Presidency, to protect the wildlife of the Pribilof Islands, which were home to hundreds of thousands of seals, which were being slaughtered in massive numbers by Russian and Japanese fishermen. The islands had just been acquired by the U.S. two years earlier in 1867, when Secretary of State William Seward arranged to purchase Alaska from Russia for $7.2 million — less than three cents an acre! Five years later, in 1872, Grant signed legislation creating Yellowstone National Park, the first "official" National Park, although it should be noted that Lincoln had protected Yosemite in 1864 and Andrew Jackson had protected the Arkansas Hot Springs in 1832.

In 1871 the Grant Administration and Great Britain signed the Treaty of Washington, which was an agreement by both countries to submit to arbitration by neutral countries the issue of Damages Caused by the Confederate Navy to American Shipping, through the utilization of ships that had been built in Great Britain during the Civil War. The issue came to be identified as the "Alabama Claims," named for the most successful of the Confederate privateers, which had captured more than sixty American ships. The international panel found in favor of the United States, and issued an award in the amount of $15.5 million as reparations for the damages caused. The amicable handling of this dispute was the beginning of a long and mostly positive relationship between the two countries, which still lasts to this day.

Following the Panic of 1873, Grant took two important steps: He vetoed a law passed by Congress that would have resulted in significant inflation and would have greatly reduced the willingness of investors to participate in the American economy. Secondly, he signed into law the Resumption of Specie Act in 1875. The new law required the Treasury Secretary to retain a sufficient supply of gold to cover all greenbacks that may be tendered after January 1, 1879. The passage of this act enhanced public confidence, especially investor confidence, in the strength of the American dollar and boosted the economy back towards prosperity.

As Frederick Douglass's quoted remarks in the second paragraph of this chapter show, Grant was a "true believer" in trying to be fair to minority ethnic groups. In 1870 he appointed the Yale-educated Ebenezer Bassett as America's ambassador to Haiti. Bassett was the first African-American ambassador in America's history. Two years later a second appointment went to James Milton Turner, to be America's ambassador to Liberia. By 1872, Douglass counted 249 black employees in one Washington, D.C. department alone. One day in 1872 Grant met with Susan B. Anthony, who was advocating for women's right to vote. Grant indicated he would not be able to get that law passed, but he wanted her to know the federal government now had over 5,000 postmistresses employed. Grant also vigorously lobbied Congress to form a Board of Indian Commissioners, composed of prominent, non-salaried persons to oversee the Indian Bureau, reduce the corruption therein, and propose much needed reforms.

During the Grant Administration there was a sharp upturn in the number of Jews the government hired. As Ron Chernow points out in his epic book, *Grant,* prominent attorney Simon Wolf estimated Grant had appointed more than fifty Jews at his request alone, including consuls, district attorneys, and deputy postmasters. Grant also advocated for Jewish rights abroad in 1869, stating "It is too late, in this age of enlightenment, to persecute anyone on account of race, color or religion." He followed up his comments with a letter of protest to the Russian Czar. Just one year later there were reports of the execution of Jews in Romania. After discussing the situation with Wolf, Grant issued a public statement: "...respect for human rights [was the] "first duty" [of any head of state, and]...the story of the sufferings of the Hebrews of Romania profoundly touches every sensibility of our nature."

The biggest issue Grant faced during his Presidency was how to physically and legally protect African Americans living in the South now that the Civil War was over. Although blacks were now free, thanks to the Fifteenth Amendment, they were still, for the most part, living in the South and very much subject to the wrath and bitterness of some of the ex-Confederate officers and soldiers, as well as non-military individuals possessed with the same measure of anger and resentment. In the area of legal protections, Grant and liberal Republicans in Congress were able to pass the Force Act of 1870 (discussed above) and the Civil Rights Act of 1875. The 1875 Act outlawed racial segregation in public accommodations, schools, transportation, and in the make-up of juries. However, eight years later the U.S. Supreme Court ruled the 1875 Act unconstitutional. Sadly, and shockingly, Congress would not pass another civil rights act until 1957!

Ku Klux Klan violence in the post-Civil War South clearly stands as the worst period of domestic terrorism in the 230-year history of the United States. Therefore, Grant dealt with it aggressively, urging Congress to expand his powers to deal with the mind-numbing horrors of the violence. Three months later, on April 20, 1871, Congress responded to Grant's request, passing the third Enforcement Act, more commonly known as the Ku Klux Klan Act. The law established criminal penalties for depriving citizens of their Fourteenth Amendment rights to hold office, sit on a jury, and cast votes. The federal government was also given the right to prosecute violators if the states refused to act effectively. The bill also gave Grant the power to suspend habeas corpus, declare martial law, and send in armed federal troops to offending areas.

Two weeks after the KKK Act was passed into law, Grant issued a statement calling the Act "a law of extraordinary public importance…" Further, Grant decried "bayonet rule," and announced that if the local courts failed to uphold the law, they would thus, "impose upon the National Government the duty of putting forth all its energies for the protection of its citizens of every race and color."

Grant meant what he said, directing his Attorney General, Amos T. Akerman, to enforce the new law. Akerman did not shy away from his responsibilities, obtaining 3,384 indictments of KKK members from federal grand juries, many of which were interracial. Although some federal judges were not sympathetic to the new law, and many of the indicted KKK members went into hiding or fled their states, still 1,143 convictions were obtained. When Akerman resigned as Attorney General in December of 1871, Grant replaced him with George H. Williams, a former United States Senator and the current Chief Justice of the Oregon Supreme Court. Williams proved every bit as energetic as Akerman had been, racking up six times as many indictments and eight times as many convictions in 1872 and 1873 as Akerman had obtained. Although it should be noted that Akerman served as A.G. for less than eight months. The campaign against the illegal activities of the KKK continued to expand for the next two years. For all the details regarding Grant's efforts to protect African-Americans and to enforce the law in the South during his Presidency, read Ron Chernow's exceedingly thorough biography, *Grant*.

On the physical side of the issue Grant repeatedly sent federal troops to states and counties where African Americans were being threatened, beaten and killed. Although some amount of violence was directed against blacks in all Southern states, the biggest problems were occurring in Louisiana, Arkansas, Mississippi and South Carolina. This was due to the number of black voters exceeding the number of white voters in those four states. Thus, the blacks, if permitted to vote, which they were now legally entitled to do, would be able to control various elective offices, from the statehouses down to the legislatures, plus many of the city halls.

In January of 1875 Grant sent troops under General Sheridan to Louisiana due to the ratcheting up of violence and threats directed against black Republicans. Grant announced his decision in the following language: "I have deplored the necessity which seemed to make it my duty under the Constitution and laws to direct such interference [of your domestic affairs, but] to the extent that Congress has conferred power upon me to prevent it, neither Ku Klux-Klans, White Leagues, nor any other association using arms and violence to execute their unlawful purposes, can be permitted in that way to govern any part of this country."

A Congressional delegation that traveled to Louisiana to gather information discovered Sheridan's investigative report of violence in Louisiana had revealed that 2,141 political murders of blacks had occurred in the state between 1866 and 1874. An additional 2,115 blacks had been wounded. Sheridan further determined that virtually all of these more than 4,200 incidents had gone unpunished. The Congressmen "solved" this problem by making a deal with Louisiana Democrats that the Republican governor would remain in office and would not be impeached, while control of the lower of the two legislative houses would revert to the Democrats.

Some specific examples of the need for federal troops in the South as the 1876 Presidential and Congressional elections were approaching include the following: In South Carolina, an estimated 150 blacks were killed in the months leading up to the elections. Governor Chamberlain requested federal assistance and Grant responded with 1,000 federal troops, which resulted in just a minimal amount of violence thereafter. In the fall of 1876 in Mississippi the fear of death was so pervasive that in Yazoo County only two black Republicans voted, while only one voted in Tallahatchie County. Grant also sent federal troops to Louisiana and Florida in advance of the 1876 election.

— Chapter 6 —

After the election, a special Senate investigative committee determined that more than sixty black Republicans had been murdered in the final weeks leading up to the election. In late January, 1877, Grant created a bipartisan commission to determine which party had won three critical Southern states, all of which had experienced massive violence in the period before election day. The committee was composed of five Supreme Court justices, five Senators and five Representatives. The group consisted of eight Republicans and seven Democrats. On February 9, the committee determined that the Republican candidate, Rutherford B. Hayes, had won Florida. One week later, on February 16, the committee found that Hayes had also won Louisiana, leaving just South Carolina. Whichever candidate won South Carolina would succeed Grant as President. Before the decision on South Carolina could be determined, a deal was struck by Hayes's operatives and the Southern Democratic leadership: Hayes would be declared the winner in South Carolina, giving him the Presidency by one electoral vote, 185-184. In return he would promise to end Reconstruction and withdraw all federal troops from the South. The final element of the deal was that Southern Democrats promised fair treatment of the black community in the future. This latter part of the bargain proved virtually non-existent, as the next seven decades would tragically and convincingly demonstrate.

Grant also launched a massive modernization project in Washington, D.C. One third of the city's streets were straightened, hundreds and hundreds of shrubs and trees were planted in public parks, many streets were paved and streetlights installed, as well as the installation of miles and miles of sidewalks, and the providing of water and gas mains and sewers. Grant also signed legislation providing for the Washington Monument to finally be completed. Strangely, it took several years for work on the Monument to resume, and it was not finished until 1888, three years after Grant passed away. Still, when it was completed it was the tallest man-made structure in the world.

In the autumn of 1875 Grant advocated on behalf of public schools, both in speeches around the country, and in his annual message to Congress in December. Grant proclaimed that "The free school is the promoter of that intelligence which is to preserve us as a free nation." Grant also advocated for a constitutional amendment that would require every state "to establish and forever maintain free public schools adequate to the education of all children...irrespective of sex, color, birthplace, or religions." This idea seems commonplace to us today, but in 1875 it was extremely far-sighted and reveals Grant's concern about America's future, as well as his belief in the salutary importance of an education for all children.

In 1884–85 in his *Personal Memoirs*, Grant wrote the following about the Civil War: "The justice of the cause which in the end prevailed, will, I doubt not, come to be acknowledged by every citizen of the land, in time... As time passes, people, even of the South, will begin to wonder how it is possible that their ancestors ever fought for or justified institutions which acknowledged the right of property in man."

Throughout much of the twentieth century a cadre of historians downgraded Grant, saying he was an alcoholic,

CHAPTER 6

a poor student at West Point, a "butcher of a general," and a corrupt President.

Let's examine those claims one by one:

#1.) Grant did turn to alcohol while stationed at a remote fort in Humboldt County, California, following his heroic performance in the Mexican War, in which Grant saw action in eleven battles and served under both General Zachary Taylor and General Winfield Scott, watching them closely and studying their battle strategies. Grant was one of only eight West Pointers from the class of 1843 to win two brevets in the War (1846–48). In Humboldt he was far away from his wife and children, who were back in Missouri. He resigned from the Army because of the situation, only re-enlisting upon the outbreak of the Civil War. However, although his binge drinking continued periodically thereafter, roughly once every three to five months, it never occurred during the planning of a military campaign or during an actual battle. In truth, he drank less frequently than many of the other Union officers engaged in the massive struggle.

#2.) At West Point there were originally eighty-two young men in Grant's 1843 class. By the end of four years it was down to thirty-nine graduates. Grant was twenty-first in his class. However, that was primarily because he simply could not learn French. If it weren't for French, he would have been in the top ten, and in fact he was second in mathematics! At one point Grant had an offer to return to West Point and teach math to the cadets, but the outbreak of the Mexican War prevented Grant from accepting the assistant professorship. Grant was also the best horseman in his class, although that didn't help his GPA. In fact, the highlight of the graduation of Grant's class came at the end of the proceedings when an eight-foot high barrier was set up at one end of the facility. The crowd watched as Grant, aboard his horse, raced toward the barrier and safely cleared it, eliciting loud and sustained cheering from the guests, as well as from Grant's fellow graduates. Grant's successful conquering of the eight-foot barrier stood as an Academy record for decades!

#3.) As for the "butcher" allegation, it is basically flat-out false. Grant occasionally did lose more men than his opposing Confederate general, but that is because attacking forces almost always lose more men than the defending forces, which are dug in and have significantly more protection than the onrushing attackers have. Additionally, if the casualties are computed on a percentage basis, Grant's troops actually suffered lower casualty rates than the Confederates in most of his battles. But the most telling statistic about the disingenuous "butcher" allegation is this: For the entire time that Grant and his troops fought in the Civil War, his units suffered 154,000 casualties, but Grant's troops inflicted 191,000 casualties on the opposing Confederate armies! Grant was also the only Union general who received the surrenders of THREE separate Confederate armies.

Chapter 6

There is, however, one major exception to the paragraph just above: The Battle of Cold Harbor in early June, 1864. After the battle was completed, Grant acknowledged that his final, major frontal assault had been a mistake on his part and that he greatly regretted his mistake. He even mentioned the mistake twenty-one years later in writing his *Memoirs*. Cold Harbor was Robert E. Lee's final victory — all that was left for Lee and his troops thereafter was to dig in and try to delay the inevitable. When Lee surrendered ten months later at Appomattox Courthouse, Grant wrote out the terms of surrender and handed them to Lee, who read them. Grant asked if the terms were satisfactory, and Lee answered: "Yes...It is more than I expected." Lee later complimented Grant for his handling of the Confederate surrender at Appomattox as "without a parallel in the history of the civilized world."

Many military historians regard Grant's victory at Vicksburg, Mississippi, as the single finest example of military tactics and strategy of any battle in the entire four years of the Civil War by any general on either side. After the war was over, in thinking back on his various campaigns, Grant said, "I could have done better in all of them, other than Vicksburg." In the Vicksburg campaign, which ended with a full Confederate surrender on July 4, 1863 (coincidentally, the same day Robert E. Lee began his retreat south from the Gettysburg battlefield), Grant had 43,000 men and lost 4,300 of them or ten percent. The Confederates were defending with a force of 60,000 men, and lost 7,200 or twelve percent! Additionally, Vicksburg marked the sixth consecutive victory for Grant and his troops over Confederate armies in Mississippi — all in a period of just over nine weeks!

The capture of Vicksburg was a major turning point for the Lincoln Administration's war effort because it gave the Union Army complete control over the Mississippi River, from the Upper Midwest down to the Gulf of Mexico, cutting the Confederacy in half. Coming as it did on the same day that Lee's forces began their southbound retreat from Gettysburg back across the Potomac River to Virginia, and following by just eight weeks the death on May 10, 1863 of the Confederates' best General, Charles "Stonewall" Jackson, by accidental "friendly fire" from his own Confederate troops, the South was thus facing a desperate situation thereafter.

#4.) There were, in fact, several scandals in Grant's second term as President, but none involved conduct by Grant himself. Additionally, Grant removed from office those members of his administration who had been involved in the improper conduct; and further, he made no efforts whatsoever to interfere with or obstruct the criminal investigations of those members of his administration who had been discharged or accused, with one exception.

It seems quite clear Grant was all too trusting of some of his cabinet officers and White House staffers, just as he was far too trusting of Wall Street wheeler-dealers in both his post- and pre-Presidency years. In May of 1884 Grant and his family were scammed out of virtually all of their savings by a young, smooth-talking, Wall Street operative. Grant suffered the major loss of his entire nest-egg as a result of his misplaced trust. That Grant was a very trusting person is actually not surprising at all. Grant's

Chapter 6

mother, Hannah Simpson Grant, was a fervent believer in the importance of trusting people, and taught all of her children to be trustworthy and to trust others.

The one exception mentioned above involved Orville Babcock, who had been on Grant's staff, both during and after the Civil War. In fact, it was Babcock who had delivered a written message from Grant to Lee at Appomattox Courthouse. Babcock was a West Point graduate who had finished third in his class. He was also a skilled engineer who had fought in both the Wilderness battle and at Petersburg. Grant and his family had grown quite fond of Babcock, a personable, thirty-nine-year-old Vermonter.

Unfortunately, Babcock, by 1875 a general, was not a person of integrity, as Grant had always believed, and as he continued to believe for a period of time thereafter. Babcock was, in fact, deeply involved in what became known as the "Whiskey Ring." In December of 1875 Babcock was indicted on fraud and conspiracy charges. Grant gave a five-hour deposition in which he expressed his confidence in Babcock's integrity and advised that Babcock had provided him with explanations regarding the various items of documentary evidence that seemed to suggest Babcock was involved in the Whiskey Ring. The jury did not witness Grant's testimony, but they did have the deposition in written form in the jury room. The jury ended up acquitting Babcock since, in the modern parlance, there was no "smoking gun."

Shortly thereafter, to his everlasting regret, Grant came to realize that Babcock was, in fact, not an honest man. This was based on the revealing of evidence to Grant that Babcock had been involved with two Wall Street swindlers in the 1869 stock market crash, which revolved around gold speculation. Grant was among the many investors who lost large sums of money in that scam. Grant, now mortified at his gullibility in having accepted Babcock's explanations, demoted Babcock to the non-White-House position of superintending public buildings in Washington, D.C. One year thereafter, Grant again demoted Babcock, assigning him the job of Inspector for the Fifth Lighthouse District, which was in Florida. Seven years later Babcock drowned while inspecting a lighthouse at Florida's Mosquito Inlet. He was forty-eight years old.

It was Grant's abject poverty following the May, 1884, stock market swindle he and his family members suffered through that led to his decision to write his autobiography, having previously refused multiple proposals for him to do so. He decided to write his memoirs because he absolutely wanted his wife to be able to live out her remaining years in reasonable financial comfort. His plan worked far beyond his wildest expectations. His autobiography was a runaway-freight-train of a success, selling in excess of 350,000 two-volume sets! Grant's wife of thirty-seven years, Julia, received a $200,000 check from Mark Twain, Grant's publisher and close friend, some seven months after Grant's death. Ultimately, the eventual total Julia received was $450,000, which was, as Ron Chernow has written, "an astonishing sum for book royalties at the time."

Grant wrote his *Personal Memoirs* in the final year of his life, battling the ever-increasing pain of throat and tongue cancer during the last four to five months of writing. He finished the memoirs literally seven days before his death. Grant's *Personal Memoirs* are regarded by many current historians as the best Presidential autobiography ever written. Grant puts his readers right on the battlefield, letting the readers know exactly what Grant was thinking at certain points, and vividly and objectively describing the actions taken, and the results obtained — pro or con.

Having read Grant's *Personal Memoirs*, I can attest to the quiet modesty he displays about his own role in his many successes. He virtually always credits his brigade and regimental commanders, together with the rank-and-file soldiers, for the successes that were achieved while typically minimizing his own significant strategic and tactical contributions to the many victories obtained. In his *Memoirs* Grant asserted that slavery was the cause of the Civil War and that he believed that cause to be: "... one of the worst for which a people ever fought, and one for which there was the least excuse."

Grant's funeral services were held in New York City. An estimated 1.5 million citizens, the largest gathering ever in the history of the city, swarmed into downtown Manhattan to be present as one of the men who, along with Abraham Lincoln, was most responsible for having saved the Union, was laid to rest.

On July 22, 1865, Grant, as the Commanding General of the United States Army, had submitted his summary report on the Union's Civil War victory to Edwin Stanton, the Secretary of War. Grant concluded the report with these words: "It has been my fortune to see [our] armies of both the West and the East fight battles...All that it was possible for men to do in battle, they have done... All have a proud record, [with] all sections...having done their full share in restoring the supremacy of law over every foot of territory belonging to the United States. Let them hope for perpetual peace and harmony…"

Late in Grant's Presidency, a delegation of Choctaws, Chickasaws, Cherokees, and Creeks met with Grant at the White House and conveyed to him the following message: "On the eve of your retirement from Office, we desire to express our appreciation of the course you have pursued towards our people while President…At all times just and humane, you have not failed to manifest an earnest wish for their advancement in the arts and pursuits of civilized life, a conscientious regard for their rights and the full purpose to enforce in their behalf, the obligations of the United States."

American poet, essayist and journalist Walt Whitman, who was a contemporary of Ulysses S. Grant, had this to say about America's 18th President: "…nothing heroic as the authorities put it—and yet, the greatest hero. The gods, the destinies, seem to have concentrated upon him." Interestingly, Whitman's personal ranking of the four greatest Americans was the following: George Washington, Abraham Lincoln, Ulysses S. Grant and Ralph Waldo Emerson.

Jewish leader and attorney, Simon Wolf, wrote the following statement during the Wilson Administration (1913-1921): "President Grant did more on behalf of American citizens of Jewish faith at home and abroad than all the Presidents of the United States prior thereto, or since."(!)

Hamilton Fish, who served as Grant's Secretary of State from 1869 to 1877 said that Grant was "…the most scrupulously truthful man he had ever known."

Chapter 6

Union General William Tecumseh Sherman said this about Grant: "...he knows, he divines, when the supreme hour has come in a campaign of battle, and always boldly seizes it...Grant is the greatest soldier of our time, if not all time."

In a separate speech about Grant in May of 1877, Sherman said this: "If the name of Washington is allied with the birth of our country, [then] that of Grant is forever identified with its preservation."

Confederate General James Longstreet, upon hearing of Grant's death said that, "[Grant] was the truest as well as the bravest man that ever lived."

One final testimonial about Grant from a contemporary, circa 1868, from General Robert E. Lee: "I have carefully searched the military records of both ancient and modern history, and have never found Grant's superior as a general."

Now for a testimonial from a twentieth-century President, Bill Clinton: "As Americans continue the struggle to defend justice and equality in our tumultuous and divisive era, we need to know what Grant did when our country's very existence hung in the balance. If we still believe in forming a more perfect union, his steady and courageous example is more valuable than ever."

In April of 2019 a statue of Ulysses S. Grant was unveiled on the Central Plain at West Point. Elizabeth D. Samet, a Professor of English at West Point, wrote the following regarding the honor being accorded to Grant: "When those archaeologists millennia hence wonder what we meant when we put Ulysses S. Grant up on a pedestal, I hope they can hear us say so clearly that there can be no mistaking it: 'This man led an army that emancipated four million people, and in so doing, saved a nation!'"

In my judgment, Grant has been the most severely underrated of all the Presidents. However, I believe he will be moving up significantly and steadily in the years to come, as an ever increasing number of historians become more aware of the information and facts contained in three recent biographies (2012–2017) on Grant's military and Presidential careers. The authors of the three new biographies are Ronald White, Ron Chernow, and H.W. Brands.

Note: In addition to reading Grant's *Personal Memoirs*, I also read both the White and the Chernow biographies, and I highly recommend each of them to anyone wishing to read about the fascinating life and accomplishments of Ulysses S. Grant. Despite being very lengthy books (659 pages for White's, and 959 pages for Chernow's), they are each surprisingly fast reads, and fully loaded with facts and details.

Chapter 7

Harry S. Truman has been, in the past, largely overlooked in terms of being an outstanding and important President, almost certainly because he grew up on a farm in Missouri and didn't have a college degree. For instance, in a 1962 survey, nine years after Truman left office, he was ranked only ninth out of thirty-one Presidents. Just above Truman in those 1962 rankings was James K. Polk, who is ranked eleventh in my 2019 rankings, and just below him was John Adams, whom I have ranked sixteenth. More recently however, many people besides myself are coming to new and more praiseworthy conclusions.

Truman, at age thirty-three while running the family farm, volunteered for service in World War I. He was accepted by the Army only because they were unaware Truman had passed the "eye test" only by memorizing the chart! In France, Truman served as an artillery officer from August of 1917 to May of 1919, rising from lieutenant to major. He and his unit, the 129th Field Artillery, saw heavy action in several battles in 1918. After the War, Truman attended the Kansas City Law School for two years but did not finish due both to family financial concerns and the offer of a good administrative position with his hometown county.

Although it is certainly true that Truman got his start in politics with the assistance of the Kansas City "Pendergast Machine," once he was in office he performed his job with integrity. He was an "every man" who communicated honestly and well with the voters, eventually being elected to the United States Senate in 1934 in an upset victory, and then reelected in 1940. Truman gained national prominence in 1944 when he chaired the Senate's Special Committee to Investigate the National Defense Program. The committee's investigation revealed that from 1941 to 1944 an estimated $15 billion of spending had been wasted by the military-industrial complex. Later as President, however, Truman came to realize that much of the funding his committee had categorized as wasted was in actuality being valuably and appropriately spent on the ultra-secret Manhattan Project's development of the atom bomb.

Truman had been selected by Franklin Roosevelt in 1944 to be his new Vice President, due in large part to both his healthy status and his prior combat experience in World War I. Truman quickly ascended to the Presidency following the death of Roosevelt in April of 1945, less than three months into Roosevelt's fourth term in office.

While attending the "Big Three" Potsdam Conference on July 26, 1945, Truman advised Japan that the United States had a new weapon that could destroy an entire city, and that it would be utilized unless they surrendered. Japan did not respond at all to Truman's message. So it was that Truman authorized the first bomb for Hiroshima, which was the site of a Japanese Army base, at which an

Chapter 7

estimated 25,000 troops were stationed. The Hiroshima base was also a point of embarkation for Japanese troops being sent out into the Pacific. Following the August 6, 1945, bombing of Hiroshima, Truman again demanded that Japan surrender or else a second bomb would be dropped. In addition to his surrender demand to the Japanese government, Truman also ordered the dropping of thousands and thousands of pamphlets explaining to the Japanese citizens why the first bomb was dropped, and why another bomb would be dropped if Japan again failed to surrender. The Japanese government once again ignored Truman's warning. Thus, Nagasaki was then bombed. Five days after the Nagasaki bombing, on August 14, 1945, Japanese Emperor Hirohito announced Japan's surrender. Had they not made that decision, a third atom bomb was fully ready and due to be shipped to the American forces in the Western Pacific on that very day. Japan's official surrender documents were signed on September 2, 1945, on the deck of the American battleship, *USS Missouri*.

Estimates of the death tolls at Hiroshima and Nagasaki range widely. There were clearly more deaths in Hiroshima than Nagasaki due to the nature of Hiroshima's relatively flat delta geography, whereas Nagasaki is located in a valley. A 1946 estimate for Hiroshima was 66,000 dead and 69,000 wounded. An estimate from a 1998 study came in at 202,000 dead. As to Nagasaki, the estimates ranged from 39,000 to 80,000 dead and tens of thousands injured.

When discussing the dropping of the atom bombs one must of course consider the alternative that was used prior to August 6, 1945. Here are some figures from World War II conventional bombings, all of which occurred during the Presidency of Franklin Roosevelt: On the night of March 9–10, 1945, the fire-bombing of Tokyo occurred. American bombers dropped 1,665 tons of incendiaries on a sixteen-square-mile area of the city. The generally accepted estimate for the number of deaths is 100,000. However, other estimates put it as high as 130,000. An estimated one million Japanese citizens were also left homeless as more than 267,000 buildings had been destroyed in the bombing. Of the 282 American B-29's that made it to Tokyo that night, twenty-seven were lost prior to delivering their payloads.

In the last week of June, 1943, the Allies, in Operation Gomorrah, delivered the heaviest aerial assault in history against the city of Hamburg, Germany. Those bombings left 42,600 civilians dead, with another 37,000 wounded. Also, in February of 1945, utilizing 722 bombers, the combined air forces of America and Great Britain dropped 3,900 tons of explosives and incendiaries on the German city of Dresden. The estimates of the deaths in the Dresden firebombing range from 22,600 to 25,000.

It has been estimated by military historians that if the American military had to defeat the forces of Japan by "island hopping," that is, by invading island after island after island, rather than by using the atom bombs, it would likely have taken two additional years of fighting. The estimated casualty figures for the "island hopping" option were 300,000 to 400,000 American military personnel, and 1,000,000 or more Japanese—mostly civilians. It is especially noteworthy that since Truman made the toughest of all decisions, a decision that ended World War II and quite likely saved well over a million lives, no other armed conflict even remotely as serious as WWII has occurred in the intervening seventy-four years.

Truman also made a number of major decisions in the post-World War II period. At the 1945 San Francisco Conference Truman led the United States in helping to create the United Nations and the U.N. Charter. The first U.N. meeting was held in London in October of 1946. In 1947 the Marshall Plan for the rebuilding of Western Europe was launched. It was an important and substantial success as the economies of the affected countries were able to rapidly regain their footings, and within three years reached levels that exceeded their pre-war high points. Also established in 1947 were the following: The Air Force became a separate branch of the military, the CIA was created, and the National Security Council came into being. Another major 1947 development was Truman's announcement of the Truman Doctrine, which provided that the United States would assist nations threatened by Soviet aggression.

On May 14, 1948, Truman officially recognized the newly created nation of Israel, literally just minutes after they became a country. Truman made his decision on Israel's nascent nationhood despite serious opposition from some cabinet members and other prominent Americans, including many Democrats. Also in 1948, on July 26, Truman issued an order fully integrating the U.S. military forces. In 1949 Truman hosted the signing ceremony of the treaty which established NATO. He also signed the Housing Act of 1949, which included urban renewal, an increase in the minimum wage, and the extension of Social Security coverage.

In 1951 the Twenty-Second Amendment to the Constitution was ratified by more than three-quarters of the states and thus became law. The Amendment had initially been passed by Congress in March of 1947, less than two years after Franklin Roosevelt's death. The Amendment limited all future Presidents to a maximum of two terms. This Amendment was clearly the direct result of wide dissatisfaction across much of America with Franklin Roosevelt having sought and served a third term in 1940, and then a fourth term in 1944. Prior to Roosevelt no American President had ever served more than two terms in office.

In 1948 Truman sought to win the Presidency on his own. His Republican opponent was the second-term Governor of New York, Thomas Dewey. The race was believed to be exceedingly close, with multiple polling firms predicting a significant Dewey victory. One prominent newspaper, the *Chicago Daily Tribune*, was so convinced that Truman would lose, they published their paper for Wednesday, November 3, 1948, before the final results were known. To make matters worse for the newspaper, they utilized a huge, bold headline across the top of the front page: DEWEY DEFEATS TRUMAN. In fact, Truman won, and he won fairly convincingly. The final results showed Truman topping Dewey in the popular vote, 24.1 million votes to 22.0 million. Truman had an even larger margin of victory in the electoral vote: 303 to 189. Truman also won twenty-eight states while Dewey captured just sixteen. The remaining four states, all in the Deep South, went for South Carolina Senator Strom Thurmond, who had been nominated by the States' Rights party.

Chapter 7

On November 1, 1950, two Puerto Rican nationalists attempted to assassinate Truman at his temporary residence, the Blair House, located not far from the White House. There was a gun battle between the two assassins and multiple Presidential guards, with one assassin and one guard being shot to death, while the other assassin and two guards were injured in the gunfire. Truman, luckily, was upstairs when the shooting broke out on the first floor of the residence. The surviving assassin was tried, convicted, and sentenced to death in 1951. Just months later, President Truman commuted the assassin's sentence to life in prison. However, twenty-eight years later, in 1979, President Jimmy Carter commuted the remainder of the assassin's sentence and he was released from Federal Prison!

President Truman made four appointments to the United States Supreme Court. The longest serving of the four was Associate Justice Thomas C. Clark, who served eighteen years on the Court. Although Truman regarded his appointment of Clark as his biggest mistake, Clark was well regarded among most members of the Bar. He wrote two prominent opinions that were taught to law students back in the mid-1970s (when I was in law school). The first was *Mapp v. Ohio*, a famous case that expanded the protections of individuals from unlawful search and seizures by law enforcement. The second case was *School District of Abington v. Schempp*, which banned prayer in public schools. Clark ultimately resigned from the Court in 1967 when his son, Ramsey Clark, was appointed by President Lyndon Johnson to be his new Attorney General. Clark's resignation from the Court was the correct ethical step for him to take, as it would have created the appearance of a conflict of interest had he remained on the Bench.

On January 31, 1950, President Truman announced his authorization for the Atomic Agency Commission to continue to develop atomic weaponry, including the hydrogen bomb. It was believed by the governments of the U.S., Canada and Great Britain that the Soviet Union was in the process of developing a hydrogen bomb of their own. Thus, Truman felt his authorization to develop the weapon was necessary in order for the country to be able to defend itself against all possible aggressors. In October of 1952 the United States conducted its first test of the Hydrogen bomb, in the area of the Marshall Islands. Not unexpectedly, the Soviets tested their first hydrogen bomb just one year later.

The Korean War (1950–1953) certainly did not progress as Truman had hoped, and eventually, on April 11, 1951, he had to relieve General Douglas MacArthur of command due to MacArthur's refusal to follow orders, thus defying the longstanding principle that it is the civilian President who has the final say over generals and admirals, even in matters of war. The principle of Presidential authority over generals and admirals dates back to December of 1783 when George Washington surrendered his sword to the Continental Congress immediately prior to heading home to Mount Vernon.

The stalemate in Korea also ate into Truman's standing with the American public, as his approval rating at the end of 1952 had fallen to a mere thirty-one percent. However, even with all the problems, a stalemate was infinitely better than the North Koreans, backed by the Red Chinese, taking over the entire Korean peninsula — as

Chapter 7

all current Americans who follow the news most certainly fully realize in 2020.

Four-Star General and Secretary of State, as well as Secretary of War, George Marshall, said this about his boss, President Truman: "There never has been a decision made under this man's administration…that has not been made in the best interest of his country. It is not only the courage of these decisions that will live on, but the integrity of them!"

In 1972, upon the death of Mr. Truman, the Republican President, Richard M. Nixon, said this about Truman's legacy: "When the death of President Franklin Delano Roosevelt thrust him suddenly into the Presidency in April of 1945, at one of the most critical moments of our history, he met that moment with courage and vision. His farsighted leadership in the postwar era has helped ever since to preserve peace and freedom in the world."

In 1952, as Truman neared the end of his Presidency, Minnesota Senator Hubert Humphrey offered the following praise: "President Truman is beloved by the American people because of his candor, honesty, frankness, and principle. He received the support of the American people [due to] the bold principles of the New Deal and the Fair Deal."

Also, most probative and most worthy of great consideration and reflection is the January, 1950, statement that Winston Churchill made to Truman at a meeting in Washington, D.C., saying, "I must confess, sir, I held you in very low regard then [1945]. I loathed your taking the place of Franklin Roosevelt. But, I misjudged you badly. Since then, you, more than any other man, have saved Western Civilization!"

Chapter 8

James Monroe was the fifth and last of the "Founding Father" Presidents, serving from 1817 to 1825. When he assumed the Presidency in 1817, Monroe probably had a greater and more varied experience in government service than any other President, before or since.

Monroe spent five years at the Campbelltown Academy in Virginia, from age eleven to age sixteen. One of his classmates at Campbelltown was the future Supreme Court Chief Justice, John Marshall. At age sixteen Monroe entered the College of William & Mary in Williamsburg, Virginia, spending nearly two years there before leaving in the spring of 1776, having just turned eighteen, to fight in the Continental Army. Later that year, still at the age of eighteen, and while serving under General Washington, Monroe was seriously injured in the crucial 1776 day-after-Christmas Battle of Trenton. There was great concern among Washington's staff, fearing Monroe's wound would prove to be fatal. Monroe, however, who was a big and physically strong young man, was able to recover in large part due to the assistance of a volunteer physician who lived in Trenton and who had just joined Washington's staff the day before. Monroe made a full recovery and was promoted to Captain by

Chapter 8

General Washington for his heroism during the battle, which had occurred prior to his injury.

Monroe and William Washington, the General's cousin, had been in the first group of fifty-two Americans to cross the Delaware River, and had captured two Hessian cannons. Monroe had been shot in the upper left chest, near his shoulder, as the Hessians were attempting to recapture the vitally important cannons. They failed to do so. The victory at Trenton was absolutely critical to the later success of the Revolution (see Chapter 2 for the reasons why the Trenton battle was of the utmost importance).

Besides Trenton, Monroe also saw action in 1776-77 in the following battles: Harlem Heights, Brandywine, and the come-from-behind victory at Monmouth, in addition to a nighttime skirmish with the enemy at White Plains, in which Monroe's unit captured thirty-six Brits and killed twenty, all without suffering a single casualty themselves! In the Battle of Brandywine, Monroe was with the Marquis de Lafayette when the Frenchman was injured. Monroe assisted Lafayette with his injury as the Americans withdrew from the action. Monroe's assistance that day turned out to be the start of a life-long friendship between the two men.

Monroe additionally spent the infamous winter of 1777-78 with Washington's army at Valley Forge, Pennsylvania. The winter encampment at Valley Forge was infamous not because it was unusually cold. It was actually a relatively mild winter, weather-wise. The infamy was due to the egregious suffering of the troops thanks to severe shortages of food, clothing and blankets, plus the presence of infectious diseases. It is estimated that 2,000 soldiers did not survive the Valley Forge winter due to those factors. Washington had ordered the soldiers to chop down trees and build small log huts. As it turned out, Captain Monroe's hut, which was just 16' by 14' by 6' high, which was the size that Washington had ordered, contained an old friend from his schoolboy days back in Virginia's Orange County—Lieutenant John Marshall, who was three years older than Monroe. Marshall would end up being one of the most prominent Supreme Court Judges in American history. After one more year of military service, Monroe resigned his commission in December of 1778. General Washington wrote the following description of Monroe's service in his army: "...He has in every instance maintained the reputation of a brave, active and sensible officer."

In January of 1780 Monroe starting "reading the law" for two years under Thomas Jefferson's tutelage, and was later admitted to the Virginia bar in 1782. Also in 1780, Governor Jefferson appointed Monroe to the position of Colonel in the Virginia State Militia, as the British Army had just recently captured the Georgia cities of Savannah and Augusta, and then had taken Charleston, South Carolina.

Monroe was elected to Virginia's state assembly in April of 1782, as was Marshall, and the two war heroes were both immediately assigned to the state assembly's executive committee, which made all the decisions. The next year saw Monroe being elected to the Confederation Congress of 1783, whose meetings were held in New York City. It was during this session of Congress that Monroe met and married his wife, the former Elizabeth Kortright.

In 1786, during the final months of the Confederation Congress, Monroe, with the assistance of South Carolina's

Chapter 8

Charles Pinckney and Monroe's cousin, William Grayson, were successful in blocking a proposed treaty with Spain that was being endorsed by John Jay. Jay's treaty would have denied western and southern Americans access to the Mississippi River for the shipment of their products for the eye-popping period of thirty years. In return, Americans would receive certain trade concessions in any commerce they might have with Spain. Jay, who was born into a wealthy merchant family in New York, was proposing the treaty on behalf of Northern merchants. Citizens in the Southern and Western areas, however, were incensed by what they viewed as a one-sided and unfair proposal. When Monroe was able to block Jay's proposed treaty, he became one of the most admired politicians in the eyes of the Western and Southern farmers, craftsmen and tradesmen.

In 1788 Monroe purchased 800 acres of land and a house in Charlottesville, Virginia. Nearly three decades later this property would become the location of the embryonic University of Virginia, which had been long advocated for by Thomas Jefferson.

In 1790 Monroe was elected to the new United States Senate, serving until 1794, when President Washington appointed him Minister to France. Monroe, who spoke nearly perfect French, and his tall, beautiful wife, Elizabeth, were both extremely popular in France. So much so that Elizabeth was able to arrange the release of the Marquis de Lafayette's wife from prison during the dark days of the French Revolution, and then make further arrangements for her to safely flee the country. Although the French loved the Monroes, Washington, who at this point in his Presidency was fully in the Hamilton/Federalist camp, came to believe Monroe was too much of a Francophile, and recalled him from France in 1797.

Monroe sailed home and moved on with his political career. At James Madison's urging, Monroe ran for Governor of Virginia, handily defeating the Federalist candidate. Although Washington had not found favor with Monroe's services in France, the vast majority of Virginians approved of the way Monroe had conducted himself in Paris. He served three terms as Governor from 1799 to 1802, during which time he established Virginia's first state-supported public schools.

In 1803 Monroe was assigned by President Jefferson to complete the critical negotiations with Napoleon regarding the Louisiana Purchase, which Jefferson later called "an empire for liberty." See Chapter 4 regarding all the details of how the Louisiana Purchase became a *fait accompli*. Jefferson next named Monroe America's minister to Great Britain. In 1806 a British officer, accompanied by his troops, had seized Buenos Aires. In a precursor of things to come, Monroe strongly advised the British Foreign Minister that "nothing be attempted without a concert with the United States." The British diplomat privately agreed with Monroe, and the British forces in South America were eventually withdrawn.

Monroe returned to Virginia in 1807 and then ran for President in 1808, but lost the Democratic-Republican Party Presidential nomination to friend and fellow Virginian James Madison. After two tense years between Madison and Monroe, they resumed their friendship at the urging of Jefferson, and with his mediation of their differences. In 1811 Monroe was elected to a fourth term as the Governor of Virginia. However, three months later

Chapter 8

he resigned the governorship after Madison appointed Monroe his new Secretary of State.

In August of 1814, Madison dismissed John Armstrong, his highly incompetent (some would say treasonous) Secretary of War and replaced him with Monroe. In the spring of 1814 Madison had warned Armstrong that preparations for the defense against a British attack on Washington City needed to be initiated immediately, as the British fleet was in Chesapeake Bay. However, Armstrong had ignored Madison's warning, claiming that, if anything, the Brits would attack Fort McHenry, not Washington.

Now doing double duty, Monroe, along with fifty cavalry soldiers, engaged in a seven-day scouting mission on horseback of the various British units' advance positions outside of Washington. During this timeframe Monroe ordered several American units to take more advantageous defensive positions. So hectic was this seven-day period that Monroe never changed his clothes even once, and slept and ate very little. As the Brits moved dangerously closer to the capitol, Monroe raced back to the President's House to initiate the immediate abandonment of the structure, as well as other nearby federal buildings.

Although Madison's staff, along with significant assistance from the President's prominent wife, Dolly, were able to safely remove important documents, as well as some of the famous paintings and statuary which adorned the President's House, much was left behind, including the nation's library — which contained over 3,000 books. The British burned the President's House (which was only 14 years old, John Adams having been its first occupant), as well as all other nearby federal buildings, except for the Patent Office, but including the Capitol. They also burned some privately owned structures. The federal government later replaced their lost library by purchasing the personal library of Thomas Jefferson, who was deep in debt and sorely in need of cash. Jefferson's personal library contained approximately 6,700 books.

However, the British plans for further advancement and destruction in the Washington City environs were quite literally washed away. A powerful hurricane/storm came roaring ashore, providentially striking the Washington area, and forcing a British retreat for the safety of their fleet. The storm also extinguished the various fires, albeit also causing much damage to many private residences. After the hurricane, Monroe immediately began preparing for the defense of Baltimore and Fort McHenry, although thankfully there was not a huge amount of work left to be done as General Samuel Smith had been long preparing for a British attack. See Chapter 14 for more details regarding Smith, Baltimore, Fort McHenry, and the *Star Spangled Banner*.

Both as Secretary of War in the Madison Administration and later on as President, Monroe worked diligently to strengthen America's military and naval powers. One example would be that as early as September 5, 1814, Monroe wrote General Andrew Jackson, warning him about the likelihood of a British attack on New Orleans. Monroe also sent 10,000 troops to New Orleans, all of which arrived prior to Jackson's own arrival on December 1, 1814. See Chapter 9 for more details regarding Jackson and the Battle of New Orleans.

With the support of both Jefferson and Madison, Monroe swept to an easy but still impressive victory in

Chapter 8

the 1816 Presidential race, blasting Rufus King of New York, who turned out to be the final Presidential candidate of the crumbling Federalist Party. Monroe won the electoral vote 183 to 34, and the popular vote by better than a two-to-one ratio: 74,000+ to 36,000+. When Monroe became President in March of 1817, he and his wife literally became the first Presidential couple to live in the "White House." This was due to the necessity of rebuilding the "Presidential House" following its burning by the British in August of 1814. After the new residence was completed it was painted a very bright shade of white, and quickly picked up the new but unofficial moniker of the "White House."

Monroe's first act was to put together an all-star cabinet in the spring of 1817. He made John Quincy Adams, arguably America's most accomplished diplomat of the era, his new Secretary of State. He selected John C. Calhoun as Secretary of War (Calhoun would later become Vice President under Adams from 1825-1829, and then continue on as the V.P. until 1833, serving under Andrew Jackson). Finally, he appointed William Crawford to be his Secretary of the Treasury. This was quite a magnanimous gesture by Monroe to appoint Crawford, as Crawford had finished as the runner-up to Monroe in the Democratic-Republican Presidential nomination caucusing.

Some observers at the time of the appointments believed that Monroe's choice of Adams for the State Department was a mistake. However, Thomas Jefferson believed they would make an excellent team, writing: "Adams has a pointed pen, [but] Monroe has judgment enough for both, and [the] firmness to have *his* judgment control." Jefferson was proven over the next eight years to have been absolutely correct in his analysis.

Monroe made two long tours of the nation, one in the summer of 1817 and one in the late spring/early summer of 1819. He traveled to all of the states during the course of the two tours, and was greeted by tens of thousands of cheering citizens in all regions of the country. Amazingly, during the 1817 tour, while in Vermont, Monroe recognized Maria Suhn Wheelock, who was the recently widowed wife of John Wheelock, the President of Dartmouth College. Monroe, however, knew her from forty-one years earlier when she had assisted Dr. Ryker, the volunteer physician, in dressing Monroe's wound following his injury during the Battle of Trenton, when Monroe was a young man still two months short of his nineteenth birthday!

With the collapse of the Federalist Party and the tremendous success of Monroe's national tours, as well as the other political successes that had been achieved, the country entered the "Era of Good Feelings," which resulted in literally no opposition whatsoever to Monroe's reelection in 1820. Many of the ex-Federalists actually supported Monroe's moderate hand on the tiller of the ship of state. They also liked Monroe personally — his tact, his courtesy, his sincerity and his accessibility. As Professor Harry Ammon, the author of the seminal book on Monroe, has pointed out, Monroe was highly successful in gaining Congressional approval for his policies. Thus it was that the electoral vote in 1820 was nearly unanimous, 231 to 1(!). New Hampshire governor William Plumer had cast his vote for Secretary of State John Quincy Adams (much to Adams's displeasure), in part because he wanted Washington to remain as the only President ever to be unanimously elected.

In 1817 Monroe proposed that if the Indians were to be moved westward, or induced to abandon their nomadic habits, they should each be given a plot of land in fee simple. However, Monroe's ideas on the Native American issue were far too advanced for most people that early in the nineteenth century, and the Senate refused to go along with his proposal. In May of 1819, the Senate did approve Monroe's proposal on improving Indian education by providing the President with $10,000 per year to supplement the preexisting educational programs already in place. Two years later, in his 1821 inaugural address, Monroe revisited the Native American issue with a vigorous proposal for a comprehensive program to bring the Indians into the American mainstream.

In 1824 the State of Georgia was adamant in attempting to leverage the federal government into forcibly moving the Cherokees out of Georgia. However, Monroe did not agree, sending a special message to the Senate, stating that the Agreement of 1802 required that the movement of Indians must be accomplished peacefully, saying: "Any attempt to remove them by force would, in my opinion, be unjust." On January 27, 1825, in the closing weeks of his Presidency, Monroe made his final proposal regarding the "land" conflict between Whites and Native Americans. Monroe proposed the adoption of a systematic and *voluntary* plan for resettling all Indians west of the Mississippi, on land set aside exclusively for them, with permanent guarantees of Indian control. He also proposed that a buffer zone surround the Indian Lands, from which Whites would be precluded from entering.

Both houses of Congress not surprisingly ignored the departing President's proposals.

In his first term Monroe had presided over the Missouri Compromise of 1820, which admitted one new slave state (Missouri) and one new free state (Maine). It also established an east-west latitude of 36'30" above which slavery would not be allowed to exist in territories/states in the future. Monroe was not happy with the 1820 settlement and the expansion of slavery into Missouri but, as he wrote in a letter to Jefferson, he was convinced the preservation of the Union was at stake.

In 1818 the Rush-Bagot agreement between America and Great Britain demilitarizing the Great Lakes was signed. This agreement had actually been negotiated by Monroe himself in June and July of 1816, when Monroe was Secretary of State, but it was not officially ratified until 1818. Also that year, the two countries agreed to the Convention of 1818, which established the permanent American-Canadian boundary from northern Minnesota to the eastern side of the Rockies. The treaty also expanded the rights of American fishermen to troll the waters off the east coast of Canada.

Another crucial decision of his first term was Monroe's appointment of Sylvanus Thayer to be the new superintendent at West Point. This was a critical and timely personnel change, as West Point was not doing at all well under Thayer's predecessor and was in danger of being closed. Thayer completely turned the institution around in his sixteen years at the helm, with improvements to the curriculum, better professors, and more decisive leadership that upgraded the Academy into both a well-respected academic and military institution.

Chapter 8

In 1821, under the terms of the Transcontinental Treaty (also known as the Adams-Onis Treaty), which had been successfully negotiated in 1819 and ratified two years later, Monroe had acquired the Florida Territory from Spain in exchange for the U.S. assumption of five million dollars of claims by American citizens against Spain due to Spain's failure to curb cross-border raids by the Seminoles into the State of Georgia. For more details, see additional information in Chapter 9 on Andrew Jackson. Spain also agreed to abandon its claims to the Oregon Territory, what is now Oregon and Washington, as well as agreeing to the Sabine River as the western boundary of the Louisiana Purchase.

The country's economy boomed during the Monroe Presidency, despite the Panic of 1819, which Monroe was able to somewhat mitigate by relaxing mortgage repayment terms on land that had been purchased from the federal government. Monroe was also able to eliminate much of the governmental debt left behind by President Madison's administration following the vast and varied expenses of the two-and-a-half-year long War of 1812, as well as Madison's failure to convince Congress to extend the charter of the First Bank of the United States, which thus expired. Subsequently, Madison was obliged to sheepishly sponsor the Second Bank of the United States. The above two factors led to the federal government actually defaulting on some of its payments in 1814, leaving the country essentially bankrupt at that point in Madison's second term.

On December 2, 1823, near the end of the third year of Monroe's second term, he issued his now-famous *Monroe Doctrine*, although it did not become known as the Monroe Doctrine until three decades later. Monroe announced the Doctrine amid the pomp and circumstance of his annual address to Congress, thus maximizing the attention it would gain both nationally and internationally. The Doctrine declared that the United States would not accept any future colonization of the Americas by any European power. Prior to issuing the Doctrine, Monroe had solicited the written opinions of all his Cabinet officers regarding the policy itself, as well as the wording to be used. The final phrasing of the Doctrine was basically Monroe's work, although he did accept John Quincy Adams's language for one of the sections. Monroe had also solicited advice from both Jefferson and Madison about whether or not the Doctrine should be issued jointly with Great Britain, or solely by the United States. Both ex-Presidents advised Monroe to submit it jointly with the Brits. However, Monroe believed it would be much more effective if the Doctrine came from the United States alone, and Adams strongly supported that belief. Historically speaking, the Doctrine has been a huge success. It has been a long-lasting major factor in restraining European attempts to interfere with Western Hemisphere countries. In fact, many historians believe it has had a greater impact in restricting the behavior of Eastern Hemisphere countries in the twentieth century than it did in the nineteenth.

In Monroe's last annual message to Congress he had not "tooted his own horn" by reviewing all the accomplishments of his eight years in office. As Professor Ammon points out, John Quincy Adams rectified Monroe's intentional omissions by listing all of Monroe's achievements in Adams's own Inauguration speech on March 4, 1825:

Chapter 8

Monroe obtained Florida by peaceful means, extended the boundaries of the nation to the Northern Pacific coast, lowered taxes while at the same time reducing the federal debt by some $60 million, strengthened the defenses of the nation by constructing a network of coastal forts, recognized and encouraged the independence of the Latin American countries, and advanced humanitarian efforts to suppress the slave trade. Adams followed up his summation of Monroe's accomplishments by pledging himself to be guided by the same goals on which the Monroe Administration had been based.

Abigail Adams, the wife of John Adams and the mother of John Quincy Adams, was not known for making overly positive statements, but when it came to Monroe and his 1817 tour, which included several days in the Boston area and which resulted in a crowd estimated at 40,000 people attending his appearance at the Boston Commons, she remarked that all who met him were taken by his "agreeable affability…[his] unassuming manners…[and] his polite attentions to all orders and ranks."

Supreme Court Justice Joseph Story, said that, "Mr. Monroe…still retains his plain and gentle manners; and is in every respect a very estimable man."

Thomas Jefferson made the following statement about Monroe in 1787, when Monroe was but 29 years of age: "Turn his soul wrong side outwards and there is not a speck on it."

Monroe died on July 4, 1831, the fifty-fifth anniversary of the signing of the Declaration of Independence. He was the third of the five "Founding Father" Presidents to have died on the Fourth of July! He was 73.

Chapter 9

Andrew Jackson was born in a log cabin in rural South Carolina, just south of that state's border with North Carolina. He was the first future President to be born in a log cabin. Jackson grew up extremely poor in Waxhaw, South Carolina, the third child of recent Scots-Irish immigrants. His father had died just prior to his birth, and his mother died when Jackson was just fourteen, while she was tending to injured and ill American soldiers in a British prisoner-of-war camp. Both of his older brothers also perished during the Revolutionary War, leaving Jackson, at age fifteen, alone in the world, although it should be noted he did have aunts, uncles and cousins living nearby.

Andrew Jackson may have been related to the highly successful Confederate Civil War General Thomas "Stonewall" Jackson, although it is far from a certainty. Both men had ancestors with the surname of Jackson that had resided in the same parish in Londonberry, Northern Ireland. This information is contained in a biography of Stonewall Jackson, written in 1898 by British military historian, G.F.R. Henderson. The claim is based on a letter that was then in the possession of Stonewall's nephew, Thomas Jackson Arnold, Esq. of Beverly, West Virginia. It

Chapter 9

should be noted that "Stonewall" was born in what is now the State of West Virginia. Related or not, both Jacksons were brilliant and aggressive tacticians/generals.

Jackson had joined the Continental Army at age thirteen! A year later, while serving as a messenger in 1781, he was captured during a skirmish with British troops. When ordered to clean a British officer's boots, Jackson refused. The officer then slashed at him with his sword, causing the teenager to throw his arm up in front of his face. The sword came down on Jackson's hand and then upon his forehead, leaving visible and permanent scars, as well as a permanent memory forever embedded in the mind of the future general.

Jackson would gain his revenge some thirty-three years later when he led the American forces against the Brits in the Battle of New Orleans, in what turned out to be the final clash of the War of 1812. That battle would also prove to be the most lopsided defeat ever suffered by the British military!

Although there were a couple of skirmishes prior to the main battle, which occurred on January 8, 1815, that final battle unbelievably consumed less than an hour! While thirteen Americans perished in the fighting and another thirty-seven were injured, the British casualty figures were otherworldly. Estimates range from over 3,000 down to 1,300. One precise figure in between the just-mentioned high and low estimates is that 2,036 British soldiers were killed (!), including three dead generals and seven dead colonels. Another 900+ Redcoats were injured, with another 800+ captured. Most of the eventual 800 captured Redcoats, upon realizing the slaughter that was taking place, had simply fallen to the ground and lay still until the shooting stopped, and then they were quite happily captured. Among the British dead was Commanding General Sir Edward Pakenham, the brother-in-law of the famed Duke of Wellington, who had ended the military career of Napoleon Bonaparte. Many of the dead British soldiers had fought with the famous Duke in the Peninsular Campaign in Spain against Napoleon, and they were collectively known as "Wellington's Heroes."

One of the surviving, but injured, British soldiers said this about Jackson's troops: "Those Americans, with their long rifles, can shoot the eye out of a squirrel."

Following the battle, Jackson spoke about the magnitude of the immense and utterly astounding victory: "It appears that the unerring hand of Providence shielded my men from the powers of cannonballs, bombs, and rockets."

One of the before-mentioned early skirmishes had occurred just prior to Christmas Day, with the Americans inflicting heavier casualties upon the British than they themselves had suffered. This caused the British generals to delay their planned attack and reconfigure their strategy. The delay was an important key for Jackson, as he and his widely varied collection of fighters, which consisted of American regulars, Tennessee, Mississippi, Georgia and Kentucky militiamen, Native Americans who were loyal to Jackson, pirates led by the infamous Jean and Pierre Lafitte, freed blacks, slaves and Louisianans, made maximum use of the extra time. They were able to strengthen and extend the "Line Jackson," which was a barrier of cypress logs, hay bales, mud, and sugar barrels. The Line Jackson stretched from the Mississippi River on the south, across a relatively flat field and into a thick,

Chapter 9

gnarled and impenetrable swamp on the northern side. The Line stood just behind a four-foot deep and ten-foot wide, muddy canal.

Jackson's riflemen were lined up three deep behind the Line Jackson. After firing a round at the oncoming British soldiers, the shooter would quickly line up behind the other two riflemen and reload. Meanwhile, the next shooter in line would be picking out his target. Thus there was a constant stream of fresh American shooters literally firing at the red coats of the British soldiers.

The Brits were aware of the Line Jackson, and they launched their attack first with their artillery pieces. Surprisingly, the British cannon bombardment caused relatively little damage to the Line Jackson. Still, the English then sent their foot soldiers forward, many of whom were carrying scaling ladders and pieces of wood to assist them in crossing the ten-foot muddy canal.

The slaughter was on. As hundreds upon hundreds of the "Lobsterbacks" fell to the ground dead, some British soldiers turned and fled, while others fell to the ground and pretended to be dead.

Now, for the rest of the story regarding the Treaty of Ghent and the Battle of New Orleans: Although the U.S. and Great Britain had signed the Treaty of Ghent on December 24, 1814, ostensibly ending the War of 1812, unbeknownst to the American negotiators and the United States government, the War was not over in the minds of the British Government!

In 2014, as the 200th anniversary of the Battle of New Orleans approached, military historian Ronald Drez of the University of New Orleans, a former Marine Corps captain, made a stunning, once-in-a-lifetime discovery among British war records found in the National Archives at Kew in London, England. As Drez told the Associated Press, "It truly is the smoking gun. They say to Pakenham: 'If you hear of a peace treaty, pay no attention, continue to fight.'" The British plan was to capture New Orleans and then colonize the entire Mississippi Valley, both as a key addition to their colony in Canada, and as a means of limiting the growing power of the United States. For more details see Michael Medved's thought-provoking book, *The American Miracle*; and Drez's book, *The War of 1812, Conflict and Deception: The British Attempt to Seize New Orleans and Nullify the Louisiana Purchase*.

Prior to the decisive battle, Jackson had requested from then Secretary of War, James Monroe, the funds necessary to cover the expenses for the men and materiel that would be required to defend New Orleans from the British. Recognizing the vital importance of New Orleans to the economy of the United States, and to the entire Mississippi and Ohio River basins, Monroe was somehow able to scrape together $100,000 despite the Federal Treasury being basically bankrupt after two-and-a-half years of war.

Prior to arriving in New Orleans, Jackson had attacked and easily captured the Spanish city of Pensacola in western Florida, thus seizing control of their magnificent bay. He had also significantly armed and strengthened Fort Bowyer, the American fort that guarded the entrance to Mobile Bay. These actions prevented the British Navy from utilizing either of the two bays as launching points for their planned attack on New Orleans.

From 1812 to 1818 Jackson had won a series of battles in the American Southeast, mostly against the Creek

Indians and the Seminoles. The largest of these battles occurred in Alabama on March 27, 1814, at The Battle of Horseshoe Bend. This battle was the direct result of the slaughter of nearly 500 soldiers and civilians seven months earlier in what is known to history as the Fort Mims Massacre. The civilian casualties at Fort Mims consisted of 239 men, women and children being killed by a group of Creeks known as the Red Sticks. The number of children killed was estimated at as many as 100. Additionally, ten children and three women were kidnapped by the Red Sticks after the fighting had ended. Among the victims at Fort Mims, other than the settlers and the soldiers, was a group of thirty to forty Creeks who did not subscribe to the Red Sticks' plan to eliminate the soldiers and settlers, and thus were staying at Fort Mims for their own safety.

Jackson's army included over 700 Cherokee, Creek, and Choctaw warriors, all of whom were enemies of the Red Sticks, as well as the twenty-one-year-old future Republic of Texas President (and Battle of San Jacinto hero) Sam Houston. Jackson directed his army to surround the insurgents and then attacked the Red Sticks from the front and the back, winning a decisive victory. In doing so, Jackson had put an end to the Red Stick Revolt, which is also known to history as the Creek War. Some 857 Red Sticks lost their lives in the Battle, with approximately 200 successfully fleeing the area. Jackson's casualties were forty-seven dead and 159 wounded, including Houston, who took an arrow to the thigh, as well as musket balls to his right shoulder and right arm (Houston surprised Jackson, as well as many others, by eventually recovering from the three wounds). The Cherokees, Choctaws and

Creeks suffered a combined total of twenty-three fatalities and forty-seven wounded.

Prior to the onset of the battle, according to two sources, Jackson had offered safe passage to the Creek women and children. His offer was declined by a Creek chief, although another source says it was accepted. Early on in the course of the fighting, according to two different sources, the Creek women and children were successfully rescued by the Cherokee and the non-Red-Stick Creek warriors.

As a result of Jackson's victory at Horseshoe Bend, which effectively eliminated the Red Sticks as a potential ally to the British in their upcoming campaign to capture New Orleans (discussed above), Madison's Secretary of War, John Armstrong, promoted Jackson to the position of Major General. Ironically, just five months thereafter Armstrong was dramatically relieved of his duties by Madison due to his utter failure to follow Madison's orders to take steps to protect Washington City from attack by the British Navy. Armstrong was promptly replaced by the current Secretary of State, and the next President of the United States, James Monroe.

Four years later in 1818, Jackson, exceeding his orders from the new President, Monroe, invaded Florida, quickly defeated the Spanish, and then turned out the Spanish governor. In February of 1819, following years of fruitless negotiations with the Spanish, Spain now suddenly agreed to sell Florida to the United States at no direct cost to the U.S. other than the assumption of five million dollars of claims by American citizens against Spain. This transaction is known to history as the Adams-Onis Treaty.

Chapter 9

Jackson's numerous military victories made him an extremely popular figure, heroic even, with most Americans. Jackson became the first Presidential candidate to win both the popular vote and the electoral college vote in three consecutive election cycles (1824, 1828, and 1832), but he served only two terms in the White House. In 1824, although Jackson had out-polled John Quincy Adams in a four-way race, 151,271 to 113,122 in the popular vote, and 99 to 84 in electoral votes, it wasn't enough to give Jackson the Presidency. This was due to the fact that no candidate had obtained a majority of the electoral votes. So, by law, the race was thrown into the House of Representatives, where Adams, with the support of Kentucky Senator Henry Clay, won the House vote with thirteen states to eight for Jackson.

However, revenge was once again sweet for Jackson in 1828 as he crushed Adams 178 to 83 in electoral votes, and 56 percent to 44 percent in the popular vote, which he won by more than 140,000 votes. The voters also gave Jackson majorities in both houses of Congress. Just as sweet were the results of the 1832 election in which Jackson shellacked Henry Clay, 219 to 49 in the electoral college, and easily defeated him by more than 216,000 votes in the popular vote. Adams had rewarded Clay for his support in the House of Representatives in the contested 1824 election by naming Clay to the powerful position of Secretary of State just two days after the House vote in Adams's favor. Thus, Jackson's victory over Clay in 1832 was the ultimate revenge for what the Jacksonians had continuously called Adams and Clay's "Corrupt Bargain."

As President, Jackson exercised great power. He vetoed more bills than his six predecessors combined. In 1832-33 Jackson's native state of South Carolina asserted the claim that states had the right to nullify federal law — in this case a tariff that South Carolinians believed unfairly favored the New England states. Jackson, in the strongest possible terms, declared that nullification and secession were not rights the states possessed, and further that if they attempted either one it would constitute treason, which would result in the shedding of "a brother's blood." The South Carolinians backed down, and the matter was ultimately resolved by making the tariffs somewhat less onerous to the South.

Another political battle won by Jackson was his "War" on the Second Bank of the United States. Jackson believed the Bank was both involving itself in national political issues and that it favored the wealthy over everyday working Americans. After much tension and political maneuvering, Jackson eventually succeeded in destroying the Bank by withdrawing all of the federal government's funds from the Bank, and placing them with state banks. The public supported Jackson's decision, as shown by the results of the 1834 mid-term elections, in which the Democrats increased the magnitude of their control of Congress.

The most controversial and regretful policy of Jackson's administration was his support for and ultimate signing of the Indian Removal Act of 1830, which passed the House by a narrow vote of 102-97, and the Senate by a more solid margin of 29-18. In response, the Cherokees hired William Wirt, who was and still is the longest serving United States Attorney General in American history. Wirt served as A.G. for eight years during the James Monroe Presidency, and then for four more years under John Quincy Adams. Wirt filed suit against the Jackson Administration, arguing that the Cherokees constituted an independent and sovereign nation. However, Chief Justice John Marshall, in an opinion handed down on March 18, 1831, rejected Wirt's argument, declaring that the Cherokees were not a sovereign nation, but rather were a "domestic dependent nation" subject to American laws, just as a ward is subject to the decisions of his/her guardian.

The Act was thus used to force most Cherokees, as well as thousands of members of multiple other tribes, to vacate their native lands in the American Southeast and to move west of the Mississippi, primarily to Oklahoma and Arkansas. Although the movement of the Cherokees to the West, which is widely known today as "The Trail of Tears" (albeit, a significant number of the Cherokees traveled west on boats for major sections of the trip), occurred in 1838-39 during Martin Van Buren's Presidency, it was Jackson's policy being carried out by Van Buren, a protégé of Jackson. Although estimates vary widely, the most accepted figure for Cherokee deaths during the long trip/march is 15 percent of the 16,543 Cherokees that started on the journey — roughly 2,500 deaths.

It should also be remembered that nearly five hundred Cherokees voluntarily went west after reaching an agreement with Jackson in an 1835 treaty, which was subsequently approved by the United States Senate. The Treaty provided five million dollars for aid in the resettlement process and as just compensation for property lost due to the displacement. For the full story on the relocation of most of the Cherokee, and the multiple intense and deadly battles between the Cherokee tribe's opposing factions, see John Sedgwick's 2018 book, *Blood Moon*.

In the fifty-year period from 1789 through 1839, more than 81,000 Native Americans were relocated to the West. Approximately 50,000 of those were relocated during the Jackson/Van Buren Presidencies. Roughly 9,000 Native Americans were not relocated, including Cherokees in North Carolina, as well as members of various tribes living in New York and other areas of the North.

In 1832 Jackson became the first President to set aside federal land for the enjoyment of the public when he signed a bill creating the Hot Springs Reservation in Arkansas, essentially America's first National Park, although that term was not in use in 1832. Jackson's Hot Springs Reservation was the forerunner of America's current National Park system, which now features some sixty National Parks, as well as a National Park Service to administer those parks, plus more than 110 National Monuments.

In early April of 1836 both houses of Congress approved $150,000 for the purpose of a three-year, worldwide voyage of discovery focusing on oceans, islands and multiple and various fields of natural history. Most observers believed Andrew Jackson couldn't care less about matters of science, and that he would quickly veto the measure. However, much to the naysayers surprise, Jackson enthusiastically endorsed the proposal and urged the Navy to act quickly, even suggesting a start date of June 9, 1836, barely more than two months off. Jackson wrote that he was, "…feeling a lively interest in the Exploring Expedition…[and] that it should be sent

Chapter 9

out as soon as possible." However, it was not to be. The Navy was unable to find a Captain willing to undertake the three-year voyage, and finally had to settle on a Lieutenant Charles Wilkes. Additionally, major modifications of the six ships that would be utilized consumed months and months, as did recruiting the non-military scientists who would be gathering specimens. Another problem was the Panic of 1837, which struck in May of that year, causing a major downturn in the American economy and also delaying the project.

Finally, on August 18, 1838, during the administration of Martin Van Buren, the six ships of the Exploring Expedition lifted anchor and sailed out into the Atlantic Ocean. Just under four years later four ships returned to New York. The oceanic exploration had been a huge success in terms of the advancement of knowledge in a wide variety of the sciences. Geographically, Wilkes and his crew had been able to discover, and name, the continent of Antarctica. More than that, they sailed along 1,500 miles of that portion of the Antarctic shoreline that lies south of Australia. They were also able to fairly accurately map the shoreline. As a result of their discovery and mapping, the specific area of Antarctica that they mapped is now referred to as Wilkes Land.

Unfortunately, all of the many scientific accomplishments and discoveries were lost sight of in the public consciousness due to the extreme animosity that existed between Wilkes and many of his officers. Wilkes was a combination of the Hollywood version of Captain Bligh (although not the actual historical version of Bligh) and Sheldon Cooper, the brilliant genius but also exceedingly annoying, know-it-all lead character on the hit TV show

The Big Bang Theory. Given the above sentence, it is quite understandable why Wilkes was detested by so many of his officers, one of whom kept a massive journal of Wilkes's mistreatment of various officers and sailors. One sailor actually came within seconds of assaulting Wilkes with a deadly weapon. Charges and counter charges flew. Multiple court-martials were held and detailed accounts of the testimony appeared in the major Eastern newspapers. It was a sad ending to what would otherwise have been a celebration of a multiplicity of prideful scientific achievements for the United States Navy and the American people.

Jackson's last official acts as President occurred during his final few days in office. Jackson sought and obtained a resolution from Congress recognizing the new Republic of Texas as an independent nation. He then appointed a *charge d'affaires* to Texas, with that appointment being confirmed by Congress on Jackson's final day in office: March 4, 1837. The first President of the nascent Republic of Texas was Jackson's former protégé, Sam Houston.

Here is a revealing and thought-provoking testimonial by a famously prominent person from a different era of American history: In 1936, then current President Franklin D. Roosevelt said the following about Andrew Jackson: "The more I learn about old Andy Jackson, the more I love him." (!)

Chapter 10

Franklin Delano Roosevelt — Just like his distant cousin Theodore Roosevelt, Franklin was born into immense wealth in New York. In fact, FDR is a descendant of Philip de la Noye, who came to the Pilgrim colony of Plymouth in November of 1621, just one year after the original Pilgrims arrived at Cape Cod. Over the succeeding decades the French surname of de la Noye was anglicized to Delano. The family relationship between the distant cousins, Theodore and Franklin, doesn't stop there. Franklin eventually married Eleanor Roosevelt, who was Teddy's niece, the daughter of Teddy's younger brother, Elliott.

FDR is extremely difficult to rank. Why? Because he was a Jekyll and Hyde president. He was strong and of great importance in the European theatre of World War II, but uneven and at times a flat-out failure with many of his domestic policies. His judgment in the run-up to Pearl Harbor has been questioned by many, but also supported by others. His handling of the post-Pearl Harbor controversies also engendered hard feelings and criticisms from many quarters; criticisms that extended for years and even decades.

Roosevelt's overseeing of American military policy in World War II, especially in Europe, was largely highly successful, considering that 1) The massive military machines that both the Nazis and the Japanese had built up in advance of the actual onset of hostilities gave them an initial colossal advantage; and 2) It was a two-hemisphere war with Japan in the Pacific and Hitler in Europe and North Africa.

FDR's early assistance to Britain in March of 1941 following the creation of the Lend-Lease program was a brilliant policy, without which the U.K. would most probably have been overrun by the Nazis. Just months later, following the Nazi invasion of the Soviet Union, their former allies, the Lend-Lease Program was similarly extended to the Soviets in October of 1941.

Roosevelt's authorization of the Manhattan Project, after having received a letter from Albert Einstein warning that the Germans were hoarding uranium and were already at work on an atomic bomb, occurred shortly after receipt of Einstein's letter in mid-1942. Its ultimate success some three years later almost certainly saved the lives of several hundred thousand American soldiers and sailors, and quite likely saved a million or more Japanese lives. An earlier letter from Einstein in August of 1940 was basically the spark that generated the forerunners of the federal government's Department of Energy, which was not officially created until 1977. The first forerunner agency was the Advisory Committee on Uranium, which was created in October of 1940. After two name changes of the Committee, the effort to build the atom bomb eventually became known as the Manhattan Project in 1942.

Chapter 10

Additionally, Roosevelt's choices of key military personnel were largely spot-on: Generals Dwight Eisenhower, Omar Bradley and George Marshall, Admiral Nimitz, General Douglas MacArthur, and then later in 1944, knowing his own health was becoming more and more fragile, he chose Harry Truman, a man of good health, as well as a WWI veteran, as his new Vice-President. This proved to be an especially important decision because FDR ended up passing away less than three months into his fourth term.

However, one key personnel choice proved to be a grossly embarrassing mistake: Roosevelt's curious appointment of Joseph P. Kennedy to be the American Ambassador to Great Britain. Appointed in the winter of 1937-38, Kennedy served until October of 1940, spending most of his time advocating for a conciliatory policy towards Hitler. As the war grew closer, Kennedy wrote to Roosevelt, urging the President to utilize appeasement with Hitler in order to avoid the looming military disaster.

Roosevelt's own Secretary of the Interior, Harold Ickes, wrote the following words regarding Roosevelt's appointment of Kennedy to the most prestigious and important of all American ambassadorships: "At a time when we should be sending the best that we have to Great Britain, we have not done so…We have sent a rich man, untrained in diplomacy, unlearned in history and politics, who is a great publicity seeker…"

In appointing an inexperienced businessman to an important ambassadorship as a major war loomed, Roosevelt was making the same mistake that President Woodrow Wilson had made during World War I. Wilson, like Roosevelt twenty-four years later, appointed a businessman to be the American ambassador to Russia from 1914–1916, and then followed that appointment with yet another businessman in 1916 rather than appointing an experienced career diplomat familiar with the vast issues and entanglements of both Russia and the myriad other European countries.

Another major area of criticism regarding FDR's WWII policies was that once it became obvious the Allies were going to prevail, he was far too lenient with Stalin, agreeing in advance to Soviet dominance over much of Eastern Europe. This is especially true in that initially Stalin and Hitler had been allies, jointly attacking and dividing up Poland. Additionally, in the early part of the war Stalin had also attacked and taken control of Finland, Latvia, Lithuania and Estonia. Shockingly, in late 1943, Roosevelt said this about Stalin: "I believe he is truly representative of the heart and soul of Russia; I believe that we are going to get along very well with him…very well indeed." In early 1944 Roosevelt added that Stalin, "hasn't got any ideas of conquest." On the trip home from the Yalta conference in February of 1945, Roosevelt's long-time foreign policy adviser, Harry Hopkins, said Roosevelt spoke often of his "respect and admiration for Marshal Stalin." What was he thinking? That he could convert Stalin to democracy?

A second, and highly controversial area of criticism of Roosevelt in the realm of military policy is the issue of misleading, untimely and incomplete information in the warnings provided by the military elements of the Roosevelt Administration to the top general and admiral based in Hawaii prior to Pearl Harbor. At least five books have been written about this issue, including one by John

Chapter 10

Toland, a Pulitzer-Prize-winning author, who wrote *Infamy* in 1982.

At the heart of this issue is the claim that the U.S. had broken the Japanese code system and had advance knowledge of the nearly certain upcoming Pearl Harbor attack. So, was the lack of detailed, timely and fully accurate warnings to the Pearl Harbor military leaders (Admiral Husband Kimmel and General Walter Short) merely inadvertent oversights by the overworked, European-theatre-centered military leaders in Washington, D.C.? Or was it intentional, based on the strong belief that actual damage of some significance needed to occur in an attack on either the American military or on the then American territory of Hawaii in order for the United States Congress and the American public to be fully supportive of American military involvement in the War in the Pacific before it was too late?

Admiral Kimmel was removed from his command shortly after Pearl Harbor and was not reassigned. However, he vociferously defended himself for the remaining twenty-five years of his life, and clearly believed he had not been fully and timely warned and was in fact scapegoated. From time to time he would vow to reveal everything he knew, at one time saying: "…those in authority in Washington for what they did… They must answer on the Day of Judgment like any other criminal."

In the 1944 Presidential campaign New York Governor Thomas Dewey, the Republican Presidential nominee, received information from an Army officer that the U.S. military had broken the Japanese code system early in 1941 and thus had advance knowledge of Japanese plans, including the December 7, 1941 planned attack on Pearl Harbor. Dewey was going to go public with the information, but was talked out of it by high-ranking Administration officials, who told him release of the information would harm the ongoing war effort. Dewey was furious, saying he knew at least twelve U.S. Senators were aware of the code-breaking information he was now being urged to withhold by General George Marshall and the military's chief of cryptography.

Having read Toland's book, as well as the recently released (2016) *A Matter of Honor: Pearl Harbor: Betrayal, Blame and a Family's Quest for Justice*, I found the facts and evidence that have been gathered and presented in both books to be substantial, logical, and persuasive. Although the nature of the evidence is basically circumstantial in nature, it is powerfully and strongly indicative of an intentional failure to warn. The United States military continued to decode Japanese messages throughout the War. This advantage almost certainly played a role in June of 1942, when the American Navy posted a decisive and momentum-changing victory over the Japanese Navy in the historic Battle of Midway.

The strong circumstantial evidence of intentional failure to timely and fully warn Kimmel and Short consists in part, of the following facts: 1) America's two most valuable and important ships at Pearl Harbor in the days leading up to December 7 were the aircraft carriers *Enterprise* and *Lexington*. Nine days before December 7, the *Enterprise* was sent out to sea to deliver airplanes to Wake Island; three days later the *Lexington* was sent out on an identical mission to deliver planes to Midway Island. 2) Multiple messages had been intercepted and

Chapter 10

deciphered by the American cryptanalysis system (which was called MAGIC) over a period of four months prior to December 7. Yet timely and specific warnings involving the possibility of an attack on Pearl Harbor were never sent to Kimmel and Short. 3) A Navy Court of Inquiry found that Chief of Naval Operations Harold (Betty) Stark's November 27 "War Warning" sent to Kimmel had not conveyed the actual dangers as was seen by the Washington military officials. 4) The aforementioned November 27 "War Warning" sent out by Stark to Kimmel in Hawaii and to Admiral Hart in the Philippines, stated that Japanese military aggression was anticipated in the next few days. It specifically mentioned the Japanese were expected to attack Thailand and/or Malaysia, and also perhaps the Philippines. It also mentioned Borneo as an additional potential victim. The message did not contain a single word about an attack on Hawaii, let alone on Pearl Harbor.

5) On December 7, at 3:00 A.M. and again at 4:30 A.M. (Washington time), Japanese messages of instructions to their Washington diplomatic corps were intercepted. The content of these messages made it a virtual certainty that Pearl Harbor was going to be attacked at 7:30 A.M., Hawaii time, (1:00 P.M. Washington time). By the time the messages were decoded and given to Stark for his review it was 9:30 on the East Coast. Marshall had also been alerted to the messages at the same time, but he had been out riding his horse and didn't arrive at his office until 11:15. Stark was advised by the director of the Office of Naval Intelligence to telephone Kimmel at Fleet Headquarters in Hawaii to give him the warning. However, Stark never called. Similarly, Marshall never

telephoned either, despite several of the military personnel who were present having recommended he phone Hawaii immediately. Instead, the information was sent by telegraph only after being laboriously encoded,. The information thus arrived in Hawaii well after the assault on Pearl Harbor had concluded and after the Japanese planes and submarines had departed the scene. If Stark and/or Marshall had telephoned immediately after determining the seriousness of the intercepted messages, Kimmel and Short would have had two to three hours to take the necessary defensive measures to prepare for the Japanese attack. 6) By orders from FDR in the months leading up to Pearl Harbor, significant military equipment had been directed to be transferred from Hawaii to the European theatre. This equipment included one aircraft carrier, three battleships, four cruisers and eighteen destroyers, which was fully one quarter of Kimmel's fleet. 7) According to Roosevelt's Secretary of War Henry Stimson, when Roosevelt read the reports of the Navy Court of Inquiry and the Army Board report, and when he saw the names they had criticized, he made the following statement: "Why, this is wicked! This is wicked!" Stimson replied he "feared the Congress would get after us, get at the papers and get at the facts." To which Roosevelt said, "We must refuse to make the reports public...they should be sealed up...a notice made that they should only be opened on a joint resolution of both houses of Congress, approved by the President, after the War."

    My own belief of what happened in the run-up to Pearl Harbor is the following: President Roosevelt was confronted with an unbelievably and agonizingly difficult decision to either warn Kimmel and Short, or to not warn them. There was no perfect solution. There were major potential downsides regardless of which option he eventually chose. I believe that after much anguished soul-searching he chose not to warn them for what he honestly believed to be in the long-term best interests of both America and the European allies. Roosevelt knew that for the American Congress to declare war on Germany or Japan, the United States would first have to be the victim of an attack by one of those countries. The reason this is so is because a vast and vociferous number of Americans were understandably dead-set against the United States getting involved in yet another "European War," especially in light of the shockingly high numbers of American military personnel that were killed and wounded in barely more than a year of fighting in Europe just twenty-two years earlier in World War I. See Chapter 19 on Woodrow Wilson for casualty figures for World War I.

And yet, Roosevelt also knew how strong the Japanese and Nazi military machines were, and how relatively weak and vulnerable Great Britain was in the face of the Nazi onslaught. He knew if the American military did not get involved soon, it may well be too late to save Great Britain, which was the last major republic left in Europe. He also knew the militaries of both Japan and the Nazis would only grow more powerful the longer they went without having to face significant opposition. He may well have viewed the Axis powers as two cancers that grew ever more dangerous the longer they were given free reign. Thus, logic dictated the process to begin the elimination of the cancers needed to begin as soon as possible.

Based on all the above factors and information, I believe Roosevelt decided not to warn, due to the overriding importance of the United States to get involved, as soon as possible, in both theatres of the War. I would add that I feel certain Roosevelt was probably trembling, mortified, sweating, and sick to his stomach when the casualty figures from Pearl Harbor became known. I also believe the deaths, injuries and damage done to the various ships and planes far exceeded his estimates as to the overall losses that were likely to accrue in the attack. However, I also believe that, in the big picture of things, he made the right decision—excruciatingly painful though it must have been.

Although I believe Roosevelt's basic decision was correct, it was also tragically incomplete. Kimmel and Short could have, and should have, been advised telephonically in the two hour period prior to the attack. Both the extreme loss of American lives and the massive damage done to American planes and ships would certainly have been lessened had the timely warnings been sent.

For those readers seeking additional factual details and circumstances regarding the decision, or failure, of the Washington government/military to send relevant and timely information and warnings to Kimmel and Short in Hawaii, read the two books cited above (*Infamy* and *A Matter of Honor: Pearl Harbor: Betrayal and Blame*). Then you can ponder for yourself what you believe most likely happened in Washington, D.C. in the early morning and mid-day hours of December 7, 1941.

Here is one last bit of significant historical information about the Japanese attack on Pearl Harbor: As is widely known, the attack on Pearl Harbor occurred without

Chapter 10

any prior Declaration of War by the Japanese government. This is why it is referred to by many as a "sneak attack." However, the final act of the Pearl Harbor story occurred some sixteen months later, on April 18, 1943. Having broken the Japanese naval codes long before, the American military was tracking the whereabouts of Admiral Yamamoto, the Commander of the Imperial Japanese Navy and the architect of the Pearl Harbor attack plan. The Navy became aware of Yamamoto's flight plans for April 18, four days earlier. President Roosevelt was so advised and understandably gave his approval for the targeted killing of Yamamoto, whose plane was subsequently shot down by one or more of the sixteen American P-38 fighter planes given the assignment. The loss of Yamamoto had a significant deleterious effect thereafter on the Japanese Navy.

One very successful aspect of Roosevelt's domestic policy during the Great Depression was the work of the Civilian Conservation Corps, which was launched by Roosevelt with an executive order in April, 1933. During its nine-year history the CCC provided employment for an estimated three million mostly young men (eighteen to twenty-five), in all forty-eight states. They planted over three billion trees around the country, constructed more than 800 state and national park facilities, and helped to build several hundred hiking trails in scenic areas around the nation. They also built more than 50,000 acres of campgrounds in the forty-eight states.

Another important, and highly warranted program, was Roosevelt's signing of the Servicemen's Readjustment Act, which is more commonly known today as the G.I. Bill. After a spirited and at times acrimonious debate regarding the bill, both houses of Congress ultimately signed off on the "G.I." bill and it was sent to the White House for Roosevelt's approval. He supported the measure and signed it into law on June 22, 1944. Although Roosevelt signed it into law, he had not initially proposed it. Interestingly, the first draft of what was to ultimately become the G.I. bill was initially proposed and written by Harry W. Colmery, a former Republican Party National Chairman!

The new law provided that veterans of the Second World War were to receive funds for their college education, as well as unemployment insurance and low-interest mortgages for housing. From 1944 through 1949 nearly nine million veterans received close to $4 billion from the bill's unemployment compensation program. The education and training provisions existed until 1956, while the insured loans offered through the Veterans' Administration remained available until 1962. The college funds portion of the bill was widely used by returning veterans; so much so that in 1947 a full 49 percent of college admissions were veterans making use of the financial provisions attendant to enrolling in college. The veterans/new collegians received a cost of living stipend, plus the first $500 of tuition was paid for by the G.I. bill.

However, as to domestic affairs other than the CCC and the G.I. bill, it was quite another story—*a consistently mistake-ridden story.* 1) True, Roosevelt inherited a weakened, *but improving*, national economy from President Hoover. However, his policies over the next seven years did very little to advance the American economy. The Great Depression was a worldwide event,

Chapter 10

however by 1938, data from the League of Nations showed that five of the other six largest economies in the world had basically recovered from the Depression, their industrial production being 23 percent above 1929 levels, while American industrial production was still down by 10 percent! Winston Churchill even publicly mocked Roosevelt for his wrongheaded financial policies. Franklin Delano Roosevelt did not bring America out of the Great Depression. It was Nazi and Japanese militarism that brought America out of its lengthy slumbering economic woes.

Here are more highly revealing facts regarding Roosevelt's "New Deal" economy: From 1932 to 1936, federal spending skyrocketed 77 percent, the national debt rose by 73 percent, and top bracket tax rates rose from 25 percent to a whopping 79 percent! In five of the other six major world economies (as of 1938), employment was 12 percent above pre-depression levels, but in the U.S. it was still down by 20 percent! In 1938, Roosevelt's sixth year in the Presidency, the unemployment rate in the U.S. was at a stunning 19 percent! In the pre-Depression period, per capita Gross Domestic Product in the U.S. was roughly 25 percent larger than it was in Great Britain. However by 1938, real per capita GDP in Britain was actually higher than in the United States! As regards the Dow-Jones Industrial Average, it reached its Hoover/Coolidge high point in September of 1929 when it hit 381.17. Contrast that with Roosevelt's 12+ years as President: The Dow-Jones high point during the Roosevelt era only reached 194 (!) in 1937, (his fifth year in office). But, by 1938 the Dow-Jones average had plunged back down into the 150's!

Roosevelt issued more executive orders during his Presidency than did all the other Presidents combined from 1945 through the year 2000!! Al Smith, the former Democratic governor of New York (Roosevelt's home state), described the economic paralysis of 1936 as a "vast octopus set up by government that wound its arms all around the business of the country, paralyzing big business, and choking little business to death." As Roosevelt assumed ever greater control of the economy, private investment collapsed, averaging only 40 percent of the 1929 level for nine consecutive years! See Chapter 17 for additional information about Roosevelt's actions and inactions, his economic policy errors in dealing with the Depression, and additional statistics and facts regarding the ongoing "Roosevelt economic depression."

2) When the Supreme Court stifled some of FDR's domestic plans, Roosevelt's proposed solution in 1937 was to pack the court with more judges. But, despite holding huge majorities of Democrats over Republicans in both the Senate and the House of Representatives, Congress overwhelmingly rejected Roosevelt's plan to pack the court with sympathetic New Dealers.

3) Roosevelt also had a major character flaw — a different type of domestic problem — repeated instances of marital infidelity. The most well-known affair was with Eleanor Roosevelt's social secretary, a woman named Lucy Mercer. The affair lasted from 1914 to 1918, when it ended due to Eleanor finding letters between the lovers in Roosevelt's luggage. FDR considered divorce, but decided to stay married to Eleanor due to strong objections and financial threats by his mother, Sara Roosevelt. Franklin promised Eleanor he would never see Lucy again. Years

Chapter 10

later, however, Roosevelt broke that promise, seeing Lucy off and on from 1941 to 1945. Indeed, Lucy Mercer (Lucy Rutherford by then), was with Franklin in Warm Springs, Georgia on the day he died (!), April 12, 1945. For more details on Eleanor, Franklin and Lucy, see Doris Kearns Goodwin's excellent work, *No Ordinary Time*.

4) Another domestic failure for Roosevelt was his mostly uncaring and passive position regarding the extreme dangers facing German Jews in the 1930s in light of Hitler's policies and treatment of people of Jewish descent. From 1933 to 1938 the federal government under Roosevelt issued roughly 30,000 visas to German Jews. Although that figure may initially sound like a positive, in fact it was a huge negative. The reason it was a negative is that the government had approximately 100,000 visas available for immigrants from Germany! In June of 1939 a vessel named *St. Louis*, which was carrying over 900 German Jews, was denied docking privileges in Cuba and in Miami. Roosevelt could easily have issued an executive order allowing the ship to dock and the passengers to disembark in America. However, he did nothing, other than to allow the *St. Louis* to sail back to Europe with nearly all passengers still aboard. Additionally, in February of 1939 a bill was proposed in Congress that would have allowed *20,000 German Jewish children* to come to the United States, over and above the annual quota for German immigrants. Eleanor Roosevelt supported the bill, but Franklin Roosevelt refused to use the "Powers of the Presidency" to lobby Congress in favor of the bill, despite having been requested to support the bill by congressmen who favored it.

Per Richard Cohen of the *Washington Post*, Franklin Roosevelt, while attending the 1943 Casablanca Conference, seemingly agreed with a suggestion by a French general that the Jews were overrepresented in Germany in the professions. FDR commented on the "understandable complaints which the Germans bore towards the Jews." Additionally, it was not until 1944 that Roosevelt even mentioned the mass murder of Jews, despite the fact that it had been ongoing for years. Also, he did little or nothing to warn Germany and its satellites that there would be a cost to pay once the War was over if they had participated in the mistreatment of the Jews.

Richard Breitman and Allan J. Lichtman, in their 2013 book, *FDR and the Jews*, write that Roosevelt, "...did not forthrightly inform the American people of Hitler's grisly 'Final Solution' or respond decisively to his crimes." It should be noted that *FDR and the Jews* is just one of a number of books that have come out in the last dozen years that deal with Roosevelt's failures and/or inaction on the unbelievably tragic subject of European Jews and Hitler's Holocaust.

5) Despite being urged repeatedly by Eleanor, who was one of the strongest of all American voices for equal rights, to fully integrate the military, FDR refused to do it. After Harry Truman succeeded Roosevelt as President, he later issued the orders in 1948 to fully integrate the military.

6) FDR also failed to listen to Eleanor on the issue of the incarceration of Japanese-Americans in the spring of 1942. She pleaded with him not to do it, repeatedly telling him, "this isn't you Franklin, this isn't you." So frequent were Eleanor's entreaties that FDR asked her

Chapter 10

to stop bringing up the subject! He went ahead with the incarceration plan anyway. Nearly 120,000 Japanese-Americans — men, women, children and grandparents — who had been living in California, Oregon or Washington, were rounded up and shipped to internment camps — some as far away as Arkansas! During their three-plus years of internment, 1,862 Japanese-Americans died in the camps! Over 6,000 infants began their lives in the internment camps. Over 5,000 Japanese-Americans were able to avoid internment by quickly moving their families eastward out of California, Oregon and Washington. *Nearly two thirds of the internees were actually citizens. All of the internees were in the country legally.* There had been zero incidents of sabotage by Japanese-Americans.

Additionally, long-time FBI director J. Edgar Hoover had advocated against the Japanese internment plan! Hoover stated there was "no Japanese problem" on the West Coast. He also warned Attorney General Francis Biddle against "public hysteria." Hoover wrote Biddle that demands for mass removal of citizens of Japanese heritage were "based primarily upon public and political pressure, rather than on factual data." Biddle then advised FDR that there was "no reason for mass evacuation." But Roosevelt remained unmoved.

Further, in June of 1942, the U.S. Navy scored a major victory over the Japanese navy in the Battle of Midway, virtually destroying the Japanese carrier fleet. This made it quite clear that the Japanese were no longer a military threat to Hawaii, let alone to the West Coast. The victory at Midway was a perfect opportunity for Roosevelt to correct his misguided and inhumane internment order, as the process of transportation of the Japanese-Americans to the internment camps was in its earliest stages. And yet, Roosevelt failed to take advantage of the rare golden opportunity to right a wrong! Regrettably, he maintained his previously issued order. Forty-six years later, in the Reagan Administration, the American Government issued a formal apology for the Internment, and paid $20,000 to each internee who was then still living.

So, you the reader, which one do you consider to be worse? Andrew Jackson, based on legislation passed by both houses of Congress in the 1830s causing 16,543 Cherokees to be mandatorily moved to Oklahoma, or FDR, on his own and without any Congressional action, merely by means of his own Executive Order, in 1942 (more than 100 years after Jackson), forcibly interning nearly 120,000 Japanese-Americans, the majority of whom were citizens, and none of whom had done anything even remotely anti-American, nor broken any laws, and most of whom spent more than three years in confinement. Which Presidential decision was worse?

Chapter 11

James K. Polk — In one way, Polk was unique among the important Presidents: When he ran for the Presidency in 1844 he told the voters he was only going to serve one term — and he stuck to his promise! President Harry Truman had this to say about James K. Polk: "A great President. He said what he intended to do, and he did it." Polk had five main goals as President, and he accomplished each of them. He was urged by many of his supporters to run for reelection following his successful first term, but Polk refused, saying he had accomplished everything he set out to do. He may also have had concerns about his health, as he passed away less than eight months after the election of 1848.

Polk had been an outstanding student at the University of North Carolina, graduating at the top of his class. In actuality, Polk was quite fortunate to even be alive to attend college. At the age of seventeen, Polk underwent an extremely dangerous and excruciatingly painful surgery, the removal of urinary stones — without anesthesia other than brandy. Although the surgery proved to be a success, it left Polk unable to father children.

Following college, Polk soon became a lawyer and then was elected to the Tennessee state legislature, where he quickly became a protégé of Andrew Jackson. Soon thereafter he met and married his future wife, Sarah Childress, as a result of his relationship with Jackson, who had been a long-time friend of the Childress family. Polk then spent ten years in Congress, eight of which occurred during the Jackson Administration. Polk was oftentimes referred to as "Young Hickory," as he faithfully supported Jackson's policies, as well as being a fellow Tennessean. Significantly, Polk served as the Speaker of the House for four years (1835–39).

In 1839 he left Congress to successfully run for Governor of Tennessee. Despite losing his reelection bid for Governor in 1841, and again losing in 1843, Polk had the full support of Jackson for the Presidency in 1844. At the Democratic Nominating Convention in Baltimore in late May of 1844, the delegates were hopelessly deadlocked after eight ballots between former President Martin Van Buren and Lewis Cass, a general during the War of 1812 as well as Jackson's Secretary of War for five years, followed by six years as the American Ambassador to France. To resolve the deadlock the delegates compromised by turning to Jackson's young protégé, the "dark horse" candidate—Polk. Jackson's support, coupled with Polk's four years as Speaker of the House, as well as the reality of the deadlock between the supporters of Van Buren and Cass, had convinced the delegates to nominate Polk, who would ultimately become the first ever successful "dark horse" Presidential candidate. Ironically, at the outset of the Convention, although Polk was hoping to somehow be nominated for President, he had felt that the most likely outcome would be the Vice-Presidential nomination.

Chapter 11

Jackson's continued support during the fall campaigning, along with Polk's catchy campaign slogan of "54'40' or Fight," in reference to a border dispute between America and the British over the location of the Canada/America border, both served to galvanize the vast majority of Democrats, who had wildly favored Jackson's aggressiveness. The result was a razor-thin victory for Polk over Henry Clay, the aging Whig Senator from Kentucky. Polk won the popular vote with 1.34 million to 1.30 million for Clay. On a percentage basis that was 49.5 percent for Polk, and 48.1 percent for Clay, with the remainder going to a third-party candidate. Polk carried fifteen states, while Clay won eleven states. Polk's margin of victory in the electoral college was a seemingly comfortable 170-105.

However, it should be noted that a swing of just 5,200 votes from Polk to Clay in the state of New York would have given Clay the narrowest of victories in the electoral college, 141-134. However, on the other hand, a swing of 5,200 combined votes in four states (North Carolina, New Jersey, Tennessee and Delaware) from Clay to Polk would have given Polk an impressively strong electoral college margin of victory of 204 to 71.

Jackson had lived to see his protégé both win the election and to be sworn into office, but he died just three months after Polk was inaugurated as President. At forty-nine, Polk was the youngest man to win the Presidency up to that point in American history.

In late December of 1845, the annexation of Texas into the Union became a *fait accompli* when the Texan citizenry overwhelmingly voted to abandon their nascent republic and join the United States, thus fulfilling one of Polk's campaign promises. Two months later Texas formally joined the Union on February 19, 1846. Mexico responded by immediately terminating diplomatic relations with the United States, and threatening war if the U.S. followed through with the annexation.

Earlier, in October of 1845, Polk approved the transfer of America's Naval Academy from Philadelphia to Annapolis, Maryland, where it has remained for more than 170 years. In 1846 Polk completed two more of his campaign goals: passing a new tariff bill that was acceptable to both the Northern states and the Southern states, and bringing order to the country's financial system by establishing an independent treasury. Polk had previously pushed through an independent treasury bill when he served as Speaker of the House, but the Whigs had repealed it in the early 1840s. Also in 1846, Polk achieved the following: he settled the Oregon Boundary issue by reaching agreement with Great Britain on establishing the boundary at the forty-ninth parallel; and he secured a treaty with opposing groups of Cherokees in the Oklahoma Territory, who were involved in a violent dispute (thirty-four deaths), over tribal governing powers.

The agreement with the Brits wherein the United States received what is now Oregon, Idaho and Washington, with Great Britain receiving what is now British Columbia, generated a massive westward exodus of Americans along what became known as the Oregon Trail. Although Americans had been travelling to the Oregon territory in significant numbers, beginning with an estimated 700 to 1,000 travelers in 1843, the 1846 agreement with Britain launched a gigantic upturn in the number of Americans moving to what are now the states of Oregon and Washington. This mass migration

CHAPTER 11

continued into the early 1850's, with as many as 50,000 travelers a year moving west. Ultimately, in the twenty-four year period from 1846 through 1869, more than 400,000 self-confident Americans had moved westward along the Oregon Trail and its multiple offshoots. In addition to the thousands of people moving to the lush environs of Oregon's Willamette Valley, far larger numbers of gold seekers traveled to California along the Oregon Trail, as did an estimated 70,000 Mormons, moving from the Midwest to Utah's Salt Lake Valley.

Another foreign affairs development in 1846 that would eventually prove extremely important to future American military and business concerns was the ratification by Congress of a treaty that Polk's State Department had successfully negotiated with the South American country of New Granada (now Colombia). The treaty guaranteed that the United States government, as well as its citizens, had free transit rights across the Panama Isthmus (Panama then being a part of New Granada) "upon any modes of communication that now exist, or that may hereafter be constructed." The United States promised in return to protect both New Granada's national integrity, as well as the neutrality of the transit zone. The treaty was entered into by Polk in order to facilitate the eventual building of a canal at some unknown point in the future.

It should also be noted that for nearly six decades the United States had honored their treaty obligations on multiple occasions by protecting New Granada/Colombia from both outside attacks, as well as from internal revolts. In fact, the first such incident of American protection came just six years later in 1852 when President

Fillmore found it necessary to deploy American troops to the isthmus. Thus it was that in 1903 when President Theodore Roosevelt was determined to get the Panama Canal built, following the utter failure of the French to build it, Roosevelt was not just carrying a "big stick," he actually had a firm legal right by virtue of Polk's prescient Treaty of New Granada, to build the canal across the isthmus.

Obtaining California, which Polk hoped to buy, as well as firming up the southern border of the State of Texas remained as Polk's last two goals. Polk attempted on two occasions to negotiate a financial settlement with Mexico in order to obtain California, but on each occasion Mexican officials refused to talk with Polk's envoys. The President's envoys each reported back to the President that there was a "clamor for war" in Mexico. A major problem for any country in trying to deal with the Mexican government in the first half of the nineteenth century was their near constant governmental changes. In their first twenty-three years as an independent nation, Mexico had experienced thirty-eight different governments! During this period the Mexican Presidency was akin to a revolving door on steroids.

Ten years earlier, in 1836, Sam Houston, a former Tennessean, had led the Texas army in a crushing defeat of General Santa Ana's Mexican army at the Battle of San Jacinto, thus gaining Texas its independence from Mexico and giving Texas the status of an independent republic for nine years (1836-1845). During this time period Texas had always claimed the Rio Grande River as their southern border with Mexico. At no time during

Chapter 11

the nine-year period of Texan independence did Mexico ever send an army to recapture the new Republic of Texas.

In the spring of 1846 both the United States and Mexico had armies in the Rio Grande Valley. The U.S. army was north of the Rio Grande, while the Mexican army was south of the river. On April 25, 1846, an American cavalry patrol was ambushed by Mexican soldiers at a location north of the Rio Grande River. Sixteen men were killed, and twenty-six were taken prisoner. On May 13, 1846, war was declared. The vote for War in Congress was forty to two in the Senate (with three abstentions), and 174 to fourteen in the House. Led by Generals Winfield Scott and Zachary Taylor, who were supported by several hundred lower officers who were relatively recent graduates of West Point (including Ulysses S. Grant, Robert E. Lee, Stonewall Jackson, William Tecumseh Sherman, George Meade—who beat back Lee's attack at Gettysburg, and Jefferson Davis), the American military won every single battle, concluding with Scott's capture of Mexico City in September of 1847.

In the American victory at Monterrey, among the many units that performed well for General Taylor was the Mounted Rifles volunteer regiment from West Texas, commanded by Colonel John C. Hays. In later years, many soldiers from this unit would gain nationwide fame for their work in law enforcement as the "Texas Rangers."

One of many individual officers who earned recognition for bravery during the Battle of Monterrey was future American President Ulysses S. Grant, then a lieutenant. Receiving word that American units were low on ammunition, Grant, who was an outstanding horseman, spurred his horse past enemy soldiers in relative safety by riding with just one leg over the horse's back, with the rest of his body hanging on the side of the horse that was away from the enemy's soldiers. Grant made it back to the quartermaster area successfully, and the fresh ammo was quickly delivered to the needy troops.

Meanwhile, Polk had dispatched smaller military forces to New Mexico and California, which still quite easily overcame very limited resistance in California, with one exception, and literally no resistance at all in New Mexico. One reason for the light resistance by the residents of California was that they themselves had launched nine rebellions in the previous fifteen years against the inept governors appointed by the Mexican government! Some of the individuals that participated in the New Mexico and California campaigns were the following: General Stephen Watts Kearney, whose forces still held the field following the December 6-7, 1846 Battle of San Pasqual, but which had suffered greater casualties than the Californios; Colonel John C. Fremont, aka "The Pathfinder" (who was later to become the first Republican Party Presidential nominee in 1856); Commodore John Sloat, Commodore Robert Stockton, *and the real Pathfinder – Kit Carson.*

If not for the bravery and leadership of Carson, Kearney and his troops would possibly have been forced to surrender to the "Californios," had they launched a second assault on Kearney's position. Carson, together with Lieutenant Edward Beale and a Native American named Chemuctah, had stealthily slipped out of camp as soon as darkness fell and made their way on foot thirty-six miles to San Diego where Stockton, with several hundred sailors and Marines, was docked. Upon

Chapter 11

receiving Carson's and Beale's reports, Stockton sent a force of 100 sailors and eighty Marines north to the San Pasqual battlefield to support the injured Kearney and his men. There was no additional fighting following the arrival of Stockton's well-supplied troops, as the Californios returned to their various ranches and homes. Kearney's casualty figures were seventeen killed and thirteen wounded. The exact casualty numbers for the Californios is unknown, but they were clearly less than Kearney's casualties.

Interestingly, Sloat and Stockton, the two Commodores, were exact opposites in terms of personality. Sloat was cautious, hesitant and by-the-book. When he was confronted by Fremont about why he had not yet taken charge of things in Monterey, California, Sloat answered by saying "I know nothing...I know nothing. I want to know by what authority you are acting." This is highly reminiscent of the character "Sgt. Schultz" in the late 1960s television show, *Hogan's Heroes*, who was constantly saying, in a faux German accent, "I know nothing, I know nothing."

Shortly thereafter, Stockton arrived to replace Sloat as the top Naval figure in California. He was highly aggressive. He was basically a naval version of World War II General, George C. Patton. Stockton, at one point "appointed" Fremont to be the new Governor of California, despite the fact that General Kearney clearly out-ranked him, and Kearney was present in the state. When Kearney pointed out his superior rank to Stockton, the Commodore initially refused to yield, and began arguing with Kearney. Ultimately, Stockton considered the possible negative consequences to his military career and acquiesced to Kearney's assertion that he was in charge.

It was a different situation with Fremont, though, who refused to follow various orders issued by Kearney and who was later found guilty of three charges following his court-martial. However, Polk dismissed the most serious charge of mutiny and ordered Fremont to report to duty, believing he deserved a second chance, especially in light of his three wildly successful expeditions exploring the American West between 1842 and 1845. Surprisingly, Fremont scorned Polk's leniency and petulantly resigned from the army. Thirteen years later, in 1861, Fremont returned to the Army after the outbreak of the Civil War. However, once again, Fremont would not follow orders, and thus he was cashiered by President Lincoln, this time for disobeying a direct order from Lincoln himself! Later, Lincoln gave Fremont yet another chance to command Union troops. However, things did not go well for Fremont's unit, which was subsequently transferred into the newly created Army of Virginia, which was commanded by General John Pope. Fremont, who hated Pope, was unwilling to serve under him and requested to be relieved of command. Lincoln granted Fremont's request, most probably exceedingly glad to be rid of the famous but egotistical and whiney John C. Fremont.

Nearly five months after Scott's capture of Mexico City, the Treaty of Guadalupe Hidalgo officially ended the Mexican War on February 2, 1848. The terms of the treaty gave California and the New Mexico Territory (which also included Arizona, Nevada, Utah, and part of Colorado) to the United States. It also fixed the southern boundary of Texas at the Rio Grande. In return, Polk agreed to

Chapter 11

provide Mexico with 15 million dollars for its lost provinces (California and New Mexico) and to assume responsibility for $3,500,000 in damage claims previously filed by individual Americans against the Mexican government. The vote in the United States Senate to ratify the treaty was thirty-eight to fourteen.

Polk's acquisition of California paid nearly immediate dividends, as the discovery of gold in California's Sierra Nevada foothills became public knowledge on August 19, 1848 (six-and-a-half months after the treaty with Mexico was signed) when a story was published in the *New York Herald* newspaper, which was the most widely read paper in the nation at the time. That news story launched the massive 1849 Gold Rush to California. By November of 1849, a state constitution banning slavery had been drawn up and was approved by California's voters by a margin of fifteen to one, although only 13,000 citizens voted. Ten months later on September 9, 1850, California was granted statehood, becoming the thirty-first state in the Union. This virtually immediate skyrocketing to statehood was due both to the ongoing political issue of slavery that was threatening to tear the Union apart, and to the rules in existence for admission to the Union during that era. In those days, a minimum population of 60,000 people was required before a territory could apply for statehood. The Gold Rush, however, had resulted in more than 100,000 people migrating to California in less than eighteen months! It was then, and remains now, the swiftest mass migration in the history of the United States.

By the mid-1850s California's population had risen to over 300,000. In the first five years of the Gold Rush over 12 million ounces of gold had been successfully mined!

The resultant circulation of the California gold led to a huge expansion of the American economy in the early and mid-1850s. Meanwhile, Polk and his wife, Sarah, left Washington in March of 1849, taking a circuitous but scenic southern route home to Tennessee, visiting various Southern towns and cities, proud of all that had been accomplished in the Polk Presidency. His goals had all been met, the country's northern and southern boundaries were extended and firmly in place, with the country also now spanning east and west from ocean to ocean. But, Polk was quite exhausted and not feeling very well upon arrival in Tennessee. Three months later he was dead at age fifty-three. Doctors believed Polk was likely a victim of a cholera epidemic that had broken out in parts of the South in the late spring and early summer of 1849.

James K. Polk had the shortest life of any American President who died of natural causes.

Chapter 12

Dwight D. Eisenhower — It is true that Eisenhower graduated just a bit above the middle of his class at West Point, 61st out of 164 in the class of 1915. However, originally the class had 301 cadets. Additionally, the class of 1915 is known as the "Class the Stars Fell On" since 36 percent of the graduates attained the rank of general – the all-time record for a West Point class. Despite his slightly above-average academic record, in the context of Eisenhower's actual Army service he proved to have outstanding skills in the fields of military strategy and organization, as well as in the evaluation of people and their individual strengths and weaknesses. All these skills served him exceedingly well in both his military career and as President of the United States from 1953 to 1961.

Advancing rapidly in rank from the late 1930s into the early 1940s, Eisenhower was promoted to Commander of all American forces in Europe in June of 1942, and then in July he was made the Commander of Operation Torch, the Allied Invasion of North Africa. Eisenhower also oversaw the subsequent Allied efforts in Sicily and on the Italian mainland. In light of his many successes in Africa and Italy he was promoted to the position of Supreme Commander of Allied Forces in Europe in December of 1943. He was responsible for the entire Allied military theater.

His biggest decision was to go ahead as planned with the "D-Day" landings in Normandy on June 6, 1944, despite some worries about weather issues. As it turned out the weather was a bit better than anticipated, and the D-Day invasions were largely highly successful, signifying the beginning of the end for the Nazis. The Allied forces suffered over 4,100 deaths during D-Day, with 2,501 being Americans (61 percent). The D-Day invasion of Nazi-occupied France (Normandy) was the largest combined sea, air, and land military operation in history. By the end of the war in Europe in May, 1945, Eisenhower had been promoted to a five-star general—as was Omar Bradley five years later in 1950. Bradley had also been a member of the famous 1915 class, graduating 42nd—some nineteen spots above Eisenhower.

After the war Eisenhower replaced George Marshall as the Army Chief of Staff, serving until 1948. From 1951 to the spring of 1952 Ike served as the Supreme Commander of NATO. He then resigned to run for President, easily defeating Adlai Stevenson in the electoral college, 442 to 89, and winning the popular vote by 6.6 million votes.

In 1956 the two candidates matched up again, with Eisenhower winning by even bigger margins: 457 to 73, and by 9.5 million popular votes. Stevenson never really had a chance in 1956, as the election occurred just months after Eisenhower had experienced a major medical issue, which had engendered great emotional support from the American public. Additionally, the election occurred just days after the Soviets had sent massive military might into Hungary, crushing the Hungarian freedom fighters' quest for independence, and slaughtering an estimated 30,000 Hungarians, with additional thousands subsequently sent to the Soviet gulags. As if that wasn't enough, Eisenhower was also dealing with the exceedingly dicey situation in the Middle East, where France and Britain, who had built the Suez Canal more than eighty years before, together with Israel, were engaged in combat with Egypt who, with the support of the Soviets, had seized control of the canal.

One of Eisenhower's first acts as President was to go to Korea and facilitate the end of the Korean War. Although no peace treaty was ever achieved, the two sides did agree to an armistice on July 27, 1953. In 1954 Eisenhower, acting in conjunction with the Mexican government, ordered more than 1,000,000 illegal immigrants to be deported back to Mexico. In June of 1956 Eisenhower signed into law the Interstate Highway act which he had proposed to Congress and had strongly lobbied them to pass. Eisenhower was well aware of the importance of highways as a result of his military experiences in Europe and elsewhere.

In 1957 Eisenhower sent federal troops to Little Rock, Arkansas, to ensure that the Supreme Court's decision to integrate public schools in *Brown v. Board of Education* was carried out. This had become necessary due to the previous actions of the Governor of Arkansas, who had called out the Arkansas National Guard in an effort to intimidate black students from enrolling. At this exact point in time Eisenhower signed into law the 1957 Federal Civil Rights Act. It was the first federal legislation on civil rights in over eighty years—since the Grant

Administration! For details regarding civil rights legislation passed during the administration of Ulysses S. Grant, see Chapter 6.

Despite Eisenhower's two 1957 actions on civil rights listed above, many historians justifiably fault Eisenhower's slowness in dealing with the issue of civil rights. At a meeting with prominent African-American leaders, Eisenhower had called for "patience" in dealing with the country's civil rights problems. Jackie Robinson, the Brooklyn Dodgers' star second baseman who broke Major League Baseball's color barrier in 1947, had attended the meeting, and soon afterwards felt it necessary to write Eisenhower a letter, stating that he had "felt like standing up and saying, Oh no! Not again," when Eisenhower had called for "patience."

Another puzzling incident occurred in 1956 when Eisenhower wrote the well-known reverend Billy Graham, encouraging him to use his prestige to lobby for more qualified blacks to be elected to political positions and to be admitted to universities. Graham, thinking he was following instructions, did so by sharing Eisenhower's letter with various prominent individuals. Strangely, however, Eisenhower later chided Graham for breaking a confidence by sharing his "personal" letter. The only logical conclusion from this incident is that, although Eisenhower supported more blacks in politics and in universities, he didn't want the general public to be aware of his beliefs in these two areas.

The biggest issue that Eisenhower faced during his Presidency was the Cold War with the Soviet Union, which didn't end until 1991. In July of 1956 the United States successfully flew their brand new U-2 Spy Plane

Chapter 12

over the Soviet Union for the first time, taking dozens of high-resolution photographs of multiple Soviet bases and other locations. The Soviets were aware of the U-2, but did not have the technology in 1956 to shoot it down.

Thirteen months later, on August 21, 1957, the Soviets, on their fourth attempt, responded with a successful launch of the first Intercontinental Ballistic Missile in world history. The missile traveled 3,000 miles. The American ICBM Atlas program was still one full year away from its anticipated launch. Just over six weeks later the Soviets again stunned the world, successfully launching Sputnik on October 4, 1957—the world's first satellite. Five days later at his weekly press conference, President Eisenhower faced the nervous and now somewhat hostile national news media, who were demanding to know if Eisenhower was concerned about "our nation's security." After initially hesitating, Eisenhower said: "Not one iota."

Perhaps Eisenhower really wasn't worried. More likely, though, is that he was trying to prevent and minimize a public panic. After all, in 1955 due to the perceived threats of communism, Eisenhower had placed 600 military advisers in Vietnam, one of whom lost his life due to a military situation. The number of American military personnel in Vietnam had grown to 800 by the time Eisenhower left office. However, it should be noted that significant numbers of American troops didn't start arriving in Vietnam until the early 1960s, during the Kennedy Administration.

Exactly one month after the Soviets' successful Sputnik launch, on November 4, 1957, Khrushchev rubbed Eisenhower's nose in additional Soviet technology: The launch of Sputnik II, which carried a dog into space, although the dog died shortly after the launch, the Soviets failed to reveal that fact to the world. What was most important about the successful launch of Sputnik II was not the presence of the dog. It was the fact that Sputnik II weighed over 1,000 pounds—more than six times as heavy as Sputnik I. The Sputnik II launch clearly established the thrust and power of the Soviets' R-7 ICBM rockets.

Eisenhower's biggest mistakes as President all seemed to involve orders issued to the CIA. In August of 1953, in conjunction with British Prime Minister Winston Churchill, Eisenhower ordered the overthrow of Iran's democratically elected President, Mohammad Mosaddegh, in favor of Reza Pahlavi, who would become the final Shah of Iran. Supported by both CIA operatives and the forces of Iranian General Fazlollah Zahedi, the revolution was accomplished in five days, with an estimated 200-300 fatalities suffered by Mosaddegh's followers. One wonders whether or not the Iranians would ever have turned to an Islamic Fundamentalist state if Eisenhower and Churchill had elected to give democracy in Iran a chance to grow and flourish, or if they had supported the democratically elected President.

Just under one year later, in June of 1954, there was yet another CIA-backed revolution authorized by Eisenhower. This one was aimed at the democratically elected President of Guatemala, Jacobo Arbenz. Although the CIA-backed rebels did not do well at all in the fighting, eventually Arbenz's army refused to fight any further, as they reasoned that the might of the U.S. Army and Navy would soon be thrown against them if they continued to fight. Thus Arbenz resigned, and a brutal dictator named

Chapter 12

Castillo Armas took control over the Guatemalan government. Great suffering then ensued among the former followers of Arbenz. Even worse, a genocide against Mayan peoples was launched in the decades that followed the 1954 takeover.

In September of 1957, Eisenhower ordered the CIA to start a revolution in Indonesia due to the widespread belief that Indonesian President Kusno Sukarno was cozying up to the Soviet Union. This "operation" was an embarrassing and public failure, which understandably caused Eisenhower to lose trust in the Agency's abilities and decision-making. Yet and still, three years later in 1960, Eisenhower once again ordered the CIA to "eliminate" the president of a small country that was receiving support from the Soviet Union. In this case it was the Democratic Republic of the Congo and its new leader, Patrice Lumumba. The CIA provided Lumumba's chief rival with $250,000 and the rival then carried out his orders, delivering Lumumba to Katangan secessionists, who were supported by the Belgians, the former colonial masters of the Congo. Four months later Lumumba was executed by the Katangans. Forty-two years after that, in 2002, the Belgians formally apologized for their role in overseeing the assassination of Lumumba.

However, the worst was yet to come: Eisenhower's biggest mistake as President came on May 1, 1960, when he authorized the CIA's request for yet another U-2 Spy Plane flight over the Soviet Union. It was to be the 24th and final U-2 flight. On this flight the Soviets were finally able to shoot down the U-2 and capture the luckless pilot, Francis Gary Powers, as well as to retrieve parts of the mostly destroyed plane. The shoot-down occurred in the Sverdlovsk area of Siberia, ironically the same city in which, forty-two years earlier, the Bolsheviks had slaughtered Russian Czar Nicholas II, the Empress Alexandra, and the couple's five children (although in March of 1918 the city was known as Ekaterinburg). Making matters even worse than they already were, Eisenhower had approved the flight knowing full well he was leaving in thirteen days for a *Détente* summit with the Soviets in Paris!

Then, things got worse. Instead of admitting the truth and mitigating the incident, since all the major powers, including the Soviets, engaged in spying, the Eisenhower Administration issued a series of four different disingenuous, misleading and contradictory statements about what had happened, trying to both excuse and disguise their conduct. Needless to say, the Paris *Détente* summit with the Soviets was exceedingly brief and utterly bereft of any hint of accomplishment.

Although the Republicans controlled both houses of Congress during Eisenhower's first two years in office, thereafter they never controlled either house for the remaining six years of the Eisenhower Presidency! Given that Eisenhower won both of his Presidential races by significant margins, the only conclusion that seems reasonable from this set of facts is that the voters liked "Ike" personally and were thankful he had done an outstanding job commanding the Allied forces in Europe during WWII, but they were not all that pleased with his administration's policies, and desired the Democratic Congress to restrain Eisenhower and/or some of his cabinet officers from succeeding with their various Republican agendas.

As per statements by Richard Helms, the former CIA Director, and supported by the official findings of

CHAPTER 12

the 1975 U.S. Senate Select Committee chaired by Idaho Senator Frank Church, there were authorized assassination attempts by the CIA against the Communist leader of Cuba, Fidel Castro, beginning in 1960 and continuing through 1965, a period covering the final year of the Eisenhower Administration, and continuing through the entirety of the Kennedy Administration, and into the first two years of the Johnson Administration. Eisenhower also authorized the initial planning for the Bay of Pigs invasion, but the final plan was okayed by Kennedy, and the invasion itself wasn't attempted until April 17, 1961, some three months after Kennedy took office, and some six months after Kennedy (then a Presidential candidate) had received a CIA briefing about the Bay of Pigs planning. More than 1,000 of the mostly ex-Cuban invaders were killed or captured/imprisoned.

Notably, in Eisenhower's parting speech to the nation on January 17, 1961, he showed amazing prescience regarding America's future, warning citizens about four specific dangers that he foresaw: 1) Overspending leading to budget deficits, 2) The corruption of the scientific process due to the ever increasing role of the federal government in funding research, 3) The impulse to "live only for today, plundering for our own ease and convenience the precious resources of tomorrow," and 4) Eisenhower chillingly warned American citizens about the dangers posed by uncontrolled defense spending and "the unwarranted influence of the military-industrial complex," characterizing it as "a potential enemy of the national interest."

The fourth point is especially noteworthy in that Eisenhower served more than thirty years in the American military!

Chapter 13

William McKinley was a genuine Civil War hero, a Congressman, a Governor, and a twice-elected President. Tragically, he was also the third President in thirty-six years to be assassinated, following Lincoln in 1865 and Garfield in 1881.

McKinley entered Allegheny College in Meadville, Pennsylvania at age seventeen, but dropped out less than a year later due to illness, as well as the necessity of helping support his family, which was, along with much of the country, still feeling the economic effects of the Panic of 1857. With the outbreak of the Civil War, McKinley enlisted in the Union Army as a private in June of 1861 at the age of eighteen. He distinguished himself in the crucial and bloody battle of Antietam in September of 1862 to such an extent that he was promoted to second lieutenant and assigned to the staff of Colonel (and future President) Rutherford B. Hayes. He remained in the army until July of 1865, by which time he was a brevet major. During his four years in the Union Army, McKinley saw action in eleven different battles and was twice promoted for bravery in battle (Antietam and Winchester). After the Civil War, McKinley studied law for a year-and-a-half and was admitted to the Ohio State Bar in March of 1867.

Turning to politics, he served six terms in Congress between 1877 and 1891. After just three years in Congress he had so impressed his fellow representatives that he was chosen for the powerful Ways & Means Committee, later becoming Chairman of the Committee. In 1892 he successfully ran for Governor of Ohio, serving until he won the Presidential election of 1896. In that election McKinley defeated William Jennings Bryan, the famous "Boy Orator of the Platte" (Bryan was only thirty-six years old.). McKinley won the popular vote by nearly 600,000 votes, and he won the electoral vote 271 to 176. McKinley's victory also included the capturing of both houses of Congress by the Republicans.

While Bryan had toured the country speaking to hugely emotional crowds, McKinley had literally done just the opposite. He ran what is now known as the "Front Porch Campaign," speaking to more than 750,000 people from thirty different states who were brought by trains to McKinley's front yard in Canton, Ohio. The ostentatiously wealthy industrialist, Mark Hanna, who was McKinley's campaign manager, was able to raise several million dollars from wealthy businessmen, who were extremely worried about the fervency of Bryan's populist rhetoric, in order to finance the Front Porch Campaign. McKinley's government experience, combined with his glittering Civil War record, plus a massive ten-to-one advantage in fundraising thanks to Hanna, proved to be far too much for the young, relatively inexperienced, and under-financed Bryan to overcome.

Four years later in 1900, McKinley sought a second term, while Bryan sought a second chance. However, the results were quite the same, although McKinley extended his margins of victory to 860,000 popular votes, and to 292 to 155 in the electoral vote. This was the largest margin of victory in any Presidential campaign since Grant's 1872 victory. McKinley had clearly and successfully launched the country into world affairs, saying: "Isolation is no longer possible or desirable... The period of exclusiveness is past."

McKinley was no doubt significantly boosted in the election of 1900 by America's highly successful and stunningly quick victory in the Spanish-American War, which lasted just over three months. Following the February 15, 1898 sinking of the American battleship, the *USS Maine*, which was sitting at anchor in a Cuban harbor (Cuba was still a Spanish colony in 1898), McKinley sent a message of "neutral intervention in the War" to Congress on April 11. This unusually phrased message was due to the vast majority of Cuban citizens trying to win their freedom from Spain. Exactly two weeks after McKinley's request to Congress, the House approved American intervention by a vote of 325 to 19, while the Senate approved the proposal 42-35, as many senators had issues with the peculiar wording McKinley had utilized.

McKinley also enjoyed the support of a clear majority of the American citizenry who, even before the sinking of the *USS Maine*, had become increasingly outraged as the Cuban revolutionaries' lengthy struggle for freedom from Spain dragged on and on, bringing ever increasing disease and starvation to the masses of Cuban people. Most of the American public was also outraged over the explosion and sinking of the *Maine*, which cost the lives of 260 American sailors. It should be noted, though, that the cause of the *Maine* disaster has never been positively determined. It may have been an enemy bomb that sent the *Maine* to the bottom, or it may have been caused by mechanical failure aboard the ship.

Just five days after the Congressional Declaration of War, Commodore George Dewey sailed into Manila Bay in the Philippines, which was also a Spanish colony in 1898. The next day Dewey engaged the Spanish Navy in battle, destroying all ten Spanish vessels and capturing the Philippines! Dewey didn't lose a single man in the combat, although nine sailors were wounded. Similarly, the American Navy also sank or destroyed all nine of Spain's naval vessels as they tried to flee Santiago Harbor in Cuba. Additionally, the ground war went well for the American army in Cuba, although 281 lives were lost in the fierce fighting there, plus 1,577 wounded. See Chapter 3 on the participation of Teddy Roosevelt and his Roughriders. After 100 days of fighting, the Spanish-American War ended with Spain's complete capitulation. Spain had lost 800 men, with another 800 wounded, plus in excess of 40,000 Spanish soldiers/sailors who had surrendered or were captured, and thus taken prisoner.

On December 10, 1898, the Treaty of Paris, which was dictated by the United States, formally ended the War. Cuba was granted its independence while Spain ceded Guam and Puerto Rico to the U.S. and sold the Philippines to America for twenty million dollars. The United States later granted the Philippines its full independence on July 4, 1946, following the victorious conclusion of World War II in the Pacific theater.

McKinley's first term as President had also been a huge success domestically, as the American economy became firmly attached to the Gold Standard and productivity

Chapter 13

boomed. McKinley's successful advocacy for an "Open Door" policy with China for trade with all Western countries also contributed to the growing American economy. Additionally, in the months leading up to the election of 1900, a bitter United Mine Workers strike had been settled, and the Boxer Rebellion had been brought to a mostly successful conclusion. An additional plus was that Cuba was in the process of holding its own constitutional convention.

Earlier, in 1898, Congress had voted to annex Hawaii into the United States, as McKinley had strongly recommended, and for which he had engaged in heavy lobbying for the support of key representatives and senators. This action reversed the position taken in 1893 by the preceding President, Grover Cleveland, when Cleveland, in his first months in office, withdrew the annexation request Benjamin Harrison had submitted to Congress in the closing months of the Harrison Presidency.

In 1899 McKinley, through his Secretary of State John Hay, established the "Open Door Policy." This program was launched for the purpose of maintaining trading rights for the United States and European countries to all engage in commerce with the Chinese, as it appeared that German or Japanese militarism might close off the major Chinese ports, thus terminating the burgeoning trade then existing. Soon thereafter, in June of 1900, what was to become known as the "Boxer Rebellion" took place. This was a violent uprising by Chinese nationalists who blamed "the West" for massive problems then being experienced in China. The result was the massacring of 200 to 250 foreign nationals (mostly Christian missionaries), as well as an estimated 32,000 Chinese citizens who had converted to Christianity.

The Boxers then laid siege to the foreign community in Peking (now Beijing). One of the Americans trapped during the siege was future American President Herbert Hoover. See Chapter 17 for the actions that Hoover took during the siege and its aftermath. In August of 1900, an eight-nation alliance was formed, which consisted primarily of military forces from the United States, Great Britain, Russia, Germany and France, as well as Japanese forces. These allied nations organized a joint rescue effort of the hostages, as well as relatively quickly extinguishing the Boxer fighters. Of the 900 foreigners who had been trapped in their compound, 69 had perished, while another 150 were injured. An estimated 3,000 combat deaths resulted in the fighting between the eight allied nations and the Boxer forces, with the vast majority of the dead being Boxers and other Chinese fighters. American military personnel suffered 53 dead and 253 injured.

The ultimate settlement of this tragic maelstrom was called the Boxer Protocol of 1901, in which the Chinese government agreed to pay $333 million to the involved foreign nations for the losses that were incurred by them in their quelling of the Rebellion. Interestingly and magnanimously, much of the American share of the Chinese reparations (which was $25 million) and some of the British share, was used to supply scholarships for Chinese students.

In 1900–01, recognizing how valuable it would be to the American economy, McKinley successfully lobbied Congress to support a deal between America, Great Britain and Nicaragua. The purpose of the agreement

Chapter 13

was to build a canal across the southernmost part of Nicaragua; although ultimately the United States would build their canal across Panama rather than Nicaragua. Read David McCullough's brilliant book, *The Path Between the Seas*, for the full and fascinating story on the circumstances of Nicaragua missing out on the isthmian canal in favor of Panama. Also see Chapter 3 on Teddy Roosevelt for details regarding the political maneuverings in 1903 which led to the building of the isthmian canal in Panama. Also see Chapter 11 for the steps taken by James K. Polk in 1846, which ultimately led to Roosevelt's legal justification for the actions he took in 1903.

McKinley would perhaps have been higher on the Best Presidents List if he had completed his second term rather than being the tragic victim of an anarchist named Leon Czolgosz, who fired two bullets into McKinley's torso while the President was standing in a receiving line at the 1901 Buffalo Pan-American Exposition. The assassination occurred just six months into McKinley's second term. McKinley's final words were to his wife, Ida: "It is God's way. His will, not ours, be done." Just seconds later he whispered the words to a favorite hymn, "Nearer my God, to Thee."

Following McKinley's assassination, Grover Cleveland, McKinley's Democratic predecessor as President, described him with these words: "William McKinley has left us a priceless gift in the example of a useful and pure life, in his fidelity to public trusts, and in his demonstration of the value of kindly virtues that not only ennoble, but [which] lead to success."

McKinley's Secretary of State, John Hay, summed up the McKinley Presidency in 1902 with these words:

"Under his rule Hawaii has come to us…Cuba is free…The Monroe Doctrine evokes now no challenge or contradiction when uttered to the world…In dealing with foreign powers, he will take rank with the greatest of our diplomatists."

Hay, who served four years as Abraham Lincoln's secretary during the Civil War, in describing how McKinley dealt with his cabinet, wrote the following: "The President rules with a hand of iron in a mitten of knitted wool…It is delightful to see the air of gentle deference with which he asks us all our opinions, and then decides as seemeth unto him good…He is awfully like Lincoln in many respects."

Chapter 14

James Madison— Although the smallest President of all, he was one of the best educated, especially in the philosophy of governments. Madison was only 5'4" tall, and his weight is reported variously from a low of 100 pounds to a high of 130. He was commonly known by the moniker "Little Jemmy Madison." Although he suffered periodic seizure episodes, he was also regarded as somewhat of a hypochondriac. Not surprising at all to his friends and family members, he ended up living to be eighty-five years old, passing away just six days short of the Fourth of July, in 1836. His friends and relatives had expected him to live to be eighty-five, or even well beyond, as Madison's mother, who had borne ten children, had lived to be ninety-seven! Only three of her ten children survived her. Madison had been the last living signatory of America's 1787 Constitution. While attending the College of New Jersey (now Princeton), Madison would routinely get just four hours of sleep per night as he pored over the strenuous and varied curriculum required of college students in the eighteenth century.

Madison is best known as being one of the three primary architects of the American Constitution, although the version of the Constitution that was ultimately passed was significantly different from what Madison had initially proposed. Notwithstanding the delegates' rejection of Madison's "Virginia Plan," some commentators and individuals from the period still regarded him as the "Father of the Constitution." Additionally, Madison and Alexander Hamilton wrote eighty of the eighty-five Federalist Papers (the other five were written by John Jay), which argued in favor of the new Constitution and were published during the period when the thirteen states were contemplating whether or not to ratify the proposed constitution. Many historians believe that without the essays written by Hamilton (fifty-one) and Madison (twenty-nine), the Constitution may well have been disapproved by the States. Madison's essay number ten is regarded as perhaps the single most influential of the eighty-five essays that were written.

Historian Douglass Adair has labeled Madison's intense studying of the work of Scottish philosopher David Hume in the months leading up to the Constitutional Convention as perhaps the most productive and consequential act of scholarship in American history. In the Virginia state-ratifying convention, Madison was able to overcome the brilliant and dramatic oratory and anti-constitution arguments of Virginia's hugely popular governor, Patrick Henry, to secure an 89 to 79 "yes" vote on the proposed new constitution from the Virginia delegates. Madison was able to win over a majority of the delegates by calmly rebutting with facts and logic each of Henry's emotional and sarcastic arguments against the proposed constitution.

Madison, at Jefferson's urging, became in 1789 the main shepherd of what was to become the first ten

Chapter 14

amendments to the Constitution—now more popularly known as the Bill of Rights. Madison reviewed more than 200 amendments that had been proposed by the various states, eventually submitting eight amendments. A select House committee reworked Madison's proposal into seventeen separate amendments. The new Senate made twenty-six changes to the House's seventeen proposals, reducing the total number of amendments to twelve. By December, 1789, three-fourths of the states had ratified ten of the final twelve that had been submitted to them. Those ten thus became part of the United States Constitution. All ten of those amendments are still with us today, along with seventeen additional amendments which have been added in the last 230 years.

Ironically, Madison's eight years as President (1809-1817) somewhat tarnished the image he had enjoyed prior to assuming the office, as he had just completed eight successful years as Jefferson's Secretary of State. This was in addition to his earlier major contributions at the 1787 Constitutional Convention, as well as his efforts in pursuing the creation of the Bill of Rights. Madison was also regarded as having been the most influential member of the House of Representatives during the first eight years of the existence of the House—this despite the fact he was not a gifted orator in any sense of the word. He was, however, smart, organized and a tireless worker despite his frail physique.

Unlike John Adams in the late 1790s, who faced the same issue with the French, and Thomas Jefferson in 1807 with the British, Madison was unwilling to avoid war with Great Britain over the issue of the Brits' continuous policy of impressments of American sailors. The

British Navy had a critical need for sailors, so they would stop American ships on the pretext of looking for British sailors who had jumped ship, and then seize a number of men, claiming they were actually British deserters. Some were, but most weren't. Basically, they were engaging in serial kidnapping of American seamen because they had the strongest navy in the world, they knew they could get away with it, and they desperately needed as many sailors as possible in their ongoing war with the French Navy and Napoleon Bonaparte. Eventually, the number of American sailors seized/impressed by the British Navy ran into the thousands! Further, America's commercial oceanic trade had also been significantly and negatively impacted by the British policy of impressments.

Madison eventually concluded that standing up to the British was the right thing to do. Thus, in June of 1812 he presented to Congress a written recommendation for war that had been drafted by Secretary of State James Monroe. Ironically for Madison, Congress, and for all Americans, and unbeknownst to them all, also in June of 1812, Great Britain had created new orders disallowing their sea captains to any longer seize American sailors, which had been the primary complaint of the United States. However, once the news of the revision of the policy arrived, both Congress and Madison decided to go ahead with the war, believing they would be successful. However, the vote in Congress to declare War was far from overwhelming, as the House voted 79 to 49 in favor, and the Senate voted 19-13 in favor, but only after much debate. Sadly, their confidence that the American military would prevail proved to be significantly misplaced, especially in the short run.

Chapter 14

America's initial attacks across the Canadian border generally proved disastrous for the under-trained and under-provisioned American army. The most puzzling early defeat was a head-shaking decision by General William Hull on August 16, 1812. Despite being ensconced within Fort Detroit and with a larger army than his British adversary, General Isaac Brock, Hull inexplicably surrendered the fort and his entire army. Hull was eventually court-martialed. The military jury found him not guilty of treason, but guilty of neglect of duty and un-officer-like conduct (cowardice), with eight of the twelve hearing officers recommending he be executed. Madison concurred in the findings of guilt, but declined to impose the death penalty recommendation. Hull's military career, which had begun in 1775 at the outbreak of the Revolutionary War, was over. He was sent home to Massachusetts.

Ironically, on August 19, 1812, just three days after the surrender of General William Hull, his thirty-nine-year-old nephew, Captain Isaac Hull, at least partially redeemed the Hull Family name. Captain Hull, aboard his ship, the *U.S.S. Constitution*, defeated the British frigate, *Guerriere*, in a one-on-one sea battle in the ocean south of Newfoundland. So badly damaged was the *Guerriere* that it was in the process of sinking. Following the British captain's surrender, Captain Hull directed his crew to work with the British crew in transferring the British sailors and their baggage aboard the *Constitution*. The *Guerriere* was then set afire. Hull received significant acclaim from both the British captain and from many Americans in his handling of the rescue of the defeated British sailors. American casualties in the battle stood at seven fatalities and seven wounded. British casualties were fifteen dead and sixty-four wounded. It was this battle that gave the *Constitution* her nickname, which still survives to this day: "Old Ironsides." The nickname arose from a British sailor observing that multiple British cannon balls had struck the hull of the Constitution, but had merely bounced harmlessly off the ship's sides. The sailor exclaimed, "Huzza, her sides are made of iron!" Old Ironsides never lost a single sea battle, and can be seen and toured even to this day in Boston Harbor. She is credited with 100 victories, albeit fifty-eight of those were surrenders by the would-be opponents upon their recognizing the identity of the ship they were up against and not wishing to suffer the same fate as the *Guerriere*.

Notwithstanding Captain Hull's naval heroics, the egregious circumstances of General Hull's capitulation in Detroit, as well as several other defeats, nearly led to Madison losing the Presidency in November of 1812 to DeWitt Clinton, the former mayor of New York City and the current lieutenant governor of New York. Madison won the popular vote by less than three percent, and the electoral vote by the relatively close margin of 128 to 89. This was in stark contrast with Madison's seemingly easy victory in winning the 1808 Presidential election by a somewhat one-sided electoral vote of 122 to 47 over the Federalist candidate, C.C. Pinckney of South Carolina. Madison's loss of popularity with the voters in 1812 was also clearly reflected in the doubling of Congressional seats won by the Federalists.

When Madison was sworn in for his second term on March 4, 1813, the federal treasury was bare. This was due to members of Madison's own party distrusting Madison's Secretary of Finance, Albert Gallatin. Thus,

Chapter 14

when Madison had proposed in 1812 to renew the twenty-year charter of the Bank of the United States, the Senate voted the proposal down. So, to finance the war Madison was forced to obtain loans totaling $9,000,000 from two German-born financiers who had immigrated to America in the second half of the eighteenth century: David Parish and John Jacob Astor, the first multi-millionaire in the history of the United States.

Besides America's military battles, things also went poorly for Astor's fur trading post near what is today the Oregon town of Astoria. When the War of 1812 broke out, as well as on many occasions thereafter, Astor requested Madison to send one American warship and a squadron of marines to protect both Astor's fledgling fur business as well as, more importantly, the United States' interests in the Oregon territory. However, the Madison Administration vacillated on the request, ultimately never sending any military personnel at all. Eventually, a British warship arrived at the mouth of the Columbia, signaling the end of Astor's dream.

At the conclusion of the War of 1812, the two countries agreed to share the Oregon Territory for the near future. Finally, thirty-two years later in 1846, during the James K. Polk Administration, the two countries agreed that the boundary would be the forty-ninth parallel, making both Washington and Oregon, plus portions of Idaho, Montana and Wyoming the property of the United States. The agreement launched a flood of settlers in the tens of thousands to begin pouring into Oregon, vastly increasing the traffic on the Oregon Trail. Given the beautiful Oregon terrain, the moderate weather, and the agricultural richness of the Willamette Valley, the massive onslaught of settlers certainly came as no surprise.

Despite the early military failures in the War of 1812, the U.S. did have three major successes in late 1813, all involving the twenty-eight-year-old Oliver Perry. The first occurred in late May when Perry and General Winfield Scott combined to execute an amphibious assault on Fort George, which was located on the southwest shore of Lake Ontario, just west of the Niagara River's entry into Lake Ontario, in Canadian territory. The American tandem captured the British fort and inflicted twice as many casualties on the British as they themselves suffered. They also captured 280 Redcoats.

Just over three months later, and roughly 150 miles to the southwest, Perry defeated a larger British fleet in the Battle of Lake Erie, which took place in the southwestern part of Lake Erie's waters, north of Port Clinton, Ohio. During the battle Perry's flagship, the *Lawrence*, was on the verge of sinking, so he ordered crew members to row him to the closest American ship, the *Niagara*, where he continued the fight. The cannon fire in the Battle of Lake Erie was so thunderous and so continuous that citizens heard it as far away as 160 miles! Eventually, the six remaining British ships surrendered under the withering cannon pounding administered by Perry's fleet, and were promptly seized by Perry's men for possible later use by the Americans.

Following his victory, Perry wrote out a brief statement to be taken by messenger to the encampment of General William Henry Harrison, whose next move depended on the success or failure of Perry's sea battle. Perhaps in part because it was brief, it is one of those

Chapter 14

classic statements that has lived on in American history. Perry wrote: "We have met the enemy, and they are ours."

Another facet of the Sea War in 1812–1814 were the 526 American privateers that roamed the high seas in search of British merchant ships. They ultimately captured 1,345 British merchant vessels. The British were thus forced to convoy their merchant vessels in order to reduce the amount of their losses. It should be noted, though, that the British privateers were also capturing American merchant vessels. Additionally, the British Navy was able to capture 148 American privateering vessels.

Perry's naval triumph at Lake Erie had also made possible America's third major attack in less than five months, which resulted in yet another important defeat of the British. The third battle was also a joint attack, this time on the British military stationed near the River Thames, in extreme Southwestern Ontario, Canada, roughly 70-80 miles north-northeast of Perry's Lake Erie victory. This attack was jointly led by Perry and General (and future President) William Henry Harrison. Just one month after the Lake Erie victory in October of 1813 at the Battle of the Thames, the American forces routed the British and their Indian allies. The "Battle" mainly consisted of Harrison and Perry's troops vigorously pursuing the fleeing forces of British General Henry Proctor for eight days before finally catching and defeating the retreating Brits and their allies. It was during this battle that Tecumseh, the most prominent, charismatic and important leader of the Indian forces, was fatally wounded.

As for Harrison, it was "déjà vu all over again" as just two years earlier he had defeated Tecumseh's younger brother, Tenskwatawa, in the Battle of Tippecanoe. That victory was to provide Harrison with one of the most memorable and victorious Presidential campaign slogans in all of American history, in the election of 1840: "Tippecanoe and Tyler too."

However, other actions in 1813 included the British Navy sailing north up Chesapeake Bay and attacking and burning multiple towns north of Annapolis. This attack apparently caused little concern to either Madison or Secretary of War John Armstrong, as no efforts at fortifying America's capitol were undertaken. Finally, on May 20, 1814, Madison ordered Armstrong "to be prepared for the worst," as he believed the British may well be looking at Washington City as a "favorite" target. However, in early July Armstrong advised Madison that the British would attack Baltimore, not the Capitol, because Baltimore was more significant militarily. Madison disagreed and demanded that Armstrong draft a plan for the defense of the Capitol, which should include 10,000 militiamen. However, once again, Armstrong dilly-dallied, and although Madison would periodically question Armstrong about "the plan," he never aggressively followed up on his order! Compounding Madison's growing dissatisfaction with Armstrong was Madison's own inspection of War Department records, wherein he discovered Armstrong was communicating with generals on matters of importance without having provided the information to Madison.

Making matters far worse was the fact that by April of 1814 the British were no longer worried about Napoleon, who had abdicated the French throne following his ill-conceived attempt to conquer Russia, as well as multiple defeats of French forces, including by the British

Chapter 14

in March of 1814 at the conclusion of the Peninsular War, which had started on the Iberian Peninsula some six years earlier and concluded in southwestern France. Thus, massive numbers of British troops were freed up to deal with America. And deal they did!

In late August of 1814 the Redcoats attacked Washington City (as it was then called), burning down the President's House, the partially completed Capitol building, as well as several other nearby federal buildings. But for the fortuitous occurrence of a powerful hurricane/storm that came roaring into the Chesapeake Bay area, the extent of the damage would certainly have been significantly greater. As it was, the storm helped to put out the multiple fires, and it also forced the British navy to hastily move their ships to safer positions within the massive confines of Chesapeake Bay, as well as sending the British ground forces marching back to their ships.

Following the burning of Washington City, Madison forced Armstrong out of office and replaced him with Secretary of State James Monroe, who then served double duty thereafter. Monroe remained as Secretary of War until the War of 1812 had been successfully concluded, resigning the position on March 1, 1815 after roughly six months of holding both crucially important Cabinet positions.

Unbeknownst to the British military, their stunningly successful attack on Washington City would prove to be their high-water mark in the entire War of 1812. To their later shock, disbelief and dismay, the final five months of the War would be mostly one crushing loss after another for the British military — a military that was fresh off defeating the forces of Napoleon, thus helping to force him into exile on the Mediterranean island of Elba in the spring of 1814.

After the hurricane/storm passed, the British turned their attention to Fort McHenry, just to the north up Chesapeake Bay and to the east of Baltimore. Unlike the Washington City area, where Secretary of War John Armstrong had failed to seriously consider the possibility that the British might attack the capitol, the federal and state militia forces in Baltimore, commanded by state Militia General Samuel Smith, had been working tirelessly to prepare their defenses for more than a year (!), Smith having anticipated that eventually the British would attack the fort. The result was a stunning defeat of the British land and sea forces. A historic secondary result of the September 13-14, 1814 artillery assault on Fort McHenry (which lives on to this very day in American culture) was the writing of a song that ultimately became the American National Anthem. Frances Scott Key, an American lawyer and amateur poet, who witnessed the entire night-long but ultimately ineffectual artillery bombardment by the British Navy from the deck of a truce vessel anchored on the Patapsco River, wrote the words to the Star Spangled Banner on the back of an envelope after seeing the Giant American flag, which was thirty feet by forty-two feet, still flying on the morning of the 14th following the conclusion of twenty-five hours of artillery bombardment.

In the attack on Fort McHenry the British forces suffered nearly double the casualties of the American defenders, both in terms of numbers killed and numbers wounded. Most importantly for the American cause, the Brits also lost their highly-respected Army general, Robert

Chapter 14

Ross, very early on during the accompanying ground attack. Once the British troops had moved to within artillery range, the American forces returned fire in an exceedingly efficient and accurate manner, thus preventing the destruction of the city of Baltimore, which was at that time the third largest city in the United States. The early death of Ross also seemed to destroy the confidence of many of the British troops, as their ground assault was not a factor thereafter once Ross had been carried to the rear on a stretcher. One of Ross's soldiers afterward said: "It is impossible to conceive the effect which this melancholy spectacle produced throughout the army."

After the British had retreated to their ships, the commander of Fort McHenry, Major George Armistead, estimated that 1,800 shells had been fired at Fort McHenry. Many were short of the mark and many had exploded in mid-air, but Armistead estimated that 400 bombs weighing between 210 and 220 pounds had fallen within the confines of the Fort. Yet amazingly, only four soldiers had been killed! And although an additional twenty-four men had been wounded, the wounds were not life-threatening, and it is believed that they all recovered.

On September 11, 1814, just three days prior to the British defeat at Fort McHenry, but several hundred miles to the north, the British Navy also suffered an even more shocking defeat in the Battle of Lake Champlain. The thirty-year-old American Commodore, Thomas Macdonough, out-prepared and out-strategized the Royal Navy, defeating the much larger British force and accepted the surrender of the British Naval officers and sailors. Macdonough's stunning victory did not go unnoticed by two prominent naval historians. Theodore

Roosevelt, in his *The Naval War of 1812*, wrote these words about Macdonough: "Down to the time of the Civil War he is the greatest figure in our naval history." Similarly, Winston Churchill, in his *History of the English-Speaking Peoples*, called Macdonough's victory: "…the most decisive battle of the War of 1812."

In the same ten-day September timeframe, the British ground assault on Plattsburg, which accompanied the naval Battle of Lake Champlain, was withdrawn as British General George Prevost believed his goals could not be accomplished without the support of the recently surrendered British Navy. In doing so, Prevost left behind large amounts of food and weapons, which the American troops were only too glad to confiscate, consume and utilize. Prevost's withdrawal also demoralized his own troops, as several hundred soldiers thereafter deserted the British Army. Additionally, on September 21, 1814, the British commander in the siege of Fort Erie, simply abandoned his seven-week-long siege and withdrew from the area.

In light of the drastic turn of events for the British in early and mid-September, 1814, and with huge war debts mounting from both the Napoleonic Wars and the War of 1812, Great Britain chose to drop all of their previous stringent demands for peace that they had been steadfastly insisting on for months in the ongoing negotiations in Belgium. Instead, they accepted virtually the entire American proposal and signed the Treaty of Ghent on December 24, 1814. However, the worst was yet to come for the British Army.

Given the slow state of communications in the early nineteenth century, neither President Madison,

Chapter 14

nor Andrew Jackson, nor the British Army, which was encamped not far from New Orleans, knew of the recently obtained peace treaty. Thus, the Battle of New Orleans was fought on January 8, 1815, with the British Army suffering the worst military defeat in their long history. See Chapter 9 on Andrew Jackson for all the details regarding the battle. Also see Chapter 9 for details regarding what the British were actually prepared to do if they had won the Battle of New Orleans! Finally, see Chapter 4 on Thomas Jefferson for Captain Stephen Decatur's uniform success in Madison's 1815 campaign against the "Barbary Pirates" of North Africa.

Perhaps not so surprisingly, Madison's popularity with the citizenry actually grew during the two years following the peace treaty. This was undoubtedly due to the extreme afterglow from Jackson's stunning beatdown of the Brits in New Orleans, the defeat of the British at Baltimore/Fort McHenry, as well as the multiple military successes along the Canadian border, plus Decatur's many successes against the "Barbary Pirates."

The American public apparently forgave James Madison for his utterly inexplicable failure, prior to May of 1814, to anticipate the possibility that the British might attack and burn the President's House, the Capitol, and additional public and private buildings. They also apparently forgave him for his additional failure to absolutely determine that Secretary of War Armstrong was actually following Madison's own directives. Washington City clearly could have been protected, just as Militia General Samuel Smith had done a short distance north at Baltimore/Fort McHenry.

Certainly, in light of the earlier British Naval attacks in May of 1813 in Maryland, just to the north of Annapolis, Madison's failure to both order the fortification of Washington City and to make absolutely sure it was accomplished was, in the parlance of the twenty-first century, "brain-dead," which is really quite surprising since Madison is justly regarded as one of the most intelligent and best educated of all the American Presidents.

Part of Madison's problem as President was that he was oftentimes indecisive. In addition to dithering about whether or not to send a warship to the Pacific to protect America's interests in the Oregon Territory and his failure to make sure that Armstrong was following his directives, Madison also had problems with his cabinet choices. He had initially determined to appoint the highly capable Swiss immigrant Albert Gallatin, who spoke perfect French, to be his Secretary of State. However, he was talked out of it and instead appointed Robert Smith, who proved to be unable to handle the position. After two years of Smith, Madison replaced him with James Monroe. Ironically, Madison had appointed the wrong Smith brother to his cabinet. If only he had appointed General (and Senator) Samuel Smith to the Secretary of War position instead of Armstrong, things would have been so vastly improved in both crucial cabinet positions. Another example of Madison's indecisiveness occurred in the final months of his Presidency. Madison had urged Congress to take up the issue of the Federal government getting involved in the building of the Erie Canal. Three months later the House and Senate reached an agreement on the canal project and submitted it to Madison for his approval. However, the Congressmen

Chapter 14

were beyond stunned when, with just one day left in his term as President, Madison vetoed the very bill he had requested of them!

Chapter 15

George H.W. Bush was perhaps the most widely experienced candidate since James Monroe in 1817 to win the Presidency. He was also only the second sitting Vice-President to be elected immediately upon the retirement of his predecessor. The first was Martin Van Buren, who replaced Andrew Jackson in 1837. Prior to Bush's crushing defeat of Michael Dukakis in the 1988 election, (426 to 111 in electoral votes, and by more than 7,000,000 popular votes), Bush had done all of the following: enlisted in the U.S. Navy on his eighteenth birthday as a seaman second class; earned his Naval wings at the age of nineteen to become the youngest pilot in the Navy; was promoted to ensign; flew fifty-eight combat missions in the Pacific, including being shot down and injured in his final mission (he was rescued by an American submarine after three hours in a rubber raft); was promoted to lieutenant; was awarded the Distinguished Flying Cross; earned his bachelor's degree from Yale in just two-and-a-half years; was the starting first-baseman for the Yale baseball team, which made the NCAA College World Series Tournament twice (albeit losing to California and USC). He also won a letter on the Yale soccer team, which won the New England Collegiate Championship; became

Chapter 15

a highly successful oilman for eighteen years, mostly in Texas; served four years in the House of Representatives; was the United States Ambassador to the United Nations; was Chairman of the Republican National Committee; was Ambassador to China; was the Director of the CIA; and served eight years as Ronald Reagan's Vice-President.

On August 2, 1990 the Iraqi forces of Saddam Hussein entered and took control of its tiny but oil-rich neighbor, Kuwait. When repeated efforts at diplomacy failed to solve the problem, a United Nations coalition of twenty-nine countries led the by the United States invaded Iraq on January 17, 1991 in Operation Desert Storm. Even a majority of the Arab League countries (twelve of twenty-one) supported the operation, including Saudi Arabia. Commanded by General Norman Schwarzkopf, the American-led forces overwhelmed the Iraqi military, winning the ground war in an astounding 100 hours! Arguably, it was the most impressive and successful war in the history of modern warfare. Many Americans were disappointed that President Bush didn't continue the war and remove Hussein from power. However, as Bush pointed out, that was not the mandate the United Nations had set forth for the operation.

Historian Herbert S. Parmet wrote the following about Bush's efforts in establishing the international coalition: "Creating such a multinational response was as fine an example of Presidential crisis management, given its scale, as can be found in the twentieth century."

President Bush was hugely gratified with the teardown of the Berlin Wall in October of 1989, and he worked hard, diplomatically, to encourage the process of German reunification, which became official on

October 3, 1990. This event had followed on the heels of the Czechoslovakian people obtaining their independence after forty years of communist rule on December 10, 1989. Six additional Eastern European countries also threw off the bonds of communism during the period from 1989 to 1992. Bush, however, generously and self-effacingly acknowledged that the groundwork had been laid during the Reagan Administration.

December of 1989 was a busy month for President Bush as he ordered a military invasion of Panama to overthrow and seize their military dictator, Manuel Noriega, who had been indicted in an American court for smuggling drugs into the United States. Noriega was arrested by the U.S. military and brought to the United States, where he was charged and ultimately convicted on numerous counts, and subsequently sentenced to forty years in federal prison. He ended up being paroled after having served seventeen actual years in prison, dying ten years later back in Panama.

Just as President Reagan had done, Bush courted Soviet leader Mikhail Gorbachev, meeting with him in 1990, as well as on three occasions in 1991. Their final meeting in Moscow concluded on August 1, 1991, with the signing of a new peace treaty to reduce both countries' stockpiles of long-range nuclear weapons. Four months later the Soviet Union dissolved, breaking up into fourteen separate republics. Bush played a major role in the dissolution, with his successful dealings with Gorbachev, continuing what Reagan had initiated with the Soviet leader during his five summit conferences from 1985 to 1988.

Chapter 15

President Bush used his veto power on forty-four Democratic-sponsored bills that related to a variety of social issues. Yet, he also had a successful domestic agenda, signing into law legislation regarding civil rights, the Clear Air Act of 1990, and the Americans with Disabilities Act (also 1990). Another promising development in 1990 was Bush's policy toward Nicaragua, which led to the collapse of the Marxist Sandinistas—at the ballot box! Bush, with the approval of Congress, provided $50 million in humanitarian aid to the citizens of Nicaragua and encouraged the Contras to participate in the upcoming elections. Surprisingly, a democratic election was held and Mrs. Violeta Chaparro won the presidency, ousting the Sandinista leader and subsequently forming a fourteen-party coalition to run the country democratically.

Among President Bush's judicial appointments was that of Clarence Thomas to the United States Supreme Court. When Thurgood Marshall, the first African American to serve on the Supreme Court retired, Bush replaced him with Thomas, who became the second African American to serve on the court. Now, nearly twenty-eight years later, Thomas remains on the bench and is currently the longest tenured member of the Court. He is greatly admired by those who believe it is the duty of judges to strictly interpret the laws Congress and state legislatures create (unless they are found to be unconstitutional) rather than to engage in "legislating from the bench" by establishing legal precedents through the issuance of decisions based on their own personal political or policy beliefs.

Among Bush's cabinet officers were Secretary of State James Baker, who had served as President Reagan's Treasury Secretary; and Secretary of Labor Elizabeth

Dole, who had been Reagan's Secretary of Transportation. Additionally, Dick Cheney, who had been the White House Chief of Staff during the Gerald Ford Administration, served as President Bush's Secretary of Defense. Cheney worked closely with General Schwarzkopf in the planning and deployment of American soldiers and materiel in the hugely successful Gulf War against Saddam Hussein in January of 1991.

In 2011, then President Obama honored former President Bush with a Medal of Freedom Award in a White House ceremony. Mr. Obama spoke the following words: "Like the remarkable Barbara Bush, his humility and his decency reflect the very best in the American spirit. This is a gentleman."

Although Bush lost his re-election bid in 1992 to Bill Clinton, it should always be remembered it was a three-way contest that also involved a conservative independent oilman from Texas/Oklahoma named Ross Perot. Bush and Perot combined to receive over 58.8 million votes, while Clinton, the only Democrat in the race, polled only 44.9 million votes. What would have happened if Perot had not been in the race? No one will ever know for sure. But the following polling data seems highly suggestive as to who would have won: Five weeks after the election, in mid-December, 1992, a WSJ/NBC News poll showed 56 percent of Americans giving Bush a positive approval rating for his handling of the Presidency! Additionally, in late January a Gallup poll showed that George and Barbara Bush were America's "most admired" man and woman.

In 1988 Atlanta Mayor Andrew Young said this about George H.W. Bush: "I've always felt there's one thing

Chapter 15

you could count on George Bush for, it's his decency and fairness."

In 1990 Sheik Jaber al-Sabah, the emir of Kuwait, said this about President Bush: "Your principled, courageous and decisive position in the face of the Iraqi aggression on Kuwait is a true expression of the unabated faith and commitment of the American people to the humanitarian morals on which, and for which, the United States of America was founded."

Bush's boss for eight years, President Ronald Reagan said this about his long-time Vice-President: "George Bush is a man of action — a man accustomed to command. The Vice-Presidency doesn't fit easily on such a man. But George Bush is a patriot. And so he made it fit, and he served with a distinction no one has ever matched."

Barbara Bush passed away in April of 2018, and George H.W. Bush's death followed seven months later on November 30, 2018. He was ninety-four-and-a-half, the longest living President of all time, although Bush's longevity record has since been eclipsed by Jimmy Carter. George and Barbara Bush were married for seventy-three years and three months — another Presidential record, although once again Jimmy Carter and his wife, Rosalyn, will quite likely break that record also.

George H.W. Bush is also one of only two Presidents to have a son follow in his footsteps and gain the Presidency. His oldest son, George W. Bush, was elected President in 2000, and then re-elected in 2004. Another one of George H.W. Bush's sons, Jeb Bush, was the highly successful two-term Governor of the State of Florida. The only other father/son Presidents were John Adams (1797–1801), and John Quincy Adams (1825–1829.)

Chapter 16

John **Adams** was an extremely intelligent man who also possessed great moral rectitude, a tremendous work ethic, and boundless courage. Unfortunately, the combination of these laudatory characteristics left him believing that anyone who disagreed with him was wrong. In the modern parlance, "he did not play well with others." Benjamin Franklin served with Adams on the Paris Peace Commission in 1783 and, being greatly frustrated by Adams, famously wrote thusly about him: "He means well for his Country, is always an honest Man, often a Wise One, but sometimes, and in some things, [he is] absolutely out of his Senses."

Similarly, Thomas Jefferson, in a letter to James Madison, circa 1783-84, wrote the following regarding Adams's mercurial personality: "He hates Franklin, he hates [John] Jay, he hates the French, he hates the English. To whom will he adhere?" Adams himself recognized his personality defects, saying at one point: "Vanity, I am sensible, is my cardinal vice and cardinal folly."

Per Historian Ron Chernow, on at least thirty occasions Adams had posed for portraits, but then "quibbled with the results" of the artists' works. Also, per Chernow: Adams was bothered by Washington's fame, at one point complaining about the "impious idolatry" of the public for Washington. Adams also began referring to him as "Old Muttonhead." In later writings, again per Chernow, Adams criticized Washington's intelligence, saying that he "could not write a sentence without misspelling some word," and that he was "but very superficially read in the history of any age, nation, or country." Adams also detested Alexander Hamilton, describing him as "the bastard brat of a Scottish peddler." Another example of Adams's temper occurred when news of the loss of Fort Ticonderoga to the British was received. Adams responded by saying: "…we shall never be able to defend a post until we shoot a general." (!)

Perhaps Adams's all-time low in losing his temper and making a mind-numbingly and shockingly offensive statement was reached in September, 1798, when Benjamin Franklin's grandson, Benjamin Franklin Bache, a Democratic-Republican journalist, passed away at age twenty-nine during a yellow-fever epidemic, some eight years after the elder Franklin had died. Hearing the news, Adams labeled Bache as a "malicious libeler" and then added, "the yellow fever arrested him in his detestable career and sent him to his grandfather, from whom he inherited a dirty, envious, jealous, and revengeful spite against me." As Benjamin Franklin had written about Adams back in 1783: "…sometimes, and in some things, [he is] absolutely out of his Senses." Clearly, by 1798, nothing had changed.

Adams graduated from Harvard College (now Harvard University) in 1755. He taught school for a year, and then began studying law under the tutelage of a prominent Massachusetts attorney. He was admitted to the bar in November of 1758. A decade later he won two major cases, one of which lives on in today's history books. His first big victory came in 1768–69 when he successfully defended future governor, as well as future President of the Continental Congress, John Hancock, against charges he had illegally smuggled wine into the Port of Boston without having paid the required duty (taxes). His second big victory, the one of historic proportions, came in his successful defense of the British soldiers and their captain, who had been criminally charged with murder for firing into a crowd of angry colonists on March 5, 1770, killing three demonstrators and wounding eight—the tragic episode that has lived on in history as the "Boston Massacre."

Adams successfully defended the unit's captain in the first trial, establishing that the captain had not ordered his men to fire into the profane crowd. In the second trial he defended the eight British soldiers, relying on the defense of self-defense. The jury ended up acquitting six of the soldiers completely, but convicted the other two, although their convictions were for manslaughter rather than murder.

Adams then served in the state legislature from 1770 to 1774. Although a state legislator, he applauded the "Boston Tea Party" of 1773, believing it was a legitimate protest against Great Britain's overbearing and unfair policy it was wielding against the colonists.

Adams's extreme sensitivity to criticism from others extended even into his Presidency and led him to the biggest mistakes of his political career: The proposal and passage of the Naturalization, Alien & Sedition Acts in the summer of 1798. The Naturalization act was aimed

Chapter 16

at foreigners who were illegally in the country. However, it also established a fourteen-year waiting period before an immigrant could gain his citizenship, which was an increase from what had been just a two-to-five-year wait. The Alien Act gave the President the power to deport any foreign-born resident he deemed to be dangerous, without any hearing or explanation being required! It should also be noted that most recent immigrants and new citizens had favored Jefferson's Democratic-Republicans over Adams's Federalists.

The Sedition act was even worse — far worse. It basically did away with the First Amendment (!) and provided for jail terms and financial penalties for anyone who criticized the government in overly strong terms (and we're not talking about the advocating of violence here). It was aimed not only at private citizens, but primarily at members of the press. Ultimately, at least twenty-six people were prosecuted under the Sedition Act, the vast majority of whom were editors of Democratic-Republican newspapers, and all of whom were strongly opposed to the Adams Administration. At least three individuals were actually imprisoned for "violating" the Act. Although Jefferson may well have defeated Adams's bid for reelection even if the Sedition Act had never been passed, it clearly helped him to deny Adams a second term.

Another factor in Adams's defeat by Jefferson were his repeated absences from Washington, D.C. At one point during Adams's Vice-Presidency he spent nine straight months at home in Braintree, Massachusetts. As President, it was more of the same: In his first year as President Adams spent a full four months in Massachusetts. By comparison, Washington was never out of the capital for more than two months. In the next three years Adams was often away from the capital. On one occasion, following a loud, emotional confrontation with a group of Federalist Senators regarding a sudden, and non-Senate-consulted diplomatic appointment made by Adams, he packed his bags and went home to Braintree, where he remained for seven straight months! Famed historian, David McCullough, commented that, "Adams's presence at the center of things was what the country rightfully expected and could indeed have made a difference." There certainly appears to be ample reasons why Adams was the only one of the first five Presidents who was not reelected to a second term.

Despite his puzzling political and constitutional blunder with the Alien & Sedition Acts, Adams accomplished much for America, both during the colonial days and after the Revolution was won. He served in the Continental Congress from 1774–1777. In the late spring of 1775 Adams proposed the creation of an American Navy for the purpose of contesting the mighty British Navy, as well as for privateering against British merchant vessels to disrupt the British economy. On Friday, October 13, 1775, the Continental Congress voted overwhelmingly in favor of Adams's proposal to establish an American Navy. By early December Adams had completed the official American Navy Manual, which was quickly approved by the Naval Committee. Interestingly, and perhaps tellingly, the Congress did not place Adams on the Naval Committee that would forthwith make all the vital decisions regarding ships, captains, shipyards, and so on.

Chapter 16

Just days later, on December 7, 1775, a twenty-eight-year-old, small in stature (but huge in courage) Scottish merchant captain was appointed the Lieutenant for the first merchant vessel to have been converted into an American ship of war, the *Alfred*. The new lieutenant for the *Alfred* was none other than John Paul Jones who, four years later, would go on to win perhaps the most improbable American Naval victory of all time; certainly the most stunning Revolutionary War naval victory.

On September 23, 1779, in the early evening, Jones, now the captain of the *Bonhomme Richard*, encountered, defeated, and captured the virtually brand new and far superior British warship, the *Serapis*, even as Jones's own ship, the aged *Bonhomme Richard*, was fatally wounded and in the process of sinking. Jones then sailed the badly damaged *Serapis* to a neutral Dutch harbor, along with the 191 captured British seamen who had survived the shockingly brutal battle in which both sides had suffered a 50 percent casualty rate of dead and wounded.

Early on in the battle, Jones's ship had taken a savage pounding from the *Serapis*, so much so that the British Captain paused his assault on the *Bonhomme Richard* and, using a megaphone-type device, asked Jones if he wished to surrender. Jones emphatically declined the offer with his now immortal seven-word response: "I have not yet begun to fight!"

One utterly improbable, but entirely true, aspect of the *Bonhomme Richard* versus *Serapis* sea battle is that it was witnessed by more than 1,000 British citizens/spectators. The battle took place barely a mile or so off the east-central coast of England, just east of a 400-foot high bluff called Flamborough Head. Although the battle was fought at night, it was easily viewed due to the bright light from a full Harvest Moon, as well as the virtual 400-foot tall natural bluff having served as a perfect viewing platform. To use a twenty-first century metaphor to describe the *Bonhomme Richard versus Serapis* battle, one could accurately state it was the Super Bowl sea battle of the eighteenth century.

As for Jones, he had other successes on behalf of the American Navy, and he also met with success years later as a Rear Admiral for Catharine the Great, in battles against the Ottoman Empire on the Black Sea (1787–88). Jones eventually passed away in Paris in 1792 at the age of forty-five and was buried there. For 113 years the location of Jones's remains was literally unknown. Then, in 1905, General Horace Porter, a wealthy Civil War hero, completed his six-year search for Jones's tomb, finding it in a tunnel underneath a French laundry! The unbelievable story finally ends on April 24, 1906 when, by order of President Theodore Roosevelt, Jones's body was retrieved from France by American warships and returned to the Naval Academy in Annapolis, Maryland, where Jones was re-buried underneath the Academy's chapel after Roosevelt had delivered a stirring eulogy praising Jones's supreme courage and brilliant naval war strategies.

Other American sea captains also met with repeated successes on the high seas during the Revolutionary War. Among these were the 6"4" John Barry, Nicholas Biddle, and Gustavus Conyngham. Barry and Conyngham were each born in Ireland in the mid-1740s, and each immigrated to the American colonies in the early 1760s — Barry at age fifteen, while Conyngham was seventeen. Biddle, who was born in Philadelphia, went to sea at age thirteen

Chapter 16

and later served three years in the British Navy. Biddle resigned his commission in 1773 and returned to the American colonies. After three highly successful years as an American Navy captain, Biddle died in March, 1778, during a battle with a British warship. Interestingly, Biddle's nephew, also named Nicholas Biddle (he was named for his famous uncle), was the third President of the Second Bank of the United States, who famously lost his battle with President Andrew Jackson, who successfully forced the closure of the younger Biddle's National Bank. See Chapter 9 on Andrew Jackson for more details regarding Jackson's war on Biddle's bank.

Some historians regard John Adams as "The Father of the American Navy" since it was his persuasive advocacy and energy that led to the formation of the Navy. However, others say the title belongs to Barry, who was the single most successful American Revolutionary War sea captain. Still others advocate for John Paul Jones as the "Father of the American Navy." Perhaps all three should be considered the "Co-Founders of the American Navy."

Adams was a diplomat for the fledgling colonies for virtually the entire period from 1778 to 1788, serving in Paris, The Hague, and London. Adams took his son, John Quincy, with him on all these assignments, with the result being that John Quincy Adams—the country's sixth President from 1825 to 1829—received a remarkable education, making him one of the most articulate and knowledgeable of all Presidents, although he too did not play well with others. In 1782 while Adams was stationed in The Hague, he secured a $2.1 million loan from the Dutch to help keep the colonies financially afloat. This was an important accomplishment, as the colonies were in severe financial distress at the time.

Later on, in 1787 while serving in London, Adams had his wife, Abigail, with him. The Adamses, primarily Abigail, spent significant time caring for Thomas Jefferson's nine-year-old daughter, Maria, growing very close to her in the process. This was due to Jefferson serving in the agitated and increasingly volatile and dangerous city of Paris. Years later in 1804, Maria passed away after giving birth to a son. Her death greatly affected Abigail, who wrote a very moving letter to the grieving Jefferson, who was now the President, about the relationship she had so enjoyed with the nine-year-old Maria. This prompted an exchange of letters between Jefferson and Abigail Adams, who some current historians regard as America's first advocate for women's rights. Eventually, the content of their letters turned to the raging rivalry between the Federalist Party and the Democratic-Republican Party — a political battle that had been burning ferociously in the 1790s and early 1800s. Abigail was outraged by the ferocity of the written and verbal attacks by both parties, writing: "Party spirit is blind, malevolent, uncandid, ungenerous, unjust and unforgiving...Party hatred by its deadly poison blinds the eyes and envenoms the heart...It sees not that wisdom dwells with moderation." An extremely wise observation, and equally as true in the twenty-first century as it was back in 1804.

After Adams finished his diplomatic career in London, he next served as Washington's Vice-President from 1789 to 1797. In late 1796 Adams squeaked out a narrow victory over Jefferson, 71-68, to capture the Presidency.

Chapter 16

The margin of victory turned out to be one vote from an elector in South Carolina and one vote of an elector from Virginia, each of whom chose Adams over Jefferson. Adams was sworn in as President on March 13, 1797 and later told his wife, Abigail, that Washington had quietly said to him after he had taken the oath of office: "Ay, I am fairly out and you fairly in. See which of us will be happiest."

In 1798, during his second year as President, Adams reactivated the Marine Corps to accompany his earlier role in the creation of the U.S. Navy. Adams also deserves significant credit for keeping the young United States out of a physical war with France in the late 1790s, which many politicians and citizens were calling for. However, Adams realized it was very likely to not end well for America. He believed the smart thing to do was to attempt to work out an agreement with the French. Adams thus sent special envoys to France, with the result being the Convention of 1800, which resolved the two countries seafaring problems, as well as dealing with several other pending issues. This conflict with France has become known to history as the "Quasi War."

Despite the political triumph of settling the "Quasi War" without actually having to fight, Adams lost the election of 1800 to Jefferson by an electoral vote margin of 73-65. Embittered at having lost the Presidency to Jefferson, his former friend but now his enemy (the results became known in mid-December), Adams embarked on what has become known to history as his "midnight judges" campaign. He urged the outgoing Federalist-dominated Congress to pass the Federal Judiciary Act of 1801, which it did. The Act created twenty-three new federal judgeships, which Adams promptly filled with, you guessed it, twenty-three Federalists. Adams was so rushed in trying to get the judicial seats filled that not all the paperwork was correctly filed. The end result was that eleven of the judges were denied their seats. Adams's motivation was to impede Jefferson's liberal policies by having a bevy of new Federalist judges to rule against as many of Jefferson's programs as possible. After Jefferson took office, a new judicial act was passed, reorganizing the entire federal judicial structure. Adams also strived to give the American military a strong Federalist flavor by naming eighty-seven additional officers on March 3 (his last full day in office), virtually all of whom were Federalists.

In 1798 Adams had appointed Bushrod Washington, a thirty-six-year-old strident Federalist, to the position of Associate Justice on the Supreme Court. Bushrod Washington was also the nephew of George Washington. However, the one judicial appointment that Adams made that was to have the most long-lasting effect was that of his own Secretary of State, the forty-five-year-old John Marshall, whom he appointed Chief Justice of the Supreme Court. This appointment was made with just thirty-one days left in Adams's Presidency! Marshall was a second cousin, once removed, of Thomas Jefferson. However, Jefferson and Marshall did not get along at all, initially due to intra-family issues, but later due to Jefferson's private criticism of George Washington (which unfortunately did not remain private) following Marshall's release of his own recently completed five-volume biography on Washington. Marshall was also an

Chapter 16

avid Federalist, which only increased the extreme distaste between Marshall and Jefferson.

Marshall ended up serving as Chief Justice for a whopping thirty-four years and was the primary mover in increasing the power of the federal court system, which established the judiciary as the third major prong of the Federal Government, alongside the executive and the legislative. In at least two cases during the Jefferson Presidency (*Madison vs. Marbury* and the *Aaron Burr Treason* trial), Marshall made significant rulings against Jefferson's positions. As Chief Justice, part of Marshall's job was to appoint one of the six Supreme Court Justices to hear and conduct various trials. In the Aaron Burr case Marshall appointed himself to preside over the sensational trial, and ultimately dismissed the charges, much to Jefferson's extreme chagrin. Was Marshall once again flexing his judicial muscles and "tweaking" Jefferson's nose? Or was he merely "calling it as he saw it?" Only Marshall knew.

One last act by Adams further showed his anger and his contempt for Jefferson, as well as his own lack of self-control. On the morning of March 4, 1801, which was the first ever Inauguration Day in Washington, D.C., Adams rose before dawn, dressed, and left Washington on the 4:00 A.M. stagecoach, heading home to Massachusetts, refusing to be present as Jefferson took the oath of office. Adams would not speak with, or write to, Jefferson for the next twelve years!

Over the centuries only five Presidents have refused to be present for their successor's swearing in: Adams was the first. His son, John Quincy was next by snubbing Andrew Jackson. The infamous Andrew Johnson refused to attend Ulysses S. Grant's swearing-in, even though he was in Washington. Woodrow Wilson refused to attend Warren G. Harding's swearing-in, although he did ride to the Capitol with him. The final one was Richard Nixon, who was flying home to California before his written letter of resignation had actually taken legal effect.

Even with all his emotional, oftentimes childish, irascible and puzzling behavior, his nearly rabid fixation with his own political positions, and his advocacy for and signing of the Naturalization, Alien & Sedition Acts, John Adams was still an important Founding Father.

Chapter 17

Herbert Hoover was the first President to have been born west of the Mississippi River, and also the first Quaker President. Hoover started life in the tiny town of West Branch, Iowa, the son of a part-time blacksmith/handyman. At six years of age, Hoover's father died. Three years later the nine-year-old boy's mother passed away. Hoover was sent to live with an uncle in a nearby Iowa town. After two years there, he was sent out west to Oregon's Willamette Valley, to be raised by yet another uncle with another brand new set of relatives. In 1891, having just turned seventeen, he was admitted into Stanford University's first-ever class, the youngest student in the class! He worked his way through the university as a newsboy, a clerk in the registration office, and also by starting up his own laundry service for fellow students. Although he did not earn high grades, mostly due to the number of hours his various jobs mandated, he did receive his degree in geology in May of 1895.

His first job in the real world was pushing ore carts in a Northern Sierra Nevada (California) mine. The job featured a backbreaking seventy-hour work week. Perhaps not surprisingly, his next job was an office job in San Francisco, after which he was hired by a prominent international British mining company in 1897. He was so immediately successful in the mining business that after just six months on the job his annual salary was doubled from $5,000 per year to $10,000 per year. After initially developing mostly highly lucrative mines in Australia, he branched out in subsequent years to develop mostly successful mining operations in China, Burma and Russia. By 1908 he had formed his own engineering company, and continued to experience huge successes around the world. His estimated worth by 1914 was $4,000,000!

However, he did have a harrowing experience in China in 1900 helping to defend the foreign community in Tientsin (a district of what is now Beijing) for more than a month during the bloody "Boxer Rebellion." The full experience included Hoover's rescue of multiple children from a burning residence, carrying them to safety even as the rioters' bullets rained down. Also, in the final days of the siege he served as a guide to Allied troops, including American Marines, who were liberating foreign civilians in various locations. He carried a Marine Corps rifle during this period, but never had to fire a shot.

With the advent of World War I in 1914, thousands of vacationing Americans were stranded in England, including Hoover and his wife. Hoover immediately contacted the American Embassy, offering to help with the obvious issues of temporary housing and arranging for transportation across the North Atlantic Ocean. His offer was accepted and Hoover jumped headlong, and hugely successfully, into solving the twin problems.

Next, he turned his attention to the far more serious and potentially devastating problems of providing food, clothing and other forms of relief to the dispossessed

Chapter 17

homeless citizens of war-torn Europe. Hoover created the CRB, the Committee for the Relief of Belgium (although residents in Northern France also received assistance). The aim of the CRB was to provide nearly the entire food supply for the people of Belgium, a country of 7.5 million, indefinitely!

Hoover quickly became well known, worldwide even, for his Herculean and largely successful efforts to save the starving Belgian people. His CRB came to an end after thirty months due to the entry of the U.S. into the War in April of 1917, thus ending Hoover's status as a "neutral." During those thirty months the CRB had spent $200 million (mostly donated by private citizens and corporations) and had shipped 2.5 million tons of food to Belgium! The citizens of Belgium never forgot everything he had done for them. They continued to honor his memory for many decades after the War ended.

British Lord Curzon described Hoover's accomplishment as, "an absolute miracle of scientific organization. Every pound of food and supplies is accounted for." The *New York Times* called Hoover's leadership of the CRB, "the most splendid American achievement of the last two years."

Hoover next served as President Wilson's "Food Czar," heading up the newly created United States Food Administration. Once the war had ended Hoover served as Wilson's economic advisor at the Versailles Peace Conference in 1919, and initially supported American participation in the League of Nations. However, when Wilson refused all attempts by the Republican Senate to compromise on various terms of the proposed League of Nations, Hoover blamed the failure of the USA to join the League on Wilson's intransigence. See Chapter 19 for more details regarding Wilson's non-dealings with the Senate Republicans.

The world-renowned economist, John Maynard Keynes, was representing the British Treasury Department at Versailles. He commented on Hoover's efforts and presence at the Conference: "....a complex personality, with his habitual air of [a] weary Titan...his eyes steadily fixed on the true and essential facts of the European situation...[He had] imported into the Councils of Paris... precisely that atmosphere of reality, knowledge, magnanimity, and disinterestedness [impartiality] which, if they had been found in other quarters also, would have given us the Good Peace."

In addition to his duties as economic adviser, Hoover was also providing food relief to the starving citizens of Europe. Hoover had, in advance, drafted for Wilson's signature an executive order creating the American Relief Administration, with Hoover himself as the executive director, which was to supply food and other materials for residents of thirty-two European countries. In conjunction with those duties Hoover had also arranged for the tours of duty of thousands of American military officers to be extended so they could be involved in the transportation and distribution of all the manifold relief supplies to the various populations of Europe, who were in dire need of virtually everything, as WWI had ended in November, and winter was bearing down hard upon millions of homeless and/or starving Europeans.

By the time the mandate of the ARA expired on July 1, 1919, Hoover's ARA had distributed $1.1 billion dollars in food and aid! Additionally, the ARA budget contained

Chapter 17

a surplus when it officially closed up shop in July, 1919, so Hoover obtained Wilson's approval to distribute that surplus to endow the European Children's Fund as a new private charity. Hoover also raised funds in America to enhance the initial budget surplus and supplement the ECF's nest egg. Thus it was that over the next five years the ECF was able to provide clothing, food, and medicine to 15 million children living in poverty in fourteen different European countries!

Back in England, after the Versailles Peace Conference had ended, Keynes said this: [Hoover was] "the only man who emerged from the ordeal of Paris with an enhanced reputation." Keynes also commented on Hoover's ARA: "Never was a nobler work of [impartial] goodwill carried through with more tenacity and sincerity and skill, and with less thanks either asked or given. The ungrateful governments of Europe owe much more to the statesmanship and insight of Mr. Hoover and his band of American workers than they have yet appreciated or will ever acknowledge...It was their efforts, their energy, and the American resources...acting in the teeth of European obstruction, which not only saved an immense amount of human suffering, but averted a widespread breakdown of the European system." Amazingly, also in 1919, Hoover found the time and energy to establish at Stanford University, the Hoover Institute on War, Revolution, and Peace.

Although Hoover was mentioned as a possible Presidential candidate in 1920, the nomination went to Ohio Senator Warren G. Harding, who easily defeated the Democratic nominee. Harding immediately appointed Hoover to be his Secretary of Commerce, an appointment that Calvin Coolidge maintained upon Harding's mysterious death in 1923. As Commerce Secretary, Hoover successfully pressed the steel industry to abandon the twelve-hour workday in 1923 in favor of eight-hour work shifts. He also advocated for a major enhancement of the St. Lawrence Seaway to increase both the speed of transport and the volume of goods that could be moved through the Great Lakes to the Atlantic Ocean. However, the Canadian and American governments were unable to reach an agreement on the proposal. Sadly, it wasn't until 1954 that the two governments reached a firm agreement and began work on the necessary improvements.

Additionally, Hoover successfully lobbied the bickering governors of the seven Southwestern states to compromise on a water distribution plan, which would result from the building of the Boulder Dam on the Colorado River. The dam was renamed the Hoover Dam in 1947 during President Truman's administration. Two more administrative creations of Hoover's Commerce Department were the Aeronautics Branch (now the FAA), and the Federal Radio Commission (now the FCC). Hoover was clearly visionary in recognizing the potential growth of these two industries, and thus the need for these areas of commerce to be brought under Federal oversight and made subject to intensive regulation for public safety purposes.

Hoover also played a major role in the Coolidge Administration, as was spelled out in a *New Republic* feature about the Presidency: "The plain fact is that no vital problem, whether in the foreign or the domestic field, arises in this administration in the handling of which Mr. Hoover does not have a real—and very often a leading—part. There is more Hoover in the administration than anyone else."

One example of what the *New Republic* was talking about occurred in 1927 when the lower 1,000 miles of the Mississippi River flooded due to massive amounts of rainfall from January to mid-April. The river was flowing at 3,000,000 cubic feet per second, and easily broke through the levees at 140 separate locations, in some places to distances of nearly 100 miles from the main course of the river! The governors of the six states most affected by the flooding begged Coolidge for federal assistance, and they specifically requested that Commerce Secretary Herbert Hoover be placed in charge of the relief effort. There was an additional reason why the six governors had requested Hoover's presence beyond what one might think: Just months before the flood Hoover had engaged in a speaking tour through the Midwest and the Southeast, touting, among other things, the need for an improved flood control system.

What would Coolidge do? Answer: the smart thing. He placed Hoover in charge of the federal government's relief effort after it became apparent there was a critical need for a massive and widespread rescue and rebuilding program. Although it was the "smart thing" for Coolidge to have done, it was also the "late thing," coming as it did seven days after the biggest of the levee breaks had occurred. After Hoover took over administering the rescue efforts the number of fatalities dropped significantly (nearly 300 deaths had occurred prior to his assignment). Hoover also launched an immediate and multi-faceted program to erect temporary housing for the thousands and thousands of citizens who had lost their homes. The prompt construction of more than 150 temporary housing units, which were kerosene-lit tent cities that contained water, sewer lines, electric lights, communal dining halls and, in most instances, medical personnel, were erected with surprising speed. Some of the tent cities contained as many as 20,000 people! Hoover's program, which was carried out by the U.S. Army Corps of Engineers, other members of the military, volunteers, businessmen, and the Red Cross undoubtedly saved hundreds, if not thousands of lives, as the flood occurred early in what had been a very cold spring.

On his first day in the flooded region Hoover became the first major American politician to address a national audience in a time of crisis, appealing to Americans across the NBC radio network to donate as generously as they could to the Red Cross. That Hoover's speech successfully tugged on the heartstrings of the American public is made clear by the amount of money received: The Red Cross's donations skyrocketed to $17 million dollars—more than triple their initial fund-raising goal!

"When a man is sick he calls a doctor," said famed comedian Will Rogers, "but when the United States of America is sick they call for Herbert Hoover."

The above accomplishments of Hoover from 1914 to 1928 are merely a brief compilation of his activities. He had boundless energy. He had a real genius for problems requiring vast organizational skills. He was constantly writing, speaking, organizing, proposing, chairing committees, et al. Thus it was no surprise when Hoover was overwhelmingly nominated by the Republicans to be their 1928 Presidential candidate, receiving 837 votes, while all other nominees combined to receive just 247! Four

Chapter 17

months later he similarly overwhelmed the Democratic nominee, Alfred Smith, the Governor of New York, winning the popular vote by more than 6.4 million votes, and the electoral college by a monstrous margin of 444 to 87.

Although the telephone had been in existence for more than fifty years, Hoover became the first President to keep a telephone on his desk in 1929. Another Presidential first for Hoover was his jump from the Cabinet position of Secretary of Commerce directly to the White House. Other than Secretaries of State or Secretaries of War, no cabinet officer other than Hoover has ever moved directly from the Cabinet to the Oval Office!

Within days of being sworn in as President, Hoover began taking steps to head off what he saw as an upcoming downturn in the economy. He campaigned publicly and privately against stock speculation; he worked with the Federal Reserve Board to pressure New York City banks regarding their dangerous and excessive lending practices due to the ongoing wild speculation in the stock market. He solicited one of the nation's most respected bank presidents to educate Wall Street brokers on the dangers of runaway speculation. Hoover also summoned the president of the New York Stock Exchange, Richard Whitney, to a White House meeting and lectured him about the extreme risks he foresaw in the vast amounts of loans being made by stock brokers. Unfortunately, Whitney did not have to answer to the President, he only had to answer to the Governor of the State of New York: Franklin D. Roosevelt!

The Washington Press Corps was stunned when they came to realize Hoover was working twelve-to-sixteen-hour days in the White House. They had grown accustomed to both Wilson's and Harding's vast numbers of hours on the area's golf courses, and to Coolidge's habit of sleeping ten to twelve hours most every night.

Seven-and-a-half months into Hoover's Presidency, New York City's Wall Street Stock Market came crashing down. Now Hoover had to deal with problems that Coolidge, Franklin Roosevelt and the New York State stock market regulators had failed to appreciate. As Secretary of Commerce, Hoover had recommended tighter controls on banks, on lending practices, on Wall Street trading rules, and especially on the rampant, sometimes mindless, speculation in the New York City stock markets. Hoover had warned Coolidge thusly: "No sensible businessman wants either a boom or a slump. Our working folk should dread a trade boom above all things, because it means an aftermath of unemployment and misery. Our farmers should resent a boom, because they inevitably get the worst of the deflation which is bound to follow." Sadly, Coolidge disagreed, making the following head-shaking and self-incriminating statement regarding Hoover's advice: "That man has offered me unsolicited advice for six years, all of it bad."

Hoover proposed numerous plans to improve the economy, but many of Hoover's proposals were rejected by Congress. Finally, in January of 1932, Congress approved the Reconstruction Finance Corporation (the RFC) and Hoover signed it into law. Beginning in March, 1932, the economy actually started improving. The RFC began bolstering private credit, thus reducing bank failures (as measured by deposits) from 200 million dollars per month to the pre-depression level of ten million dollars, in a period of just six months. Also belatedly, Congress authorized additional funds for the Federal Land Bank System, and also passed the Glass-Steagall Act, which allowed for a broader definition of acceptable collateral, thus allowing expanded credit to member banks nationwide. By the time autumn had arrived the boom in the economy that had started in the spring was approaching pre-depression levels in many areas of the economy.

Three weeks before the 1932 election, Hoover knew he was going to lose. This is because he had received the results from the first scientific national election poll in American history. The survey contacted 5,000 people in fourteen metropolitan areas, from all regions of the country. The huge surprise in the poll was the reason so many Republican voters were defecting from their party and planning on voting for Roosevelt. It was the issue of Prohibition (the Eighteenth Amendment) that caused 83.6 percent of the defecting Republicans to vote against Hoover, who was a supporter of Prohibition. Significantly, 68 percent of this group felt Hoover had acted in a manner that made the depression less severe. Similarly, 64 percent of Republicans believed the depression was the fault of financiers and businessmen, not the government. Additionally, 82 percent of defecting Republicans believed unemployment rates would continue to decline; and 65 percent of all respondents agreed "that business in general is picking up." So, the economy, although certainly a factor in the voting, was clearly not the primary reason that Hoover lost.

Interestingly, after Roosevelt won the Presidential election in early November, the economy started heading downhill again. Hoover proposed immediate legislative measures to arrest the slide to the Democratic-dominated

Congress, but they ignored virtually every proposal. Hoover also appealed directly to FDR in writing to get involved and assist in assuaging the growing panic of the general public. Roosevelt never responded, although he later claimed he had issued a written statement, but his "secretary neglected to send his response" to Hoover!

Various newspaper editorial boards proclaimed Roosevelt had a "personal and moral responsibility" to meet and work with the outgoing President. But FDR turned a deaf ear to those entreaties to work together immediately, choosing to sit on his hands instead. The *New York Times* wrote that Roosevelt had ignored Hoover's magnanimous proposal for "unity and constructive action." But, newspapers weren't the only ones who believed that FDR should meet immediately with Hoover for the good of the nation's economy. Two prominent Democrats, Bernard Baruch and Carter Glass, along with the Federal Reserve Advisory Board, all called on Roosevelt to meet with Hoover. Note that in the 1930s, as it had been since 1793, the President wasn't sworn into office until March 4—some four months after the fall election. So there was a very real probability the country would suffer as a result of FDR's unwillingness to "hit the ground running," even though Hoover was inviting his involvement for the good of the American public.

Meanwhile, the Senate finally agreed to Hoover's long-standing recommendation for an investigation of the stock exchanges. Once the investigation was completed it yielded new rules that were passed into law early in the Roosevelt administration. Subsequent to the passage of the legislation, Senator Frederic C. Walcott of Connecticut wrote to then ex-President Hoover: "You, more than anyone else, were responsible for the constructive reforms eventually adopted."

Raymond Moley, who had been a part of FDR's "Brain Trust" in 1932–33, when later asked by Hoover why Roosevelt had refused to cooperate in the 1933 banking crisis, answered thusly in writing: "Roosevelt either did not realize how serious the situation was, or that he preferred to have conditions deteriorate and gain for himself the entire credit for the rescue operation. In any case, his actions during the period of February 18 to March 3 could conform to any such motive on his part." For more details on the multiple paragraphs above, see the two Hoover biographies listed in the bibliography; the most recent work is by Kenneth Whyte, while the earlier biography is by Eugene Lyons.

In April of 1933 Roosevelt took America off of the gold standard in favor of a policy of inflation through the issuance of paper money. In the period of June/July, 1933, the London Economic Conference was held. It involved all the major European economies plus the USA. However, Roosevelt refused to personally attend, choosing instead to take a vacation with Vincent Astor on Astor's yacht rather than confer with the other leaders of the Western World. Instead, he sent Moley, Secretary of State Cordell Hull, and others in his place. When the conference had reached an agreement on stabilizing international monetary policy, Moley, after much effort, was finally able to contact a U.S. Naval vessel to track down Astor's yacht and deliver a radio message regarding the proposed agreement. Roosevelt messaged back his condemnation of the agreement and continued on his floating vacation, thus missing out on personally witnessing the anger and disgust of the European leaders. For all the details about FDR's economic policies see *The Great Deformation*, by David Stockman, especially chapters 8 and 9: "New Deal Myths of Recovery" and "The New Deal's True Legacy: Crony Capitalism and Fiscal Demise."

"When we all burst into Washington," wrote Raymond Moley, "we found every essential idea" had been considered or proposed by the Hoover Administration. Another New Dealer, Rexford Tugwell, stated that a long list of New Deal programs "owed much to what (Hoover) had begun," either when he was Secretary of Commerce, or as President.

In 1937 and 1938, which were Roosevelt's fourth and fifth full years in office (!), the unemployment rate in America went UP from 16.9 percent to 19 percent! Further, those figures are misleading because 3.5 million people that were counted as being "employed" were actually in federal government "make-work" jobs, not legitimate jobs in private industry or in business. Roosevelt's disingenuousness was apparent during the "Roosevelt Depression" of 1937–38, in that as new tent cities were springing up around the country, the New Dealers continued to call them "Hoovervilles." "Disingenuous" is perhaps too polite a word. "Dishonest" would be a more accurate descriptor.

Famed columnist Walter Lippmann wrote that, "the New Deal does not have any program, good, bad, or indifferent, which even pretends to have any relation to the economic crisis."

Hoover had a witty and ironic take on Roosevelt's obvious economic problems with the economy, saying the New Deal had resulted in "two families in every garage."

Chapter 17

Does Hoover share some of the blame for the depression not being mitigated more quickly and more completely? Certainly. But so do the Congressmen who served from 1930 through 1932, who were largely uncooperative with Hoover's proposals. And Hoover's share of the blame is certainly far, far less than is Roosevelt's share of the blame.

During his Presidency, Hoover appointed three Supreme Court Judges, two of whom are recognized as being among the most outstanding jurists of the twentieth Century: Chief Justice Charles Evans Hughes and Associate Justice Benjamin Cardozo.

Once Hoover left the White House, he retired to his home in Palo Alto, California, not far from the Stanford campus. He was somewhat of a non-entity on the political scene during Roosevelt's terms in office (March, 1933 through early April, 1945), but thereafter he remained amazingly active, engaging in the following activities: He was appointed by President Truman in 1946 to coordinate the Food Supply for World Famine following World War II; he was also appointed Chairman of the Organization of the Executive Branch of the Government, which quickly became known as the Hoover Commission, (1947–49). The commission made nearly 300 suggestions to streamline government, make government more efficient, and reduce financial waste. Over 70 percent of the Hoover Commission's recommendations, in whole or in part, were adopted by Congress. In 1953 President Eisenhower appointed Hoover to head up a second Hoover Commission, which again made over 300 recommendations, about 60 percent of which were approved, in whole or in part. The *New York Times* called the Second

Hoover commission, "a milestone in the history of American government."

In his last five years of life, with his wife having previously passed away, and now at the age of eighty-five years and too old for fishing, Hoover turned to writing in a very big way: seven books, including one that contained four separate volumes! His most successful book was the story of Woodrow Wilson's pursuit of peace at Versailles and on his whistle-stop campaign in the United States in 1919. It actually made the bestseller lists. It also stands as the first book ever written by a former President about another former President.

In 1959 the *Saturday Evening Post* said the following in an editorial: "It is too often forgotten that Herbert Hoover, who celebrated his eighty-fifth birthday August tenth amid glowing tributes from people of all shades of political opinion, was the victim of one of the most vicious, expensive and skillfully engineered smear campaigns in the country's history."

In August of 1960, on the floor of the United States Senate, Mike Mansfield, the Democratic Whip from the State of Montana, said this about Herbert Hoover: "He is now looked upon as a revered elder statesman. In the light of history, I believe he was a great President; and I think future historians will bear out that statement."

Author Kenneth Whyte, *a life-long Canadian*, wrote a comprehensive biography of Hoover that was published in 2017. In the biography Whyte summed up Hoover with the following lines: "His capacities and achievements are obvious and awe-inspiring. Among [America's] forty-four chief executives, he stands with the most intelligent and erudite, and none worked harder.

Chapter 17

He was the only President to have enjoyed two brilliant careers before the White House, and next to John Quincy Adams he was its most cosmopolitan inhabitant, having lived two decades abroad and circled the globe five times before the age of aviation. He was also a man of enormous goodwill, supporting with countless acts of charity his needy friends and relatives, not to mention the family of a colleague who was jailed for swindling him (Hoover) out of a large sum of money. The number of lives Hoover saved through his various humanitarian campaigns might exceed 100 million, a record of benevolence unlike anything in human history."

Here is one last telling, and especially ironic, testimonial about Herbert Hoover: "He is certainly a wonder, and I wish we could make him President of the United States. There could not be a better one." These words were delivered in 1920 by then Assistant Secretary of the Navy Franklin D. Roosevelt!

Chapter 18

John Quincy Adams, similar to Herbert Hoover in Chapter 17 just above, makes my list in large part because of his accomplishments both before and after his Presidency, rather than for his limited achievements during his four years as President.

Adams was arguably the most independent-thinking President in American history in terms of not loyally following his party's political doctrine. Originally, Adams was a Federalist, but he grew dissatisfied with some of their policies and became a nominal Democratic-Republican. Even at this point his political belief system still contained strong strains of the federalism of his father, John Adams (although not nearly strong enough for the strict federalists of New England). On the other side of the political spectrum, although Adams admired and respected James Monroe, a Democratic-Republican, and served as Monroe's Secretary of State for seven-and-a-half years, he thought very little of the two most famous Democratic-Republicans of the nineteenth century: Thomas Jefferson and Andrew Jackson. Indeed, he came to despise Jackson. As he grew older, Adams flirted with the short-lived Anti-Masonic Party, as well as with the Whigs.

Chapter 18

Adams was also one of the best educated and well-spoken of all the Presidents. Adams spent the majority of his childhood in Europe (France, England and the Netherlands), while his father served as the American ambassador in those three countries. His father also arranged for young John to attend the best private schools in each country. Thus it was that Adams ended up speaking five languages fluently, as well as two additional languages moderately well. Adams was also intensely interested in the esoteric subject of weights and measures, and conducted detailed and voluminous research into the subject. Along this line, he wanted to know exactly how tall he was, even though he was not a tall man. The answer was, to the nearest quarter inch: 5'6¾".

With all the above in mind, it is not surprising that Adams became the most prolific Presidential diarist in the more than 230-year history of the American Presidency. At the time of his death at age eighty, Adams's personal journal amounted to over 15,000 pages! That is the equivalent of fourteen copies of *Gone with the Wind*! Adams's son, Charles Francis Adams, ultimately edited his father's journal and then published twelve massive volumes. The journal is hugely revealing, both in his criticisms of his political rivals, and also in his self-criticisms regarding his own perceived character flaws. Adams also describes periods of extreme personal depression, including the terrible loss of his only daughter in early childhood, as well as his extreme disappointment with his two older sons: George and John.

In 1794, at the age of twenty-seven, Adams was appointed by George Washington to be the American ambassador to the Netherlands. Three years later

Adams's father appointed John Quincy to the ambassadorship of Prussia, where he served for four years. Returning to Massachusetts in 1801, Adams was elected to Congress. He served one term and then was elected to the United States Senate. As a senator Adams supported Jefferson's Louisiana Purchase as well as his Embargo of 1807. Interestingly, he was the only "Federalist" in either house to support both of those initiatives. However, those two acts of support proved to be too much for the Federalist-dominated Massachusetts legislature, which voted in 1808 to replace Adams as senator. In those days it was the state legislators, not the citizens, who elected the Senators.

However, in 1809 President Madison named Adams the new American Minister to Russia, where he served until 1814. Adams was able to establish a close working relationship with Czar Alexander, which led directly to financial benefits for America's nascent commercial shipping industry. In mid-1814 Madison sent Adams to London to serve as the chief American negotiator for the Treaty of Ghent, which ended the War of 1812. He was able to obtain what he thought were surprisingly generous terms from the British. This was due to his being unaware of the major losses the Brits had suffered in mid-September. See Chapter 14 for details regarding the disastrous month of September for the British military.

The final humiliation for the British military in the War came three weeks after the signing of the treaty, when General Andrew Jackson's forces annihilated the British in the Battle of New Orleans (see Chapter 9 on Jackson). Neither side was aware that the Treaty of Ghent had been signed, as the news of the treaty had to go by boat from England to Washington, D.C., and then on to New Orleans. Following the Treaty of Ghent, Adams remained in London until midway through 1817, serving as the American Ambassador to England.

Adams next experienced significant success as Monroe's Secretary of State, completing a treaty with Great Britain in 1818 that established American fishing rights in certain important areas off the coast of Canada. Shortly thereafter Adams finalized another treaty, this one with Spain, which established the details of Monroe's acquisition of East Florida. For more details on both treaties see Chapter 8 on James Monroe.

Adams also supported Monroe when it came to the issuance of the "Monroe Doctrine." Jefferson and Madison had each recommended to Monroe that he issue a joint declaration along with Great Britain. Adams, however, argued that the declaration should be America's own stand-alone doctrine. Monroe agreed with Adams on this point, and issued his Monroe Doctrine on December 6, 1823 in the name of the United States only. The Doctrine was quite strenuously worded, and it is possible Adams lobbied Monroe to make the terms as stringent as possible in order to protect the numerous burgeoning young republics in Central and South America.

In the Presidential election of 1824, Adams finished second to Andrew Jackson in both popular votes (42 percent to 32 percent), and electoral votes (99 to 84). However, due to two additional Presidential candidates (Henry Clay and William Crawford) having received a combined 78 electoral votes, Jackson did not have a majority of the electors. Thus, for the first and only time in the more than 230-year history of American Presidential elections, the contest was to be determined in the House of Representatives, with each state having one vote. So it was that on February 9, 1825, Adams was elected President when Clay threw his three states to Adams, and the House members from three additional states that had been won by Jackson in the November voting also voted for Adams at the urging of Clay, who had been the long-time Speaker of the House and was generally well respected by most of the House members.

Two days later, Adams announced the appointment of Clay to be his new Secretary of State. In the twenty-first century that would not be a significant talking point, but in 1825 it was HUGE. The previous three Presidents (Jefferson, Madison, and Monroe) had all been Secretary of State prior to achieving the Presidency, and Adams's election in 1824 made it four in a row. Thus, what was going to be a difficult Presidency for Adams in any event, given the popular vote, became exponentially more difficult in light of his appointment of Clay to the second most important position in the federal government. Those two factors, plus Adams basically being philosophically independent rather than a loyal party member, when combined with Adams's rather superior "I'm-smarter-than-you" personality, led to a disastrous four years in which precious little was accomplished. Although Adams did manage to get the "Tariff of Abominations" passed in 1828, the high tariff rates were subsequently rolled back.

At times Adams could be his own worst enemy. A classic example of this occurred in 1825 in Adams's initial annual message to Congress, in which he urged the legislators to not be "…palsied by the will of their constituents." Needless to say, the Jacksonian press had a

Chapter 18

field day with Adams's stunningly thoughtless, impolitic comment to the members of Congress.

George Dangerfield, a prominent British historian, described Adams's Presidency quite correctly as: "...a rather conspicuous example of a great man in the wrong place, at the wrong time, with the right motives and a tragic inability to make himself understood."

So, was there a *quid pro quo* arrangement between Adams and Clay? Was the Secretary of State position offered in return for Clay's support in the House's Presidential voting? It certainly seems quite likely in that the two politicians twice met privately in the month of January, just prior to the House vote in early February. Following the second meeting, Clay wrote to a friend that although Adams had made no promises, it was clear to him (Clay) that he could have whatever position in an Adams Administration he wanted.

There are multiple, significant reasons highly indicative of a deal having been struck: Adams and Clay had a significant prior history going back more than ten years, much of which was negative. They did not like each other, nor did they share common interests. They had different values and different lifestyles. With Clay being from Kentucky and Adams being from Massachusetts, their constituencies had vastly different interests and concerns.

The two men had each been on the American team during the peace talks with Great Britain at Ghent in 1814. Their rooms were right next to each other. Clay was a night owl who enjoyed gambling and card-playing, while Adams was an early riser who spent his free time reading and writing. On multiple occasions Adams would rise at 4:00 A.M. and head out for his morning stroll, only to meet Clay, who would just be getting back from his night of revelry. A major concern for Adams during the peace talks was the retention of American fishing rights on the Grand Banks, whereas Clay's primary issue was for America to have control of the Mississippi River. Clay and Adams also argued over matters of terminology. Another issue between the two men had arisen in 1816 when Monroe was considering both men for the Secretary of State position, along with Albert Gallatin. Clay told Monroe that Adams was not suitable for the post. Adams additionally believed that in 1822, during the run-up to the 1824 election, Clay had attempted to damage Adams by having an associate obtain all the correspondence from the Treaty of Ghent negotiations in an attempt to show that Adams was trying to help New England, while at the same time hindering Western commerce.

Ironically, their biggest blowup came after the Treaty of Ghent was signed, and the Americans were getting ready to head home. The two men completely lost their tempers over the seemingly innocuous question of which one would take the documents back to Washington, D.C. Adams wrote an insulting letter to Clay and the other two treaty team members, which resulted in Clay, in the modern parlance, "completely losing it." Clay shouted at Adams: "You dare not, you cannot, you shall not, insinuate that there has been a cabal of three members against you…no person shall impute anything of that kind to me with impunity." It appeared to those present that Clay, who had engaged in dueling several times before, was going to challenge Adams to a duel. Ultimately, no challenge was issued, and the parties agreed to divide up the documents among themselves.

Chapter 18

So, given that history, why in the world would John Quincy Adams want to spend the next four years working with Henry Clay, unless it was the only way he could gain the office of the Presidency? Adams was a man of great principles, no doubt. But it appears most likely that on this occasion he relaxed the rigidity of his principles in order to assume the Presidency, and thereby, hopefully, accomplish greater good for the American people.

In the autumn of 1828 Adams sought a second term as President, although realizing he had very little chance against Jackson, the wildly popular former hero of the Battle of New Orleans. Additionally, Adams was being opposed only by Jackson, with no other major candidates to muddy the waters. Not surprisingly, Adams was defeated, and this time it was not close. He lost the popular vote (56 percent to 44 percent) and the electoral vote (178 to 83). Detesting Jackson as he did, Adams refused to attend Jackson's swearing in as President, just as his father had refused to attend Jefferson's swearing in back in 1801!

In 1830 Adams was returned to Congress, representing his hometown district in southeast Massachusetts. He remained in Congress for the rest of his life, literally dying in the office of the Speaker of the House on February 23, 1848, after having suffered a stroke two days earlier (immediately following his casting of a very loud "NO" vote to a proposal to honor certain American generals who had served in the Mexican War). The Speaker of the House appointed a Committee of Arrangements to make preparations for the funeral. Among the House members appointed to the Committee was a freshman

Congressman from Illinois, who was serving his first and only term in Congress—Abraham Lincoln.

While in Congress Adams had argued repeatedly and at length, advocating for the rights of slaves to petition Congress, arguing against the "gag" rule, against the Mexican War, against Jackson's elimination of the Bank of the United States, and against slavery. In 1841, at the age of seventy-three, while serving as co-counsel, he successfully argued on behalf of the "slave mutineers" in the infamous case of the Spanish slave ship *Amistad*. The Supreme Court ruled 7-1 in favor of both Adams and the illegally-abducted West Africans, granting them their freedom. Two years later, in 1843, Adams issued his now famous visionary statement about American slavery, saying: "I am satisfied slavery will not go down until it goes down in blood."

Adams also vigorously and successfully advocated for creating what would become the Smithsonian Institute. James Smithson, an Englishman, had left a half million dollars of gold to the United States for the purpose of "disseminating knowledge." Other Congressmen had favored dividing the gold up among the various states, and letting them do with it what they would. Fortunately, Adams's arguments and larger vision carried the day.

In November of 1833, Adams, for the first time in his life decided to travel to Washington, D.C. by train for the upcoming Congressional session. Near Hightstown, New Jersey, one of the passenger-car axels broke and the car overturned. Two passengers were killed and twenty-one were injured, but not Adams. However, among the injured was Cornelius Vanderbilt, who vowed never to ride on another train. Irony of ironies, he later changed

Chapter 18

his mind and bought numerous railroads, eventually becoming the richest man in America!

In 1815, while Adams was serving as America's Ambassador to Great Britain, having stayed on following the conclusion of the War of 1812 and after the signing of the Treaty of Ghent, he learned of Captain Stephen Decatur's unique treaty with Tripoli that ended the "Barbary Pirates" War. See Chapters 4 and 14 for more details regarding the Barbary Pirates. The unique aspects of the treaty were that Decatur had insisted that the Tripolitan dey must release all of his jailed sailors, regardless of their nationality, not just the American sailors, and further that there would be no tribute whatsoever paid. Adams then sent a letter to Decatur, stating in part the following: "I most ardently pray that the example, which you have given, of rescuing our country from the disgrace of a tributary treaty, may become our irrevocable law for all future times."

This written comment by John Quincy Adams shows both his wisdom and his visionary nature, as the paying of tribute to rogue nations in various parts of our "modern" world has been a major problem for the past forty years, bedeviling multiple American Presidents. It is a problem that is still with us as America starts the third decade of the twenty-first century.

Chapter 19

Woodrow Wilson was a brilliant student, professor and orator who switched from academia to politics at the age of fifty-four. Recruited from his job of eight years as the President of Princeton to run for Governor by New Jersey "Bosses," Wilson agreed to run on a "progressive reformist" platform. He won the election and then proceeded to ignore the "Bosses" as he vigorously and largely successfully pursued his own progressive agenda. Within twelve months of assuming the governorship of New Jersey, the National Democratic Party was courting him to run for President against the current White House occupant, William Howard Taft, who was viewed as being quite vulnerable to being turned out of office.

Wilson received the Democratic nomination, and quite luckily for him, Theodore Roosevelt, who had been President for nearly eight years immediately preceding Taft, was also intensely displeased with Taft, so much so that he formed the Bull Moose Party and also ran for President. Wilson ended up winning the election with 6.3 million votes, while Roosevelt was second with 4.1 million and Taft third with 3.5 million. So the Republicans, with 1.3 million more votes than Wilson, ended up with nothing to show for it while Wilson waltzed into the White

House. Most historians believe if Taft had not sought reelection, Roosevelt almost certainly would have won.

Wilson continued his progressive reforms as President, signing into law the following highly important legislation: the creation of the Federal Trade Commission, the Clayton Anti-Trust Act (which strengthened the Sherman Act of 1890), the Federal Reserve Act, and the Underwood-Simmons Tariff Act, which also included the first graduated income tax.

However, now comes the negative side of Wilson: Born in Virginia in 1856, he was raised in Georgia and the Carolinas from the age of two. Unfortunately, he was never able to escape his upbringing in terms of race relations. While President, Wilson instituted formal segregation of the races in federal facilities, such as the post office, which were already integrated and running very smoothly! Wilson also viewed, in the White House, the film *Birth of a Nation*, which glorified the activities of the KKK. After the viewing, Wilson praised the film as, "history written with lightning."(!)

In the same vein, Wilson's 1902 book *History of the American People,* attempts to portray Southern slavery as a positive and caring experience for the slaves: "…black people had multiplied among them…hired labor had been, once for all, driven out…the care of the slaves, their maintenance like a huge family of shiftless children, remained a duty and a burden which the master could not escape, good season or bad, profit or no profit… where the master was himself at hand, there was almost always moderation, a firm but not unkindly discipline, a real care shown for their comfort and welfare."

Wilson also meddled with Mexico on two occasions: In 1914 he sent 800 troops to Veracruz to seize the customs house, believing Mexican officials might seize property belonging to American citizens. Then, in 1916, after the Mexican revolutionary Poncho Villa led a raiding party into the southern New Mexico town of Columbus, provoking a gun-battle that left seventeen Americans dead, but also more than 100 Mexicans dead, Wilson ordered General John J. Pershing to conduct a punitive pursuit of Villa. Pershing, with a force of nearly 14,000 men followed Wilson's orders, penetrating 350 miles south into Mexico, searching in vain for Villa. The search ended in February of 1917—just two months before the U.S. entered World War I. The commanding general of American forces in Europe in World War I was, wait for it, General John J. Pershing!

World War I started in late July of 1914. On May 7, 1915, a German U-boat (submarine) sank the *Lusitania*, a passenger liner with nearly 1,200 people aboard, including 128 Americans. German U-boats thereafter continued to sink passenger and/or merchant vessels, always claiming there were weapons aboard, or that the ship had been sunk by mistake. In the summer and fall of 1916 Wilson ran for re-election, utilizing the slogan, "He Kept Us Out Of The War." Wilson narrowly won re-election over former New York Governor and Supreme Court Justice Charles Evans Hughes, who spent just one day campaigning in California, and that was without California's hugely popular Republican Governor, Hiram Johnson, at his side. The result was a narrow victory in California for Wilson (less than 4,000 votes). Quite clearly, Wilson would have lost California, and the Presidency, if Hughes had merely spent a couple days in California, touring the state with Johnson, who was himself running for the U.S. Senate that autumn.

On February 2, 1917, Wilson presented to the members of his cabinet a bizarre and insulting new reason for America to not get involved in WWI (at that time known as The Great War): Wilson argued that if the U.S. joined the war the result would be that "white races" would experience "a depletion of manpower," and that might lead to an attempt by "yellow races to take advantage of it and attempt to subjugate the white races." What? Really?

Twenty-six days later, on February 28, 1917, Wilson revealed information to the country that he had been aware of since January of 1917, to wit: that Germany was soliciting Mexico to join in the war by promoting the possibility they could possibly recover their old territories of Texas, New Mexico and Arizona, which they had lost on multiple fields of battle between 1836 and 1847, and which were confirmed by the Treaty of Guadalupe Hidalgo in 1848.

During just the second week of March, 1917 alone, German U-boats sank four American commercial vessels. There was no action or word from Wilson, as he was physically sick for nine days during this period. On March 20, 1917, Wilson met with his entire cabinet, which unanimously advised him that the U.S. needed to join the War. Thirteen days later, on April 2, Wilson took action, addressing Congress and requesting a declaration of War. Four days later Congress approved Wilson's request by margins of 82-6 in the Senate, and 373 to 50 in the House.

Once American troops were fully trained and in position in France, the Allies were able to defeat Germany in less than nine months, with the armistice coming on November 11, 1918. However, the American casualty figures were shockingly high: 116,000 dead and nearly 200,000 wounded. On a per-month basis (for a period of eighteen months), Americans died at a faster rate in World War I than they did in the Civil War, when both sides were American!

During the four years of the war the German U-boats sank 200 American merchant vessels, including ten off the coast of North Carolina alone! There were also U-boat attacks off the New Jersey and Delaware coasts, as well as off of Cape Cod.

The end of the War did not come soon enough for Wilson, though, as the nation's voters returned control of both the Senate and the House to the Republicans in the 1918 mid-term elections held on November 5. This was hugely significant because it meant Wilson would have to work with the Republican-controlled Senate Foreign Affairs Committee when it came time for approval of any treaties which Wilson might propose.

The total number of deaths as a result of World War I is estimated at between 15 to 19 million people, with 23 million wounded military personnel. The number of military deaths is estimated at 9–11 million, while the number of civilian deaths is estimated at 6–8 million.

If Wilson had made his request for a Declaration of War to Congress earlier, as many people had urged him to do, how much sooner would the war have ended? How many millions of lives would have been saved? We'll never know the answers to those questions. One can only ponder and wonder…reflecting on what might have been.

Chapter 19

On September 25, 1919, while Wilson was in Pueblo, Colorado, nearing the end of his barnstorming tour around the country on a train, while attempting to drum up public support for the League of Nations, he suffered what is believed to have been a mini-stroke. The remainder of the tour was cancelled, and Wilson returned to the White House on September 28. Four days later Wilson suffered what is believed to have been a full stroke. His personal physician, upon examination of Wilson, exclaimed, "My God, the President is paralyzed." In fact, Wilson's left side was severely paralyzed, and he was partially blind in his right eye.

However, the nature, extent and depth of seriousness of Wilson's health issues was concealed from both the public and the Congress. In fact, as a PBS documentary in 2015 pointed out, Wilson and his wife, Edith, basically "embarked on a bedside government that essentially excluded Wilson's staff, the Cabinet and the Congress." PBS went on to say that as historians have continued to dig into this issue over the last century, "it has become clear that Edith Wilson acted as much more than a mere 'steward.' She was, essentially, the nation's chief executive until her husband's second term concluded on March 4, 1921."

Ironically, Wilson's barnstorming tour had been all for naught, as The Treaty of Versailles, which included the League of Nations (an institution which Wilson passionately supported), was never ratified by the United States Senate, which was controlled by Republicans. Massachusetts senator Henry Cabot Lodge, the Chairman of the Senate Foreign Relations Committee, had proposed various compromise measures to the treaty, but Wilson had adamantly refused all proposals, saying: "I shall consent to nothing. The Senate must take its Medicine."(!?!?)

Had Wilson been willing to compromise on some of the punitive and stringent terms of the Versailles Treaty, perhaps the next World War, which began just twenty years later, would have been far less tragic. However, Wilson was one of those men who believes he's the smartest guy in whatever room he's in. It was not in his nature to either admit to mistakes nor to participate in compromises. Wilson was that way as the American President, and he was that way in Versailles, and he was that way as the President of Princeton. For more information on Wilson's behavior at Princeton see Chapter 21 on Grover Cleveland, as well as Scott Berg's excellent biography on Wilson for all the details regarding Wilson's behavior at Princeton—and note that Berg is himself a Princeton graduate!

Colonel Edward House, who had been Wilson's primary foreign affairs advisor for the majority of Wilson's Presidency, in 1919 said the following of Wilson: "The President is the most prejudiced man I ever knew, and likes but few people."

French President Georges Clemenceau, who was on the treaty committee with Wilson at Versailles, said in 1919: "He (Wilson) thinks he is another Jesus Christ come upon the earth to reform men."

As historian Kenneth Whyte has said: "President Wilson had left the nation a shambles, socially, politically, and economically. Demobilization had been bungled, with some $35 billion in government contracts and commitments canceled without plans for economic reconstruction, and 13 million workers and servicemen

Chapter 19

dumped into the job market without a plan for their reintegration...Those who could find jobs were paid low wages in a time of high inflation and soaring corporate profits. The cost of living had almost doubled since the prewar years with food and clothing leading the way... Four million workers took part in labor actions in 1919."

The Country's voters had clearly grown tired of Wilson and his policies, as well as with his utter intransigence, and his blatantly apparent pathological inability to work with others and compromise in order to get things accomplished. Voters wanted a change in Washington, and they got it. In the 1920 election Wilson's "coattails" were non-existent as the Republican ticket of Warren G. Harding and Calvin Coolidge drew 16.1 million votes versus a scant 9.1 million votes for the Democratic ticket of James Cox and Franklin D. Roosevelt. Additionally, the Republicans won shockingly huge gains in both the Senate and the House. In the Senate the Republicans now held a whopping 70 to 26 advantage, while in the House the margin was nearly just as eye-popping: 303 to 131.

It should be noted, though, that Wilson does however hold one Presidential record: Most rounds of golf played while serving as President—an estimated 1,200 rounds; Eisenhower is second with an estimated 800 rounds, while Barak Obama is third with an estimated 600 rounds.

In 2017, C-SPAN conducted a survey of historians as to their ranking of the American Presidents. Wilson came in eleventh. I believe that ranking is significantly too high, and I further predict he will continue to tumble down the rankings in future surveys. In the 2000 survey Wilson had been ranked sixth; so the tumbling has already begun.

Being academically successful is absolutely not a guaranty of being a great or good President. See Appendix IV for data regarding the non-correlation of academic success with Presidential success.

Chapter 20

James Garfield—it may seem incongruous for a man who was President for only six-and-a-half months to be ranked twentieth, but the story of James Garfield is so amazing and so utterly tragic on multiple levels that I can only think that he would have, had he lived, gone on to be an outstanding President. The above opinion is based not only on what he accomplished in his brief period as President, but also on the successes of his political career before the Presidency, the success and bravery of his service in the Civil War, the manner in which he and his wife raised their children, and the multiple successes that those children enjoyed as adults.

Garfield was born into abject poverty in 1831 in Cuyahoga County, Ohio, growing up in a log cabin, the last of the American Presidents to grow up in a log cabin. He was the youngest of four children (of those who lived to adulthood). His father died when he was two years old. His mother was a strong woman, but she struggled to run the family farm. After failing as a canal worker, having fallen overboard fourteen times in six weeks, Garfield took his mother's advice and enrolled in a local academy, as he had been an avid reader as a boy. From there he attended the Eclectic Institute in Hiram, Ohio, working his way through school as a janitor. He then attended Williams College, where he was significantly influenced by Mark Hopkins, the Williams College President. He graduated with honors and was selected to give the commencement speech.

Garfield served as an Ohio State Senator from 1859 to 1861. When the Civil War broke out he joined the Union Army in August of 1861, serving through December of 1863, and rising from the rank of lieutenant colonel to major general. At thirty-one years of age, Garfield was one of the youngest generals in the Union Army. Garfield saw action in the Battle of Middle Creek and at Shiloh. In the Battle of Chickamauga, Garfield, under enemy fire, rode an injured horse from flank to flank to convey information and orders from Major General William Rosecrans to subordinate commanders. Garfield resigned his commission in December of 1863, having been elected to Congress (at thirty-two, he was the youngest member). Initially, Garfield had planned to turn down the voters and remain in the army. However, President Lincoln personally urged Garfield to take the position in Congress, believing he would be of more help advancing the cause of the North in Washington, than he would be on the battlefield.

Garfield then went on to serve in the House of Representatives for eighteen years. During the Grant Administration Garfield was selected to be the Chairman of the House Banking and Currency Committee, as well as the House Appropriations Committee. Early in 1880 he was elected to the U.S. Senate, but declined the seat when he won the Presidency some months later.

Chapter 20

At the Republican Convention in 1880 Garfield gave a brilliant and moving speech in nominating Ohio Senator John Sherman for the Presidency. Sherman was the younger brother of the famous Civil War General, William Tecumseh Sherman. There were two other primary candidates contesting for the nomination, James G. Blaine of Maine and Ulysses S. Grant, whom many Republicans wished to have returned to the White House. Grant had retired from the Presidency in 1877 after having served two full terms. After thirty-three ballots (!) the voting was still deadlocked, with Grant in the lead, but short of the magic number required for nomination. Suddenly, voters started switching to Garfield, despite his having unequivocally stated he was not a candidate. Sixteen delegates switched on the thirty-fourth ballot, and then thirty-four more on the thirty-fifth ballot. On the thirty-sixth ballot, Blaine and Sherman threw their delegates to Garfield, and he had won the nomination with 389 votes to Grant's 306.

Although beaten for the nomination by Garfield, Grant campaigned doggedly on behalf of his fellow Ohioan. Grant was extremely concerned about what might happen in the South if Garfield's opponent, General Winfield Hancock, a well-known Civil War hero, were to win the election. The results of the November voting were impossibly close in the popular balloting, with Garfield nipping Hancock by less than 10,000 votes out of over nine million ballots cast. However, in the electoral vote Garfield won relatively handily, 214 to 155. Each candidate had won nineteen states, however Garfield won all the big northern states, while Hancock won the smaller southern states, plus New Jersey. Following Garfield's victory,

Grant, who was quite pleased and extremely relieved by the election results, issued the following statement: "The country, in my judgment, has escaped a great calamity in the success of the Republican party."

As President, Garfield selected William Robertson for the plum position of Collector for the Port of New York, which was then the busiest port in the nation. This choice outraged Roscoe Conkling, the powerful New York senator, who was the foremost practitioner of what was then known as "the Spoils System." Nowadays Conkling would be known as "the King of Pork." Robertson and Conkling were archrivals. Conkling pressured Garfield to withdraw the appointment, however Garfield wouldn't budge on his nomination, as one of his governing principles was to attack corruption in national politics. Conkling then tried the childish ploy of resigning his Senate seat, thinking this would rally people, including powerful legislators, to his side. It didn't happen. The resignation turned out to be the end of Conkling's financially-motivated political career. Garfield had struck a major blow against the "patronage" system (as Grover Cleveland would also do a few years later during his terms as President).

Garfield also supported his Postmaster General, Thomas James, in an investigation he was conducting regarding bribery by some Republicans in the letting of contracts for rural mail delivery. Garfield refused to terminate James's investigation, despite pressure from various prominent Republicans to do so.

Garfield and his wife, Lucretia, had five children who lived to adulthood. They were all successful: three sons were lawyers, while the fourth son was a prominent

Chapter 20

architect, with degrees from Williams College and M.I.T. Garfield's daughter married an investment banker, who had previously been Garfield's Presidential Secretary. Garfield's son, Harry, was the first professor of politics at Princeton University, working under then dean and future President, Woodrow Wilson. During the first World War Harry served as an administrator in the Wilson Administration, and was later awarded a Distinguished Service Medal.

The most successful of the Garfield boys was the second son, James Rudolph Garfield. James was also a graduate of Williams College, and took his law degree at Columbia University in New York City, graduating in the same class as his older brother, Harry. James spent four years in the Ohio State Senate, and then two years with the U.S. Civil Service Commission. From 1903 to 1907 James served in Teddy Roosevelt's Department of Commerce and Labor, and was a major factor in promulgating Roosevelt's antitrust policies. In the final two years of Roosevelt's second term James Garfield served as the President's Secretary of the Interior, and was a vitally important player in helping Roosevelt carry out his massive program of conservation and preservation of federal lands. Roosevelt later wrote of James Garfield that "…he was beyond all comparison, the best we have ever had."

On July 2, 1881, just short of four months after taking office, President Garfield was shot in the back by a disgruntled and mentally ill job-seeker. It should not have been a fatal wound. However, the doctors treating him were negligently unaware of the work of British scientist and doctor Joseph Lister, who had spoken to dozens of American doctors during his appearance at Philadelphia's

Centennial Exhibition five years earlier, in 1876. Lister advised them of the life-or-death importance of antisepsis in medical surgeries/working areas. The American doctors largely, and tragically, turned a deaf ear to Lister! Meanwhile, in England, and over much of Europe, the doctors were already well aware of Lister's work on antisepsis, and were actively practicing safe medical procedures, utilizing antiseptic conditions to the best of their ability. If only Garfield had been shot while on vacation in London!

Garfield had been a robust and strong man, six feet tall and 200 pounds. He remained alive until September 19, 1881. When he finally passed away his weight was down to 130 pounds!

Former President Rutherford B. Hayes, who had immediately preceded Garfield in the White House, said in 1880 (prior to Garfield's being shot): "The truth is no man ever started so low that accomplished so much in all our history. Not Franklin, or Lincoln even."

In 1881, *The Nation* magazine wrote the following: "As far as knowledge of public questions and experience of public business go, no President since the younger Adams has been so well prepared to get along with second-rate men as Mr. Garfield. He does not need cabinet officers to teach him, or 'keep him straight' on any point whatever. There is not one of the departments of which he is not himself fully competent to take charge."

For all the details regarding Garfield, his death, Lister, and American doctors, see Candice Millard's excellent and moving book, *Destiny of the Republic*, 2011.

Chapter 21

Grover Cleveland is best known as the only President to be voted out of office, but then later returned to the Presidency by the voters. He is also one of only three Presidents to win the popular vote in three consecutive Presidential elections. The other two are FDR — four straight, and Andrew Jackson — three straight. It should also be noted, though, that FDR and Jackson, unlike Cleveland, also won the most electoral votes in each of their various Presidential campaigns.

Cleveland's career in public service began as an assistant district attorney in Erie County, New York from 1863 to 1865. After being defeated for the County District Attorney position in 1865, Cleveland returned to private practice. Strangely, he was nominated for, and accepted, the position of Erie County Sheriff, serving from 1871 to 1873. At the end of his two-year term he returned to private practice.

Eight years later, in 1881, Cleveland accepted the Democratic Party's request to run for the position of Mayor of Buffalo, which he handily won, running on a "reform and honesty in government" platform. He immediately and vigorously started eliminating graft and corruption in the city, as well as improving the city's sewage system, which had led to an outbreak of typhoid fever and several hundred fatalities. Buffalo had suffered 1,378 deaths due to epidemics the year before, with typhoid fever being the leading cause of deaths in the epidemic category. After just six months on the job the *Buffalo Sunday Times* was promoting Cleveland for Governor of New York! The New York State Democratic Party agreed, and so did the voters of New York, as Cleveland rolled to the biggest gubernatorial victory in state history up to that time, defeating Republican Charles Folger by nearly 193,000 votes.

Cleveland took office in Albany on January 1, 1883, and again went right to work cleaning up state government. He turned down patronage requests, instituted a merit system for job openings, imposed strict scrutiny on state banking procedures, and signed into law a new state civil service bill sponsored by a brash, young twenty-four-year-old state assemblyman by the name of Theodore Roosevelt. Cleveland also took steps to preserve 1.5 million acres of state land around Niagara Falls.

His first eighteen months as Governor of New York were so impressive that Cleveland was one of the favorites for the Democratic Presidential nomination in July of 1884. It didn't take long for the convention delegates to decide on Cleveland, and he won the nomination by a landslide on the second round of balloting. Four months later, however, it was a different story as Cleveland squeaked out a narrow win over James G. Blaine of Maine, winning the popular vote 4.87 million to 4.85 million, and the electoral vote, 219 to 182. A swing of 700 votes from Cleveland to Blaine in the State of New York would have given Blaine the electoral college victory!

Chapter 21

The biggest weapon Blaine had utilized against Cleveland during the campaign was the possibility that back in 1874, Cleveland (who never married until 1886), had fathered a child with a single woman. Cleveland didn't know if he was the father or not, but the other men that had engaged in sexual relations with the woman were all married, so Cleveland acknowledged a relationship with the woman and agreed to, and did, assume financial responsibility for the child. However, the story eventually had a happy ending as the young boy was adopted by a prominent New York family and grew up to become a physician.

It had been a meteoric rise for Cleveland. In the space of just four years he had gone from a private attorney in Buffalo, New York, to President of the United States! In 1887 Cleveland signed into law the Interstate Commerce Act and the Hatch Act. The ICA created the Interstate Commerce Commission to regulate the railroads. The ICC was the first federal regulatory agency. The Hatch Act provided federal funds for agricultural colleges around the nation to do research to improve American agricultural output. It was an enhancement to the Morrill Act, which was created in 1862 during the Lincoln Administration. Also in 1887 Cleveland incurred the wrath of the powerful railroad owners when he ordered an audit of their Federal land grants. The audit revealed the railroads had taken far, far more acreage than they were entitled to under the laws that had been established in 1862 and 1864 to provide incentives to the railroads to extend their lines across the breadth and width of the country. Thus, the railroads were forced to return a whopping 81,000,000 acres to the federal government!

In Cleveland's third annual message to Congress in December of 1887 he called for a reduction in the various tariff rates to assist farmers and ranchers across the country who were struggling to make ends meet, in part due to the high tariff rates. This advocacy for lower tariffs was one of the factors that caused Cleveland to lose the Presidency to Benjamin Harrison in the election of 1888. High tariff rates were generally popular in New York, which had the busiest port in the nation. New York had narrowly voted for Cleveland in 1884, but switched to Harrison in 1888.

The other factor that hurt Cleveland was his decision to hire a surrogate for $150 to serve in his place in the Civil War. Cleveland had made the decision due to his being, at age twenty-five, the supporter of his widowed mother and two younger sisters, ages eighteen and fifteen. In the 1884 election Blaine had not been able to attack Cleveland on this issue because Blaine himself had also paid his way out of the Civil War. Harrison, however, had served with distinction in the War, leading the 70th Infantry, a volunteer brigade from Indiana that Harrison had helped recruit and train. The 70th was especially recognized for their participation in the lengthy and major battle of Atlanta in 1864. Of the eight Presidents who served America between 1869 and 1909, Cleveland was the only one who did not serve his country in either the Civil War or the Spanish-American War.

Even though Cleveland had beaten Harrison in the popular vote by more than 90,000 votes, Harrison had flipped both New York and Indiana from Cleveland's 1884 victory column to Harrison's side. This gave Harrison the electoral victory, 233 to 168. Four years later Harrison and

Cleveland were matched up again in the 1892 election. Harrison stood firmly behind the existing high tariff rates, while Cleveland again called for appropriate reductions in some of the rates. Cleveland also won a large share of the "labor" vote by decrying government interference with legitimate union organizing. Cleveland more than reversed the results from 1888, besting Harrison by more than 370,000 votes and capturing the electoral victory by an impressive margin of 277 to 145. The presence of a third party in the race, the populist People's Party which polled more than one million votes, was another factor in the final results, almost certainly drawing more votes away from Harrison than they drew from Cleveland.

Just weeks before the start of Cleveland's second term, the Panic of 1893 began with the collapse of the Philadelphia & Reading Railroad in February of 1893. The resultant depression lasted for four years. Cleveland attempted to arrest the "Panic" in several ways. Believing that the Sherman Silver Purchase Act was one of the factors causing the panic by siphoning off the federal gold supply, Cleveland called Congress into special session in August of 1893, and prevailed upon them to repeal the Act, which they did just two months later, but which also caused a significant split among Congressional Democrats. In 1895–96 Cleveland twice sold gold bonds to J.P. Morgan's syndicate of Wall Street bankers at a discount, in exchange for their cooperation in minimizing the withdrawal of gold from the federal treasury. After the second purchase, the drainage of gold from the Federal Treasury was successfully reversed. He also encouraged a lowering of the tariff rates, which took effect in 1894.

However, the rates weren't lowered by nearly as much as Cleveland had advocated.

Early in his second term Cleveland blasted American involvement in the over-throwing of Hawaiian Queen Liliuokalani, and thus he recalled from the Senate the treaty for annexation of the islands that had been previously submitted by Harrison in the final weeks of his Presidency. Cleveland also invoked the Monroe Doctrine to force the British to agree to arbitration in a dispute between the Brits and Venezuela over the location of the boundary between Venezuela and British Guyana. Interestingly, Great Britain agreed to ex-President Benjamin Harrison serving as the arbitrator of their boundary dispute with Venezuela.

Cleveland had two additional Presidential "firsts." He was the first President to be married in the White House. A lifelong bachelor, Cleveland finally took the plunge on June 2, 1886, at age forty-nine, marrying the soon-to-be twenty-two-year-old Frances Folsom, the daughter of longtime friend, and fellow Buffalo lawyer, Oscar Folsom. Cleveland and his wife had five children, born between 1891 and 1903. The oldest was Ruth, who was quite quickly dubbed "Baby Ruth" by the media. Nearly thirty years later, in 1921, she would enter history when the Curtiss Company named a candy bar after her: the Baby Ruth bar. The Curtis Company was most probably also hoping to capitalize on the soaring fame of George Herman "Babe" Ruth, the record-breaking home run hitter who had just joined the New York Yankees the year before (1920). The next child born to the Clevelands was a daughter named Esther, and her birth was also a "historic first" as she is the only child of a President to actually be born in the White House itself.

It should be noted that Cleveland was the only Democrat elected to the Presidency in the fifty-two-year period from 1860 through 1911! In retirement, the Cleveland family moved to Princeton, New Jersey. Four years later, in 1901, Cleveland accepted a position as a trustee for the university, a position he held until his death in June of 1908. During the course of his trusteeship, Cleveland and his fellow trustees had to rule on a dispute between the Graduate School Dean, Alexander West, and the University President, Woodrow Wilson, over the location of the new graduate school complex. Cleveland and the trustees sided with West in October of 1907, and again in the spring of 1908. Shortly thereafter, West visited Cleveland, as the latter's health was clearly failing. West later wrote that Cleveland told him that, "Your plan is sound. Hang on to it like a bulldog." West additionally wrote that Cleveland "then went on to express his distrust of Princeton University President Wilson at some length, and in no uncertain terms."

Cleveland was an unusual President in that he believed in doing what he thought was right, even if it was going to cost him politically. He was a lot like John Quincy Adams in that respect, but only in that respect. And for the most part, Cleveland stuck with that belief system, even though it most likely caused him to lose the electoral college vote in 1888.

In 1906, two years before Cleveland's death, Mark Twain said/wrote the following: "Your patriotic virtues have won for you the homage of half the nation and the enmity of the other half. This places your character upon a summit as high as Washington's…When the votes are in a public man's favor the verdict is against him. It is sand, and history will wash it away. But the verdict for you is rock, and it will stand."

Chapter 22

Calvin Coolidge was born in south-central Vermont in the tiny hamlet of Plymouth, on the Fourth of July in 1872. Growing up he was educated in both Plymouth and the nearby town of Ludlow. He was initially denied enrollment at Amherst College in Massachusetts, but took additional college prep classes and was admitted the next year. Although he struggled early on at Amherst, he improved rapidly, graduated *cum laude*, and was chosen by his classmates to give the "Class Speech" at graduation ceremonies.

The first of Coolidge's ancestors to leave England and come to Massachusetts was John Coolidge, Calvin's seven-time Great Grandfather, who came to the Massachusetts Bay Colony in 1630. The adult Calvin Coolidge, as one might expect, reflected his Puritan ancestors. He was a religious person, as well as a very serious person. He believed in hard work and in a brevity of speech, which ultimately earned him the nickname, "Silent Cal." He had a somewhat unusual, quirky personality (what today would likely be called nerdy), and he almost certainly would not have been a successful politician in today's world. However, in the America of the early twentieth century he was a very successful politician. From 1899 to

1924 he won all twenty elective positions he sought except for one—on a school board. He rose steadily from City Council to State Legislature, to Mayor, to State Senator, to Lieutenant Governor, and then to the Governor of the State of Massachusetts.

In September of 1919, during his first year as Governor, approximately 75% of the Boston Police Department walked off the job. Their actions led to rioting in the city which lasted several nights and led to multiple fatalities. On the second day of the walkout Coolidge sent additional state militia to the city, and further, he upheld the police commissioner's decision not to rehire any of the striking officers. A.F.L. president Samuel Gompers urged Coolidge to reconsider. Coolidge refused, sending Gompers the following famous telegram: "There is no right to strike against the public safety by anybody, anywhere, any time." Two months later the citizens of Massachusetts re-elected Coolidge governor by a substantial margin (his victory one year earlier had been quite narrow).

Seven months later Coolidge was a favorite-son candidate for the Republican Presidential nomination, but drew only limited support. However, after the convention had chosen Ohio Senator Warren G. Harding as their Presidential nominee, the mass of delegates surprised the party big-wigs by overwhelmingly choosing Coolidge to be the Vice-Presidential nominee (674 votes to 146 over Irvine Lenroot, a Wisconsin senator). Five months later Harding and Coolidge hammered the Democratic nominees, James Cox and Franklin Roosevelt. For the jaw-dropping details of the Democrats' blockbuster defeat in the Presidential and Congressional races of 1920,

Chapter 22

see the second-to-last paragraph on Woodrow Wilson in Chapter 19.

In the summer of 1923 President Harding and his wife set off on a tour of the northwestern states, Alaska and then California. On August 2, while at the Palace Hotel in San Francisco, Harding (where he had been for five days after taking ill), suddenly passed away. This struck many people in the Presidential party as odd, since he had been steadily improving and was planning on going fishing the very next day at Catalina Island.

Eventually, Coolidge was contacted at 2:47 A.M., inside his father's home in Plymouth, by his chauffeur, his stenographer, and a local reporter, who had received a wire news report of Harding's death. Coolidge's father, who was a notary public and a justice of the peace, then administered the oath of office to his son in the home's sitting room. Coolidge then went upstairs to sleep, prior to waking at 6:00 A.M. and returning to Washington.

Coolidge's initial problem was dealing with the widely varied scandals of Harding's administration. Although several officials had already resigned, the Attorney General, Harry Daugherty, who was refusing to cooperate with Congressional investigators, had stayed on. Coolidge demanded, and received, his resignation early in 1924. Coolidge then made an excellent choice for his new Attorney General with the selection of Harlan Stone. During Stone's tenure as Attorney General, he reorganized the FBI and appointed a twenty-nine-year-old lawyer as its new director: J. Edgar Hoover.

Also in 1924, the federal government granted Native Americans full citizenship. Additionally, a modified agreement with Germany regarding the pay-down of their reparations from World War I was achieved, thus stabilizing the German economy, and earning the American negotiator, Charles Dawes, a Nobel Peace Prize. The achievement also earned Dawes a spot on the 1924 Presidential ballot as Coolidge's Vice-President. The American voters clearly liked what they had seen of Coolidge in his first fifteen months as President, so they resoundingly elected him to a full four-year term in November of 1924. Coolidge received 15.7 million votes, while the Democratic candidate (John W. Davis) polled 8.3 million votes. A Progressive Party candidate, Wisconsin Senator Bob La Follette was a distant third in the race with 4.8 million votes.

As President, Coolidge wrote all his own speeches and was the first President to hold regular press conferences—510 press conferences in the 67 months of his Presidency! In 1928 Coolidge and his Secretary of State, Frank Kellogg, successfully concluded the Kellogg-Briand Pact. It was an international treaty signed by virtually all the major countries in the world, plus several developing countries, denouncing the initiation of war as a matter of national policy. What the various world leaders did not want to see happen again was what had occurred in World War I: a number of major countries had interlocking treaties with each other wherein they promised to join their partner in war should the partner be attacked by a third country. So, once the first country was attacked, declarations of war flew fast and furious due to the previously established obligations set forth in the various interlocking treaties. The signing of the 1928 treaty ultimately earned Kellogg a Nobel Peace Prize,

Chapter 22

giving the Coolidge Administration two Nobel Prizes in the span of five years.

During Coolidge's tenure as President (1923 to 1929) the National debt that had been inherited from Wilson was cut by 36 percent. Taxes on Americans were cut back four times between 1921 and 1928. The rate of growth in federal spending was cut back hugely (only 13 percent over the course of six years) and unemployment fell precipitously from the end of the Wilson Administration, down to just 3-5 percent. In 1921, when Wilson left office, 5.7 million Americans were out of work. By 1929 that figure was down to 1.8 million! Additionally, each year's federal budget always ended with a surplus. During Coolidge's Administration workers' wages rose while borrowing rates came down. And perhaps most significantly, the nation's economy grew at a huge rate. In 1921 the nation's Gross Domestic Product was $672 billion. By 1929 America's GDP had grown to $977 billion. That is an increase of 45 percent in just eight years!

Coolidge had only one appointment to the Supreme Court, but it was a great one—Harlan Stone in 1925. Sixteen years later in 1941, President Franklin Roosevelt appointed Stone to the position of Chief Justice. Stone served as Chief Justice until his death in 1946.

Coolidge, like Lincoln, Jefferson and several other Presidents, experienced great personal tragedy while serving as President. During Coolidge's campaign for re-election in the summer of 1924, his younger son, Calvin, Jr., who was the President's favorite, and who loved the game of tennis, played his older brother for several hours on a hot afternoon without having worn socks. He developed a blister on the middle toe of his right foot, which ultimately became infected with Staphylococcus. Coolidge and his wife consulted multiple doctors, had lab work done, and had their son transported to Walter Reed Army Medical Center, which was an excellent facility for the 1920s. Penicillin could have saved Calvin, Jr., but it had not yet been invented. Sadly and shockingly, the Coolidges' young son succumbed to the infection in less than a week. Many historians believe Coolidge lost his interest in the Presidency after the death of his son. Coolidge's wife, Grace, went even further, saying that Coolidge had, "lost his zest for living."

In August of 1927 Coolidge surprised the American political world by announcing he would not seek another term as President in 1928. Herbert Hoover, who had been Coolidge's highly successful Secretary of Commerce, ultimately received the 1928 Republican nomination for the Presidency and, thanks in part to Coolidge's "long coattails," he swept to the Presidency with a crushing victory over Alfred E. Smith, the governor of New York. Hoover outpolled Smith 21.4 million to 15.0 million in the popular vote, and 444 to 87 in the electoral vote.

However, many historians believe Coolidge shares some of the blame for the Stock Market Crash in the autumn of 1929 (seven months after he left office), and for the resultant ten-year depression in America (1930-39). But it would certainly be a smaller share of blame than Franklin Roosevelt, who failed to revive the American economy for the first seven years of his Presidency! For more information on Roosevelt's failings in handling the American economy from 1933 through 1939, see Chapter 10 and Chapter 17. As for Coolidge's culpability in the depression, Hoover (the Secretary of Commerce

Chapter 22

from 1921 thru 1928) had repeatedly warned Coolidge regarding the dangers of "boom" economies, as well as of lax controls on banks and financing. However, Coolidge failed to take any action regarding Hoover's warnings, later ironically making the following hugely revealing, as well as unintentionally self-incriminating statement about Hoover's many warnings: "That man has offered me unsolicited advice for the last six years, all of it bad." For more specifics regarding Hoover's economic policies, see Chapter 17.

Coolidge died suddenly in early January, 1933, at age sixty, less than four years after leaving the Presidency. Alfred Smith, the defeated Democratic Presidential candidate from 1928, said this about Coolidge: "Mr. Coolidge belongs in the class of Presidents who were distinguished for character. His great task was to restore the dignity and prestige of the Presidency when it had reached the lowest ebb in our history."

In 1981, President Ronald Reagan said this about Coolidge: "You hear a lot of jokes about 'Silent Cal Coolidge.' [But]...the joke is on the people who make the jokes. Look at his record. He cut the taxes four times. We had probably the greatest growth and prosperity that we've ever known."

Appendix 1

DATES OF SERVICE OF THE 22 BEST PRESIDENTS

1. Abraham Lincoln (Illinois) March 4, 1861 to April 15, 1865
2. George Washington (Virginia) April 30, 1789 to March 13, 1797
3. Theodore Roosevelt (New York) September 14, 1901 to March 4, 1909
4. Thomas Jefferson (Virginia) March 4, 1801 to March 4, 1809
5. Ronald Reagan (California) January 20, 1981 to January 20, 1989
6. Ulysses S. Grant (Ohio) March 4, 1869 to March 5, 1877
7. Harry S. Truman (Missouri) April 12, 1945 to January 20, 1953
8. James Monroe (Virginia) March 4, 1817 to March 4, 1825
9. Andrew Jackson (Tennessee) March 4, 1829 to March 4, 1837

10. Franklin D. Roosevelt (New York) March 4, 1933 to April 12, 1945

11. James K. Polk (Tennessee) March 4, 1845 to March 5, 1849

12. Dwight D. Eisenhower (Kansas) January 20, 1953 to January 20, 1961

13. William McKinley (Ohio) March 4, 1897 to September 14, 1901

14. James Madison (Virginia) March 4, 1809 to March 4, 1817

15. George H. W. Bush (Texas) January 20, 1989 to January 20, 1993

16. John Adams (Massachusetts) March 13, 1797 to March 4, 1801

17. Herbert Hoover (California) March 4, 1929 to March 4, 1933

18. John Quincy Adams (Mass.) March 4, 1825 to March 4, 1829

19. Woodrow Wilson (New Jersey) March 4, 1913 to March 4, 1921

20. James Garfield (Ohio) March 4, 1881 to Sept. 19, 1881

21. Grover Cleveland (New York) 1885 to 1889 and 1893 to 1897

22. Calvin Coolidge (Vermont) August 3, 1923 to March 4, 1929

Appendix 2

The Eleven Most Important Events In United States History

1.) The Declaration of Independence & the Winning of the Revolutionary War (1776-1783)

2.) Lincoln's decision to put Grant in charge of all Union forces in the Civil War, with full victory achieved in just 13 months; and Lincoln's freeing of the Slaves (1861-1865)

3.) Bringing an end to World War II by defeating the Nazis in Europe and the Japanese in the Pacific (1940-1945)

4.) Winning the Cold War & the Collapse of the Communist Soviet Union (1985-1991)

5.) The Louisiana Purchase & the resultant excitement following the success of the Lewis & Clark Expedition, followed by the rush to settle the newly acquired territory (1803-1820)

6.) The annexation of Texas and the Acquisition of the American Southwest (1845-1848)

7.) Teddy Roosevelt's launching of the American Conservation & Preservation movement; and his preeminent role in the building of the Panama Canal (1901-1914)

8.) The Triumph of the Democratic-Republicans over the Federalists—the 24 year run of the three consecutive Virginian Presidents: Jefferson, Madison & Monroe (1801-1825)

9.) Seward's "Folly"—the purchase of Alaska for $7.2 million (it cost under 3 cents an acre)

10.) Andrew Jackson's stunning crushing of the Brits in the Battle of New Orleans, thus retaining control of New Orleans and the all-important Mississippi River; and the Monroe Doctrine, which curtailed European interference in the Western Hemisphere (1815-1823)

11.) The building of the Trans-Continental Railroad connecting the Atlantic Coast with the Pacific Coast (1862-1872)

Appendix 3

The "Spacing" Pages of the Best 22 Presidents

In ranking the Presidents from first to twenty-second it was by no means similar to the "spacing" of, say, 22 consecutive thick wooden support beams which underlie railroad tracks. Those support beams are evenly spaced for reasons having to do with safety. Whereas, my Presidential rankings are not evenly spaced at all. What I mean by that is that there are significant gaps between some of the Presidents, even though they are numerically ranked right next to each other. Conversely, some of the Presidents who ranked immediately next to each other numerically, were actually exceedingly close to each other in terms of how I evaluated their pluses and minuses. Thus, to give the reader an idea of which ranking placements were relatively easy for me to make (after having done all the reading and research), and which ranking positions were so close that I spent significant time evaluating the comparative pluses and minuses of the more or less "equal" Presidents, I offer the following "spacing" pages, so that readers will be clear as to just how tight some of the rankings were.

1. Abraham Lincoln
2. George Washington

3. Theodore Roosevelt
4. Thomas Jefferson
5. Ronald Reagan
6. Ulysses S. Grant

7. Harry S. Truman
8. James Monroe

9. Andrew Jackson
10. Franklin D. Roosevelt

11. James K. Polk
12. Dwight D. Eisenhower

13. William McKinley
14. James Madison
15. George H.W. Bush

16. John Adams
17. Herbert Hoover
18. John Quincy Adams

19. Woodrow Wilson
20. James Garfield
21. Grover Cleveland
22. Calvin Coolidge

Examining the "spacings" it becomes immediately apparent that numbers 3 through 6 involved the most

Appendix 3

analysis and evaluation, as well as the largest amount of time to determine what order seemed most appropriate for those four Presidents. The second most time-consumptive group were the four Presidents from 19 to 22. I also did a lot of thinking and comparing on those four.

Another way to evaluate the Presidents would be to use the power of descriptive terms, which would involve the utilization of a smaller number of groups. Using this method, here is how I would group the "22 Best" Presidents:

THE ALL-TIME GREATS (6): Lincoln, Washington, Theodore Roosevelt, Jefferson, Reagan and Grant

THE NEAR GREATS (4): Truman, Monroe, Jackson & Franklin Roosevelt

IMPORTANT PRESIDENTS (5); Polk, Eisenhower, McKinley, Madison & G.H.W. Bush

ABOVE AVERAGE PRESIDENTS (7); J. Adams, Hoover, J.Q. Adams, Wilson, Garfield, Cleveland & Coolidge

Prior to reading the 98 books and doing the additional research, here is how I had grouped the Presidents:

The All-Time Greats: Lincoln, Washington & Jefferson

The Near Greats: Both Roosevelts, Reagan, Monroe, & Jackson

The Important Presidents: Truman, Eisenhower, Polk, Madison, Wilson & G.H. W. Bush

The Above Average Presidents: Both Adamses, Grant, McKinley, Cleveland & Coolidge

The Effect of the Reading & Research:

Clearly, the biggest beneficiary of my reading and research was Ulysses S. Grant, who moved from the "Above Average" category into the "Near Great" category. Also moving up were Truman (from "Important" to "Near Great"), Theodore Roosevelt (from "Near Great" to "All-Time Great"), McKinley (from "Above Average" to "Important"), and Hoover and Garfield, who moved up to "Above Average," after not originally being in any category.

As for downward movement, only one President dropped to a lower classification: Woodrow Wilson moved down from "Important" to "Above Average."

Appendix 4

Non-Correlation Between College Success & Presidential Success

Contrary to what many readers probably believe, or at least assume, the thirteen most highly-rated Presidents on my list were not nearly as successful in their college careers as the nine lower rated Presidents, (numbers 14 through 22).

The Top Thirteen Presidents:

Excellent College Students: (3) Thomas Jefferson, Teddy Roosevelt and James K. Polk

Average College Students: (4) Ronald Reagan, U.S. Grant, Dwight Eisenhower, and FDR

Partial College Students: (2) James Monroe (Monroe left William & Mary in the spring of his sophomore year, having just turned 18, and joined the Continental Army. William McKinley (McKinley left Allegheny College prior to the end of his first year due to health problems.)

Did Not Attend College: (4) Abraham Lincoln, George Washington, Harry S. Truman, and Andrew Jackson (Truman did attend two years at a law school, however he did not finish the course of study.)

Presidents #14 Through #22:

Excellent College Students: (7) James Madison, G.H.W. Bush, John Adams, John Quincy Adams, Woodrow Wilson, James Garfield, and Calvin Coolidge (As for Coolidge, he struggled at Amherst in his first two years, but in his final two years he achieved significant academic success and graduated *cum laude*.

Average College Student: (1) Herbert Hoover (As for Hoover, it should be noted that he had lost both of his parents by age 9, was raised by relatives, and was quite poor when he entered Stanford. He held three jobs while attending Stanford in order to pay his tuition, support himself, and remain in school; so his grades, quite understandably, suffered significantly.

Did Not Attend College: (1) Grover Cleveland (It should be noted that Cleveland was planning on attending college, but with the death of his father when young Cleveland was 16, he began working in order to help support his mother and his two younger sisters, as well as himself.)

Reviewing the above data, it is abundantly clear that success in college is not an indicator, at all, of whether or not a President will be great, good, or above average.

Annotated Bibliography

Note: The following annotated bibliography lists all ninety-eight books I read prior to making my final rankings. The books will be listed in groups based on how informative and readable I found them to be. If the subject of the book is not obvious from the title, I will indicate which President(s) it dealt with. Also listed will be the author, the year of publication, an indication of historical focus, plus occasional evaluations of quality.

Highly Informative, Eminently Readable, and Strongly Recommended Books

Goodwin, Doris Kearns. *Team of Rivals: The Political Genius of Abraham Lincoln.* New York: Simon & Schuster, 2005. If you can only read one book on this list of ninety-eight books, this is the one. Although it contains 754 pages, they fly by. This book starkly, but with subtleness, reveals the greatness of Lincoln, his wisdom and his strength, both in terms of policy, and in the way in which he was able to deal with the widely variable personalities of his brilliant cabinet members — his hand-picked "Team of Rivals."

Chernow, Ron. *Grant*. New York: Penguin Press, 2017. At 959 pages, *Grant* stands as the second longest book I read. It also stands as my second favorite among the 98 books I read. Chernow focuses on all aspects of Grant's life. It is a memorable account of redemption, and of overcoming hurdles that Grant repeatedly faced throughout his life, as well as a detailed account of his military genius. The book also covers in great detail Grant's efforts to reign in the KKK violence in the Post-Civil War period, as well as the many other accomplishments of the Grant Presidency.

White, Ronald. *American Ulysses: A Life of Ulysses S. Grant*. New York: Random House, 2016. Although "only" 659 pages, this is also an excellent account about a great general, who was unfairly and wrongfully maligned for decades. White's book is very strong on the military aspects of Grant's career, both in the Mexican War and in the Civil War. The book also contains clear, detailed maps of key battle sites, as well as depicting the troop movements of the opposing armies, adding to the reader's understanding.

McCulloch, David. *Truman*. New York: Simon & Schuster, 1992. At 992 pages, this is the longest book I read, but it is well worth it. No college degrees for Truman, but he was still an extremely important President, who made some of the most critical decisions of the twentieth century. Truman also saw action in multiple engagements in World War I, which is well covered by McCulloch, who won a Pulitzer Prize for *Truman*, just as he did for his book, *John Adams*.

Goodwin, Doris Kearns. *No Ordinary Time*. New York: Simon & Schuster, 1994. FDR's many accomplishments and failings are covered in this memorable account. Also covered is Eleanor Roosevelt's role in the Roosevelt Administration, as well as her repeated entreaties to prevent FDR from making one of his most tragic and severely regrettable decisions. Sadly, she was unable to persuade him to alter his inexplicably chosen course. This book is 636 pages.

McCulloch, David. *Mornings on Horseback*. New York: Simon & Schuster, 1981. McCulloch covers Roosevelt's life from birth to his late 20's. If you read this book you will have a perfect understanding of exactly why Teddy was the highly energized and passionate outdoorsman, Rough Rider, conservationist and President that he was. It also tenderly covers the death of his young wife, in her early 20's. At just 370 pages, this is the shortest of my "Top Group" books.

Brands, H.W. *Reagan: The Life*. New York: Random House, 2015. This is an important book (757 pages) by one of America's best current historians. Reagan grew up poor and graduated from a tiny college in central Illinois, but later emerged as one of America's most transcendent Presidents at a very shaky, scandal-ridden, yet most important time in American history.

McCulloch, David. *The Path Between the Seas: The Creation of the Panama Canal*. New York: Simon & Schuster, 1977. If you have time to read three books, this would be the third one. It details the gross failings of the French attempt to build the Panama Canal, the American Army's subsequent striking success in actually building it, and Roosevelt's integral role in the United States taking over responsibility for the Canal. This book is 617 fascinating pages.

Brands, H.W. *Andrew Jackson: His Life & Times*. New York: Random House, 2006. This is an excellent and well-balanced account of the unique, irascible, rugged and highly successful frontier general, and later a President who vastly expanded the power of the Presidency. This book is 560 pages.

Berg, Scott. *Wilson*. New York: Putnam Publishing Group, 2013. Berg writes in great detail about Wilson's academic & political achievements, as well as his puzzling and glaring character flaws and blunders, which sadly led to a Presidency that was, clearly, not as accomplished as it could have been. This book is 743 pages.

Morris, Edmund. *Theodore Rex*. New York: Random House, 2001. This well-researched and well-written book covers primarily Roosevelt's Presidential years, and it does so in a highly detailed and page-turning fashion. Lots of facts; a surprisingly fast read, even at 555 pages.

Chernow, Ron. *Washington: A Life*. New York: Penguin Press, 2010. This is a full biography, covering all aspects of Washington's youth and young adulthood, his French & Indian War heroics, his role as a step-parent and adoptive parent, as well as his subsequent military and political life. Very detailed and a well-deserved Pulitzer Prize winner for Chernow. This book is 817 pages.

Sides, Hampton. *Blood and Thunder: An Epic of the American West*. New York: Doubleday, 2006. Sides covers James K. Polk, Kit Carson, John C. Fremont, Commodore Stockton, Stephen Watts Kearney and the exploration, obtaining, and settling of the American Southwest. This is a hugely energetic and informative account. I did not want to put it down. Highly recommended. This book is 497 pages.

Randall, Willard. *Unshackling America: How the War of 1812 Truly Ended the American Revolution*. New York: St. Martin's Press, 2017. Willard writes about Madison, Monroe, and Jackson. This is an excellent account of the War of 1812 — both the heroes and the villains, as well as the high points for America *and* her many low points. Randall's thesis that Great Britain conducted a "40-year War" on the Colonies/United States is well-supported in this book. Like *Blood and Thunder* (immediately above), this book is an edge-of-the-seat, page-turner, and is also highly recommended.

Fischer, David Hackett. *Washington's Crossing*. Oxford, UK: Oxford University Press, 2004. Fischer writes about both George Washington and James Monroe. His book covers Washington's battles and decisions from April of 1776, through March, 1777. The first seven months saw the Americans lose four straight battles in New York, five if you count the abandonment of Fort Lee. However, the next 14 weeks saw a string of successes in multiple battles, both large and small, all in New Jersey, beginning with

Washington and his troops crossing the Delaware River on Christmas night, 1776. This book is quite detailed, despite being just 379 pages. It also contains excellent maps of the various military encounters. Fischer justifiably won the Pulitzer Prize in History for this book.

Also Highly Informative, and nearly as readable as the First Grouping:

Chernow, Ron. *Alexander Hamilton*. New York: Penguin Press, 2004. Chernow writes about Washington, John Adams, and Thomas Jefferson. Although not quite as brilliant as Chernow's later biographies of Ulysses S. Grant and George Washington, *Hamilton* is still an outstanding biography of the most important non-President in the period of 1787 to 1804. Hamilton tragically and inexplicably let "honor" overcome both his common sense and his obligations to his large family (seven children, five of whom were 12 years old or younger), when he was killed in a duel with Vice-President Aaron Burr. This book is 731 pages.

Donald, David. *Lincoln*. New York: Simon & Schuster, 1995. A complete biography by one of America's foremost historians, as well as a recognized Lincoln scholar. It is 599 pages, but they are all definitely worth it, even if you've also read *Team of Rivals*.

Randall, Willard. *George Washington: A Life*. New York: Henry Holt & Co., 1997. This bio is very detailed and well-written. Randall is especially knowledgeable on this period of American history. It is well worth reading.

Brinkley, Douglas. *Wilderness Warrior: Theodore Roosevelt and the Crusade for America*. New York: HarperCollins Publishers, 2009. The focus is mainly on the wildlife and wilderness-preservation sides of Teddy Roosevelt's Presidency. This is a very detailed book of 817 pages.

Meacham, Jon. *American Lion: Andrew Jackson in the White House*. New York: Random House, 2008. The drama of Old Hickory's White House is the primary focus of this book, but other aspects of his life, military career, and his Presidency are also well covered.

Goodwin, Doris Kearns. *The Bully Pulpit: Theodore Roosevelt, William Howard Taft, and the Golden Age of Journalism*. New York: Simon & Schuster, 2013. Teddy Roosevelt and William Howard Taft—their long friendship and then their shocking breakup after Taft gained the Presidency; plus the huge political impact of the emerging print media in the Gilded Age, and the role they played in Roosevelt's progressive policies. This book is 750 pages.

Unger, Harlow Giles. *The Last Founding Father*. Boston, Massachusetts: Da Capo Press, 2009. This is an enthusiastic biography of perhaps the least known of the Founding Fathers, James Monroe. Unger details Monroe's amazing life of public service, beginning with his Revolutionary War years as an eighteen-year-old, his nearly fatal injury sustained in the Battle of Trenton, and culminating in his highly successful eight years as America's fifth President; an interesting and fast read at 347 pages.

Isaacson, Walter. *Benjamin Franklin: An American Life*. New York: Simon & Schuster, 2003. This is a full biography of the brilliant inventor, statesman, author, diplomat and scientist who played such a major role in America's history from 1775-1789, along with George Washington, John Adams, and Thomas Jefferson. The book is 493 pages.

Meacham, Jon. *Destiny and Power: The American Odyssey of George Herbert Walker Bush*. New York: Random House, 2015. This is a full biography covering George H.W. Bush's youth, his WWII years, his years at Yale, his private business successes in Texas, and his numerous governmental positions, concluding with his highly successful Presidency.

McCulloch, David. *John Adams*. New York: Simon & Schuster, 2001. The intense passions of our highly-opinionated and easily-angered second President. There are loads of facts and details, as well as numerous quotes from letters by both Adams and his wife, Abigail. McCulloch won his second Pulitzer Prize for this biography of perhaps our most irascible and emotional President. This book is 651 pages.

Traub, James. *John Quincy Adams: Militant Spirit*. New York: Basic Books, 2016. This is an enlightening and full biography of JQA—warts and all, but still an amazing man—in 537 pages. There are, however, several historically incorrect facts in the book. One example occurs on page 16, wherein General Washington is credited with "a smashing victory over Burgoyne at Saratoga." In fact, General Horatio Gates and future traitor, Benedict Arnold, were the key generals at Saratoga. Ironically, while the two battles at Saratoga were being fought, Washington was several hundred miles south in Pennsylvania, losing the battle of Germantown. However, despite the three or four misstatements, this is still an informative and moving biography. Highly recommended.

Meacham, Jon. *Thomas Jefferson: The Art of Power*. New York: Random House, 2012. The political side of Thomas Jefferson is the primary focus of this book, but there is also significant information about Jefferson the man; a very interesting and thought-provoking read.

Wood, Gordon. *Friends Divided: John Adams and Thomas Jefferson*. New York: Penguin Press, 2017. This is a dual biography of America's second and third Presidents and their on-again-off-again friendship, from 1776 to their deaths — which improbably occurred on the same day: July 4, 1826 — the fiftieth anniversary of the signing of the Declaration of Independence. Wood is perhaps the country's foremost expert/historian on Jefferson.

Merry, Robert W. *A Country of Vast Designs: James K. Polk, the Mexican War, and the Conquest of the American Continent*. New York: Simon & Schuster, 2009. This is well-written and full of facts about America's least known transformative President. This is a fast, interesting and informative read. Polk nearly died as a teenager, but survived a very dangerous surgery to become a President who accomplished every single one of the Presidential goals he had set forth in his 1844 Presidential campaign—and then some. Highly recommended.

Whyte, Kenneth. *Hoover: An Extraordinary Life in Extraordinary Times*. New York: Knopf, 2017. This is a full biography of Hoover's truly amazing storybook life, plus an analysis of both Hoover's & Roosevelt's actions, and non-actions, during the 1929-1939 Great Depression, especially the crucial period from the autumn of 1932, to March of 1933. Whyte is a life-long Canadian, and his comparison of Hoover and FDR's behaviors/decisions during the depression is objective and unbiased. Highly recommended, this book is 614 pages.

McDonough, James Lee. *William Tecumseh Sherman: In the Service of My Country*. New York: W.W. Norton & Company, 2016. Very detailed and factual, this is a terrific read about a complex man who could well have succeeded Grant as President in 1876, had he merely chosen to accept the Republican nomination. Sherman was the older brother of Senator John Sherman, who nearly won the Republican nomination for President in 1880. The book is 721 pages.

Nevins, Allan. *Grover Cleveland, a Study in Courage*. Norwalk, Connecticut: Easton Press, 1932. This book provides an abundance of detail about an interesting and highly principled man, & his meteoric rise to the Presidency. Nevins's writing style is a bit old school—no surprise for a 1932 biography of 766 pages.

Millard, Candice. *Destiny of the Republic: A Tale of Madness, Medicine, and the Murder of a President.* New York: Doubleday, 2011. This book is a biography of James Garfield, but it also deals in detail with the incompetence and conceit of American doctors from 1876 into the early 1880's. It is a terrific read, but heartbreakingly sad.

Merry, Robert W. *President McKinley: Architect of the American Century.* New York: Simon & Schuster, 2017. Very detailed and well-written, this book is a pretty fast read. It covers McKinley's repeated acts of heroism during his four years of Civil War service, his rise in politics in Ohio, his largely successful Presidency, and his tragic assassination.

Medved, Michael. *The American Miracle: Divine Providence in the Rise of the Republic.* New York: Crown Forum, 2016. This is a factual, very interesting and fast read, whether you believe Providence was involved or not. There are chapters on Washington, Lincoln, Jackson, Polk, Jefferson, Adams, the Pilgrims, the 1787 Constitutional Convention, Sam Houston and the Texas Revolution, the Louisiana Purchase, and the acquisition of California and its subsequent Gold Rush. The book is 374 pages.

McCullough, David. *1776.* New York: Simon & Schuster, 2005. Primarily about the highs and lows of Washington's first 18 months as General of the Continental Army; lots of interesting facts about the military successes, as well as the more frequent losses. James Monroe also plays an important role in several of the battles with the British.

Parrett, Geoffrey. *Eisenhower*. New York: Random House, 1999. This is a very informative and detailed full biography of Eisenhower, from growing up in Kansas, to West Point, to his Army career, to Supreme Allied Commander in WWII, and then on to the Presidency and the issues that Eisenhower dealt with in his eight years in the White House. The book is 608 pages.

Ammon, Harry. *James Monroe: The Quest for National Identity*. Newtown, Connecticut: American Political Biography Press, 1971. This is a full biography with lots of facts about an honorable and highly principled President, who spent nearly 50 years serving his country and his state. It also contains details about the "Era of Good Feelings," as well as the creation of the Monroe Doctrine. Additionally, the book provides information about Monroe's Revolutionary War battlefield experiences; it is 573 pages.

Ambrose, Stephen. *Nothing Like it in the World*. New York: Simon & Schuster, 2000. Ambrose covers Lincoln and the building of the Trans-Continental Railroad—1862 to 1869, plus the resultant rivalry between the Central Pacific Railroad and the Union Pacific RR in the building of the "line," form the essence of this book. Ambrose's writing style is straight-forward and highly factual, which results in an intense page-turner. He focuses on the hard-working men who labored diligently, oftentimes in highly dangerous conditions, to accomplish what most people felt was not accomplishable.

Sea of Glory: America's Voyage of Discovery, The U.S. Exploring Expedition, Nathaniel Philbrick, 2003, *(Andrew Jackson and Martin Van Buren),* (This book is the oceanic version of the Lewis & Clark land exploration. Commanded by Navy Lieutenant Charles Wilkes, all the world's oceans were sailed (initially) by six American naval vessels between 1838 and 1842, with significant discoveries in multiple fields of science, ranging from geography to botany. Unfortunately, Wilkes's personality was a combination of the movie version of Captain Bligh (although not of the historical Bligh), and television's annoyingly brilliant Sheldon Cooper, (of *Big Bang Theory* fame). Despite the animosity among many of the officers, Philbrick's book is a fascinating read, and in places, an edge-of-the-seat, page-turning thriller.

Ellis, Joseph J. *Founding Brothers: The Revolutionary Generation.* New York: Alfred A. Knopf, 2000. Ellis won the Pulitzer Prize for this book. It was an interesting read, but surprisingly short at only 248 pages. My only disappointment with the book was that Mr. Ellis does not include the fifth President, James Monroe, among his "Founding Brothers." Monroe, unlike Jefferson, Adams and Madison, actually fought in the Revolutionary War with George Washington, seeing action in five battles, spending the winter of 1777-78 at Valley Forge, and nearly losing his life at age eighteen, during the crucial victory at Trenton on December 26, 1776.

Taliaferro, John. *All the Great Prizes: The Life of John Hay, From Lincoln to Roosevelt.* New York: Simon & Schuster, 2013. This is a vivid account of John Hay's amazing life—from four years as Lincoln's secretary during the Civil War, to his brilliant years as Secretary of State for Presidents McKinley and Roosevelt four decades later. The book is 552 pages.

Thomas, Evan. *First: Sandra Day O'Connor*. New York: Random House, 2019. This is a full biography of the first woman to serve as a Supreme Court Justice. Well-written and detailed, the reader comes away from the book with high admiration for both O'Connor and Evan Thomas, the author. O'Connor grew up on a cattle ranch in extreme southeastern Arizona, attended school in El Paso, Texas, and then spent six years at Stanford earning her B.A. and then her J.D. She dealt with the extremely difficult task of being the first woman on the Supreme Court with character and courage. Thomas had to walk a fine line, given the many difficult issues, but he did so with integrity and objectivity. Highly recommended.

Beschloss, Michael. *Presidential Courage*. New York: Simon & Schuster, 2007. There are multiple chapters on crucial situations confronting nine different presidents, which required those Presidents to make tough decisions, even though the decisions would be politically unpopular. The Presidents included are George Washington, John Adams, Andrew Jackson, Abraham Lincoln, Theodore Roosevelt, Franklin Roosevelt, Harry Truman, John Kennedy, and Ronald Reagan.

Kiernan, Denise. *The Girls of Atomic City: The Untold Story of the Women Who Helped Win World War II*. New York: Atria Books, 2012. This book deals with the presidencies of Harry Truman and Franklin Roosevelt through the lens of the vast multitude of women who worked at the Oak Ridge, Tennessee facility during World War II, as the American Army furiously engaged in the development of the atomic bomb. The book also covers the men that played major roles in the process, as well as the scientists that were intricately involved in discovering the secrets of uranium.

Valuable and Interesting, but slightly below the Second Grouping:

Groom, Winston. *Kearny's March: The Epic Creation of the American West, 1846-1847*. New York: Knopf, 2011. Although only 277 pages set during the time of James K. Polk, it's a real page-turner that deals with the Mexican War in Mexico, California and New Mexico; plus the Donner Party, the Mormon migration to Utah, Native Americans of the Southwest, John C. Fremont and Kit Carson.

Peterson, Merrill. *Thomas Jefferson and the New Nation: A Biography*. Oxford, UK: Oxford University Press, 1970. This author was a prominent historian and professor. There is an abundance of information in this book, but his writing style is from the 1950s (or earlier), so reading the book is, at times, slow going — I actually read just the chapters I was most interested in due to the semi-ancient writing style.

Ambrose, Stephen, *Undaunted Courage: Meriwether Lewis, Thomas Jefferson, and the Opening of the American West*. New

York: Simon & Schuster, 1996. Jefferson sends Lewis and Clark west to the shores of the Pacific Ocean. This is a stunning, almost unbelievable, story of discovery; as well as one of physical and mental endurance. Well written. The pages fly by.

Hersh, Seymour. *The Dark Side of Camelot*. New York: Little, Brown and Company, 1997. JFK and his brothers and their repeated shenanigans (to use an exceedingly mild euphemism) both before and after JFK gained the Presidency. Quite detailed at 456 pages.

Burstein, Andrew & Isenberg, Nancy. *Madison and Jefferson*. New York: Random House, 2010. This is a dual biography that also includes significant information about Washington, Adams, and Monroe. Through the year 1811 the book is highly informative. However, in 1812 Madison's re-election bid is barely mentioned, even though the election was relatively close and in serious doubt. I read the 2013 paperback copy, which makes me wonder if there was some type of a printing error therein. Additionally, the authors' coverage of the War of 1812 was not nearly as detailed as I would have expected, especially given the controversial nature of Madison's initial decision to engage in the War, and the Brits' subsequent calamitous attack on Washington, D.C. The book is 653 pages.

Baier, Bret. *Three Days in Moscow: Ronald Reagan and the Fall of the Soviet Empire*. New York: William Morrow, 2018. Although this book is narrow in scope, it is still very interesting and quite well written. Covers the development of the relationship between Reagan and Mikail Gorbachev in detail. Definitely worth reading.

Lyons, Eugene. *Herbert Hoover: A Biography*. New York: Doubleday, 1964. Very informative with lots of details, about a President who was truly a self-made man, and who accomplished amazing things in his life; although Lyons's writing style is somewhat old school.

Stark, Peter. *Astoria: John Jacob Astor and Thomas Jefferson's Lost Pacific Empire*. New York: Ecco, 2014. An interesting book and a quick read. Like *Undaunted Courage*, this is a book that reminds one just how unbelievably tough and rugged people were back in the early 1800s.

Beschloss, Michael. *Presidents of War: The Epic Story, from 1807 to Modern Times*. New York: Crown, 2018. Multiple chapters on Presidents that had to deal with wars, or the prospect of war: Thomas Jefferson, James Madison, James K. Polk, Abraham Lincoln, William McKinley, Woodrow Wilson, Franklin Roosevelt, Harry Truman and Lyndon Johnson.

Rove, Karl. *The Triumph of William McKinley: Why the Election of 1896 Still Matters*. New York: Simon & Schuster, 2015. This book primarily deals with the unparalleled political strategy of McKinley's "Front Porch" Presidential campaign of 1896, which was masterminded by millionaire Ohio Senator Mark Hanna.

Nagel, Paul. *John Quincy Adams: A Public Life, a Private Life*. New York: Knopf, 1997. This is a good, solid objective biography of an unquestionably unique person (and exquisitely well educated man), who gained the Presidency in a unique and highly controversial, some would say questionable, manner. The book is 419 pages.

Kilmeade, Brian and Yeager, Don. *Andrew Jackson and the Miracle of New Orleans*. New York: Penguin Publishing Group, 2017. Lots of facts and drama—a real page-turner, but at only 240 pages it makes one wish it was much longer. Still, it's an incredible story.

Sedgwick, John. *Blood Moon: An American Epic of War and Splendor in the Cherokee Nation*. New York: Simon & Schuster, 2018. Tons of research went into this book, and it is well worth the read. The careful reader will have a much clearer understanding of the various interests of different groups of whites, as well as the conflicts between two rival Cherokee leaders and their followers, which ultimately led to the "Trail of Tears" for 16,000+ Cherokees.

Thomas, Evan. *John Paul Jones: Sailor, Hero, Father of the American Navy*. New York: Simon & Schuster, 2003. This book covers Washington and John Adams, plus the naval career of Jones before, during and after the Revolutionary War. It's an excellent book with a thrilling account of Jones's most famous, and utterly unbelievable, David-versus-Goliath naval battle just a mile or two off England's eastern coast. More than a thousand English citizens had virtual front-row seats atop a 400-foot high bluff overlooking the most historic and improbable sea battle of the Revolutionary War.

Annotated Bibliography

Thomas, Evan. *Ike's Bluff: President Eisenhower's Secret Battle to Save the World*. New York: Little, Brown and Company, 2012. This book is centered around Ike's efforts to prevent nuclear war during the period of the Cold War. It also covers the 1960 CIA U-2 spy plane incident involving American pilot Francis Gary Powers, and the mistakes that were made by Eisenhower in dealing with the aftermath of the Soviets having shot down Powers and his U-2.

Taylor, Alan. *American Revolutions: A Continental History, 1750-1804*. ,New York: W.W. Norton & Company, 2016. This book combines "traditional" facts regarding the leading politicians and generals of the period 1750-1804, with the lesser-known lives of women, Native Americans, slaves, the poor, and the Loyalists, and how the Revolutionary period, the Articles of Confederation period, and the Republican/Constitutional period, largely negatively affected the latter, mostly powerless groups. The book is 480 pages.

Ellis, Joseph J. *American Sphinx: The Character of Thomas Jefferson*. New York: Alfred A. Knopf, 1998. This is not a full biography. Instead, it focuses on five separate two-to-five year periods in Jefferson's life. The book is written in an exceedingly academic style.

Updegrove, Mark. *The Last Republicans: Inside the Extraordinary Relationship Between George H.W. Bush and George W. Bush*. New York: Harper, 2016. This book is about George H.W. Bush primarily, but also George W. Bush. It examines the traditional "Republicanism" of the

Bushes, their relationship and interaction with each other before and during their Presidencies, and contrasts them with the mostly far-right ideology of Donald Trump.

Cheney, Lynn. *James Madison: Life Reconsidered*. New York: Penguin Books, 2014. Madison was a brilliant student and constitutionalist, who was a prominent leader in the early Congresses of America, and who also served Jefferson well as his Secretary of State. However, he had an uneven, at times shaky, and at time disastrous, eight years as President. Well researched by Ms. Cheney.

Shlaes, Amity. *Coolidge*. New York: Harper, 2013. This is a well-researched and interesting biography of quite an unusual man—both politically and personally. Besides covering his Presidential years, it also covers his youth and initial schooling in small-town Vermont, as well as his college days and his political career in Massachusetts, followed by his sudden assumption of the Presidency upon the surprising and mysterious death of Warren G. Harding.

McGrath, Tim. *Give Me a Fast Ship: The Continental Navy and America's Revolution at Sea*. New York: Dutton Caliber, 2014. This is a highly detailed account of the American colonies and their continuous attempts to contest the mighty British Navy on various oceans and bays during the Revolutionary War. It covers John Paul Jones, as well as multiple other successful captains, plus some captains who did not exactly cover themselves with glory; plus the activities of various privateers on both sides of the conflict. Well worth reading.

Stark, Peter. *Young Washington: How Wilderness and War Forged America's Founding Father.* New York: HarperCollins, 2018. This book deals nearly exclusively with Washington up to 1759, age twenty-seven. Quite detailed and a fast read. Mr. Stark demonstrates significant objectivity in describing Washington's strengths and weaknesses in his late teens and into his late twenties.

Brands, H.W. *Heirs of the Founders, The Epic Rivalry of Henry Clay, John Calhoun and Daniel Webster.* New York: Doubleday, 2018. Although I found Brands's books on Reagan and Andrew Jackson highly informative and very well done (see above), this one misses the mark just a bit, although it is still well worth reading. This book is primarily about Henry Clay. If you are a Clay fan you should absolutely read it. It is 370 pages.

Stiles, T.J. *Custer's Trials, A Life on the Frontier of a New America.* New York: Doubleday, 2015. Although a brilliant tactician, absolutely courageous as a leader of Union Cavalry, and highly successful in the vast majority of his battles/skirmishes during the Civil War, Custer was mostly unsuccessful in all other aspects of his life, both before the Civil War while attending West Point, and afterwards in numerous other endeavors that he undertook.

McCullough, David. *The Wright Brothers.* New York: Simon & Schuster, 2015. The hugely improbable but amazing successes of Wilbur and Orville Wright in the early 1900s in becoming the "First in Flight." They succeeded on a shoestring budget, besting the publicly-financed efforts of the Smithsonian Institute, as well as the efforts of various well-financed Frenchmen, to prove that man, like the birds, could also fly. It is a fast and interesting read.

Philbrick, Nathaniel. *In the Hurricane's Eye: The Genius of George Washington and the Victory at Yorktown*. New York: Penguin Books, 2018. Very interesting, detailed, fast read. Philbrick has a flowing and informative writing style. This book is definitely worth reading.

Philbrick, Nathaniel. *Bunker Hill: City, a Siege, a Revolution*. New York: Penguin Books, 2013. A detailed and quick read regarding the start of the Revolutionary War, the Massachusetts Minute Men and their early successes, as well as Washington's first triumph as the Continental Army's General-in-Chief: forcing the Redcoats to abandon Boston. Also well worth reading.

Philbrick, Nathaniel. *Valiant Ambition: George Washington, Benedict Arnold, and the Fate of the American Revolution*. New York: Penguin Books, 2016. This book covers only that period of the Revolutionary War from the spring of 1776, when Washington is preparing to confront the British in New York, to Benedict Arnold's treason in the early fall of 1780. The book also details the many failures and shortcomings of the Continental Congress.

Buck, Rinker. *The Oregon Trail: A New American Journey*. New York: Simon & Schuster, 2015. This book deals with James K. Polk, John Tyler, Zachary Taylor, and Millard Fillmore, combining the history and geography of the Oregon Trail with the author's own journey along the

Trail in 2011 with his brother. They used a buckboard and a team of three mules to follow the ruts of the trail for nearly 2,000 miles! The book makes nervously clear both the dangers and the difficulties of traveling the Trail, while at the same time containing multiple humorous incidents.

Morgan, Ted. *Wilderness at Dawn: The Settling of the North American Continent.* New York: Simon & Schuster, 1993. This book covers the initial settling of the Americas across the Bering Land Bridge; the explorations of the continent by the Spanish, French, British and Dutch; the colonization of the continent and the subsequent interactions with Native Americans, and the lives of ordinary settlers. There is also some focus on government officials, but not much.

Langguth, A.J. *Union 1812: The Americans Who Fought the Second War of Independence.* New York: Simon & Schuster, 2006. This book primarily covers the post-Revolutionary War period through the Presidency of Andrew Jackson. It's a fast and factual read, but at only 409 pages, not as detailed as many readers might expect. Two volumes of 350 pages apiece, say 1783 through 1808 (Jefferson's Administration), and then 1809 to 1837 (Madison's administration through Jackson's), would have allowed for more detailed coverage of that mostly tempestuous period of American history. Still, lots of facts.

Wood, Gordon. *Revolutionary Characters: What Made the Founders Different.* New York: Penguin Press HC, 2006. This book focuses on the characters of four Presidents

(Washington, John Adams, Jefferson, and Madison), plus Alexander Hamilton, Benjamin Franklin, Thomas Paine, and Aaron Burr. It also highlights the affect that the burgeoning number of American newspapers had on the manner in which political campaigns were conducted in the 1790s and early 1800s.

Ellis, Joseph J. *American Creation: Triumphs and Tragedies at the founding of the Republic*. New York: Knopf, 2007. This is an interesting book that deals with what went right and what went wrong in America's Founding (1775-1803). There is, however, one glaring factual error in the book: On page 204 the author asserts that John Adams sent James Monroe to France as the American Ambassador. In actuality, it was George Washington who sent Monroe to France in 1794 — three years before Adams became President.

Toland, John. *Infamy: Pearl Harbor and its Aftermath*. New York: Doubleday, 1982. This book explores the question of whether or not FDR had advance knowledge of the December 7, 1941 attack. Read this book and form your own opinion on the strength of the evidence presented. The author, John Toland, was a Pulitzer Prize winner. But, also read the book just below on Pearl Harbor, written 34 years later. Was it gross incompetence in Washington, D.C., or was it a strategic decision to get America into World War II?

Summers, Anthony & Swan, Robbyn. *A Matter of Honor: Pearl Harbor: Betrayal, Blame, and a Family's Quest For Justice*. New York: Harper, 2016. This book is about FDR,

Pearl Harbor, scapegoating, and extreme military bureaucratic incompetence. An interesting read.

Colacello, Bob. *Ronnie & Nancy: Their Path to the Whitehouse – 1911 to 1980*. New York: Warner Books, 2004. Both Ronald and Nancy Reagan's lives through 1980 and a good read, quite detailed. It covers in significant depth their childhoods, their careers in stage and movies, and Reagan's many successes as California Governor during the turbulent period of 1967 through 1974. It also relates Reagan's razor-thin loss to Gerald Ford for the 1976 Republican Presidential nomination, as well as his subsequent crushing of Jimmy Carter, the incumbent President, in the 1980 election. It does not cover Reagan's eight years as President.

Remini, Robert V. *Andrew Jackson and his Indian Wars*. New York: Viking Adult, 2001. The title tells it all, in that the main focus of this book is devoted to the Native American policies that Jackson promulgated. The book also covers Jackson's mostly tragic first fifteen years of life. The book is 281 pages.

Millard, Candice. *River of Doubt: Theodore Roosevelt's Darkest Journey*. New York: Doubleday, 2005. This book is about Teddy Roosevelt, post-Presidency, still in love with outdoor adventure and still engaging in extreme risk-taking. Teddy being Teddy!

Wren, Christopher. *Those Turbulent Sons of Freedom: Ethan Allen's Green Mountain Boys and the American Revolution*. New York: Simon and Schuster, 2018. Washington, both in the Revolutionary War, and later as President, has to deal with agitated Vermonters. This is a surprising and interesting read.

Montgomery, M.R. *Jefferson and the Gun-Men: How the West Was Almost Lost*. New York: Crown, 2000. This book deals with the Lewis and Clark Expedition, plus Aaron Burr's and General James Wilkinson's conspiracy to separate the American West from the original thirteen colonies, as well as Zebulon Pike's two expeditions of discovery. This book is 327 pages.

O'Reilly, Bill & Dugard, Martin. *Killing England: The Brutal Struggle for American Independence*. New York: Henry Holt & Co., 2017. This book is a very fast read that hits most of the salient high points of the Revolutionary War, but it could certainly have been more detailed regarding the battles and the lives and backgrounds of the major players.

O'Reilly, Bill & Dugard, Martin. *Killing the Rising Sun: How America Vanquished World War II Japan*. New York: Henry Holt & Co., 2016. Same exact comment as above, except that this book relates to the War in the Pacific from 1941 to 1945.

O'Reilly, Bill & Dugard, Martin. *Killing Lincoln: The Shocking Assassination That Changed America Forever*. New York: Henry Holt & Co., 2011. This book deals in great detail with the fifteen days leading up to the assassination, and the search for and capture of the various conspirators. It is a fast and interesting read, but it could easily have been expanded by 100 pages.

Annotated Bibliography

Baier, Brett. *Three Days in January: Dwight Eisenhower's Final Mission*. New York: William Morrow, 2017. This book is about Eisenhower and his farewell speech to the nation. It is well researched and gives the reader pause to think. It also deals with Eisenhower's contacts with Kennedy, both before and after the election of 1960. A solid book.

Kilmeade, Brian. *Thomas Jefferson and the Tripoli Pirates: The Forgotten War that Changed American History*. New York: Sentinel, 2015. Just as with Bill O'Reilly's books, more details and more background would give a more complete picture. However, the second half of this book is a real page-turner, in part because of the similarities between the early 1800s and the last forty years.

Shlaes, Amity. *The Forgotten Man--A New History of the Great Depression*. New York: Harper Perennial, 2008. Ms. Shlaes makes the depression years (1929-1940) come to life by coverings dozens of individuals and businesses and how they were affected by the oftentimes mistaken policies of FDR, Hoover and Coolidge. This is both a thought-provoking book, and a surprisingly fast read at 396 pages.

O'Reilly, Bill & Dugard, Martin. *Killing Reagan: The Violent Assault that Changed a Presidency*. New York: Henry Holt & Co., 2015. Although this book deals with the shooting of President Reagan, it is more of a biography than the other "Killing" books. It also postulates that the shooting led directly to an early diminishment of the President's mental faculties during his second four-year term. An interesting read on several levels.

O'Reilly, Bill & Dugard, Martin. *Killing Kennedy: The End of Camelot*. New York: Henry Holt & Co., 2012. This book provides significant info on Kennedy's youth and college days, as well as an excellent account of Kennedy's legitimate heroism in the South Pacific during WWII. However, its "take" on the assassination of JFK ignores substantial amounts of evidence that has been in the public domain for decades.

Stockman, David. *The Great Deformation: The Corruption of Capitalism in America*. New York: PublicAffairs, 2013. I read only Part III covering FDR, Hoover, the Great Depression and economic statistics regarding the performances of both Presidents and their attempts to improve the U.S. economy.

Kilmeade, Brian & Yaeger, Don. *George Washington's Secret Six: The Spy Ring that Saved the American Revolution*. New York: Sentinel, 2014. The focus of this book is specifically on six spies in the New York City area. Their successes and failures are set forth in some detail.

Oller, John. *The Swamp Fox: How Francis Marion Saved the American Revolution*. Boston, Massachusetts: Da CapoPress, 2016. This book is about Washington and the Revolutionary War, mainly in South Carolina; and the amazing successes of Francis Marion—the Swamp Fox. It's a very interesting read about the unusual way in which the war was fought in the swampy Carolinas. Also a fast read.

Markle, Donald. *The Fox & the Hounds: The Birth of American Spying*. New York: Hippocrene Books, 2014. Details and statistics regarding Washington's cadre of spies in multiple colonies.

Kaplan, Fred. *John Quincy Adams: American Visionary*. New York: Harper, 2014. This book is immensely informative about JQA's passion for literature and writing. However, the author, a New Englander as well as an English professor, is unable to conceal his extreme admiration for both JQA and his father, John Adams, America's second President.

A Category All His Own

Grant, Ulysses S. *Personal Memoirs*. Published by Mark Twain in 1885. This was the final book I read, and it was after the rankings were established. Although the information in Grant's memoirs did not affect the rankings, some of his written comments which appear in the memoirs are included in the chapter on Grant. It is an exhilarating book to read, albeit nineteenth-century writing styles are greatly convoluted when compared with twenty-first-century styles. Some of his sentences are way too long, and some nineteenth-century words no longer carry the same meaning now as they did back then. Still, Grant's honesty, magnanimity and his desire to spread the credit around, comes shining through.

Works of General Reference

DeGregorio, William. *The Complete Book of U.S. Presidents.* Fort Lee, NJ: Barricade Books, 2005.

McPherson, James. *To the Best of My Ability.* New York: Dorling Kindersley, 2001.

All of the Presidential election vote totals, and many of the testimonials regarding the various Presidents' strengths, weaknesses, and character traits may be found in one or both of the above reference books. DeGregorio's book also provides detailed information on all the Presidential cabinet officers, all Supreme Court appointees, family genealogies, wives and children, important legislation passed, scandals, etc. It is very impressively detailed. McPherson's book, in which he serves as the general editor, is a series of mini-bios about the Presidents, from Washington up to Bill Clinton. It also provides information about historical and cultural events that occurred during the various Presidents' administrations. A variety of authors wrote the different mini-bios, and most of those were objective and well done.

CPSIA information can be obtained
at www.ICGtesting.com
Printed in the USA
LVHW080709170520
655781LV00010B/416/J